Sources
of
Hermeneutics

SUNY Series in
Contemporary Continental Philosophy

Dennis J. Schmidt, Editor

Jean Grondin

Sources

of

Hermeneutics

STATE UNIVERSITY OF NEW YORK PRESS

Production by Ruth Fisher
Marketing by Terry A. Swierzowski

Published by
State University of New York Press, Albany

© 1995 State University of New York

All rights reserved

Printed in the United States of America

No part of this book may be used or reproduced in any manner whatsoever
without written permission. No part of this book may be stored in a retrieval
system or transmitted in any form or by any means including electronic,
electrostatic, magnetic tape, mechanical, photocopying, recording, or
otherwise without the prior permission in writing of the publisher.

For information, address the State University of New York Press,
State University Plaza, Albany, NY 12246

Library of Congress Cataloging-in-Publication Data

Grondin, Jean.
  Sources of hermeneutics / Jean Grondin.
    p. cm.
  Includes index.
  ISBN 0-7914-2465-0 (hard : alk. paper). — ISBN 0-7914-2466-9
(pbk. : alk. paper)
  1. Hermeneutics—History. 2. Heidegger, Martin, 1889–1976.
3. Gadamer, Hans Georg, 1900– . I. Title.
BD241.G697 1995
121'.68—dc20   94-22339
                                                          CIP

10 9 8 7 6 5 4 3 2 1

For
Emmanuel and Paul-Matthieu, the primary sources

CONTENTS

INTRODUCTION

In recent debates, contextuality and objective truth have been seen to form an irreconcilable contradiction. Philosophers who stress the historicity of our experiences of truth are conveniently labeled and dismissed as relativists. The charge is rendered all the more credible by authors—in both the Continental and the Analytic fields—who even gleefully adopt the relativist label. Indeed, this "happy" relativism is particularly evident in the American tradition of pragmatism.

By uncovering the sources of hermeneutic thought, the present book wishes to call into question some of the presuppositions of this unhistorical understanding of truth and the relativist mind-set associated with it. Truly, hermeneutics strives to understand what is said by going back to its motivation, or its context. However, this is not done in order to relativize the truth claim contained within a given statement. On the contrary, it is only if one inquires into the underlying motivation of what is being said that one can hope to grasp its truth. In other words, what is the urgency that speaks through an utterance which alone makes its truth claim understandable? This is the prime question of hermeneutics. If one ignores this question, as modern scientific method urges us to do, one risks missing the true meaning of what is being said. Contextuality and truth belong together in a way that does not entail any kind of relativism, because the truth that emerges out of a given situation and urgency remains one that can be shared by others, provided they are attentive to the unsaid side of the discourse.

Hermeneutics is the discipline of thought that aims at this un-said life of our discourses. What this unsaid amounts to is often trivial. To a large extent, it concerns the motives and the intentions that can be easily grasped through the words that are stated explic-itly. In this regard, it is clear that one cannot abstract from this "con-text" if one wishes to get at the truth of what is being said, even if almost every sentence can be distorted from its original intent. In-deed, most human misunderstandings stem from such distortion. However, the unsaid also extends to a dimension which exceeds the motivations of the speakers and to tensions of which they are not immediately aware. It is even questionable whether understanding is necessarily related to words at all. For example, it is undeniable that we also seek to understand events, the silence of the suffering, the cries of an infant, the meaning of a work of art, and the immi-nence of death. And despite the fact that such instances might es-cape words, something calls for understanding.

This dimension will be alluded to in this volume under the very antiquated notion of the "inner word." It will defend the thesis that human speech can only be adequately understood if one takes into account the "interior word" out of which it proceeds and that it strives to convey. The meaning of language cannot be reduced to the realm of the utterances and words that circumstances have brought to the fore. Behind or, rather, "in" language lies a meaning which surpasses the limited scope of the perceptible sounds or the visible signs. The interiority referred to here does not designate some nebu-lous spiritual realm of the soul. The interiority of the word is rather an invitation to venture into what is said, what is uttered, but at the same time in what is silenced, if one hopes to get at the truth of what is always only babbled. Behind every manifestation that calls for understanding, something else is going on which can only be al-luded to by the words or traces it leaves behind. This interiority is not that of the soul, but that of meaning itself. It is the interiority of what is signified, but also hidden, by the words that present them-selves to us more than we come to them. There is no method to get at this unsaid, only understanding. Indeed, the fact that this un-said always exceeds what can ever be said is what ultimately con-stitutes our finitude.

Hermeneutics is attuned to this dimension of the unsaid inso-far as it has traditionally defined itself as an attempt to understand meaning out of its context (stressing the prefixe *cum* that refers to everything meant "with" or by a text, but which remains unspoken). In like manner, hermeneutics itself should be grasped out of its own context. Again, not in order to "contextualize" and thus relativize it, but to bear out its truth potential. There is no question that contemporary hermeneutics received its most forceful and coherent exposition in the work of Hans-Georg Gadamer. His hermeneutics has, however, been received in a rather one-sided way in the English-speaking community, its understanding being somewhat overshadowed by the figures of Rorty and Derrida, who do not always render justice to Gadamer's endeavor nor to the sources of his thought. This can be corrected if one becomes reacquainted with the forgotten historical sources of hermeneutical thought: Plato, Augustine, Humanism, the early Heidegger and Husserl.

Even if everyone is speaking of hermeneutics today, its sources and tradition remain largely unexplored. This volume will, therefore, begin with a general characterization of the relationship between hermeneutics and the philosophical tradition of metaphysics (Chapter 1), which will be followed by a forensic investigation into the meaning of hermeneutics in Antiquity (Chapter 2). This will enable us to evaluate the hermeneutic impulse which is essential to the phenomenological movement of the 20th Century, even if its proponents did not always understand themselves as hermeneuts. The third essay will therefore undertake the delicate task of ascertaining Husserl's own "silent" contribution to hermeneutics. There is no question that hermeneutical thought was unsympathetic to him and especially to his foundationalist account of philosophy. Nevertheless, his own return to the "things themselves" was itself hermeneutical since such "things" are only given by way of the intentionality of the inquiring subject. In this respect, there are no "things themselves" for Husserl. Rather, there are "dialogical intentionalities," which are immersed, like us, in a sea of meanings.

It is this conception of the "given" which so fascinated Heidegger in his hermeneutic appropriation of Husserl. Having also worked through the work of Dilthey, he characterized Husserl's notion of intution as "hermeneutic" as early as 1919, which marks the very first appearance of the term "hermeneutic" in his thought.[1] For Heidegger, this meant that human understanding (*Verstehen*), indeed self-understanding, is involved in every encounter with Being. We are always there (*da*) in the guise of understanding when the world becomes manifest. This insight opened the way for Heidegger's hermeneutic of facticity as it was developed in his early Freiburger and Marburger lectures. Chapter 4 will stress the ethical dimension of this early hermeneutics which was to a certain extent overshadowed by the stronger ontological orientation given to *Being and Time* in 1927. But the early Heidegger is not the only one who influenced the unfolding of contemporary hermeneutics. There is also a hermeneutic dimension to Heidegger's second philosophy, even if Heidegger refrained from using the term *hermeneutics* to describe his philosophical endeavor. Chapter 5 will attempt to sort out this hermeneutic dimension of the turn by recognizing in it a radicalization of human finitude. The notion of finitude was, of course, already present in *Being and Time*, but it did not yet affect the rather traditional conception of philosophy Heidegger still espoused in 1927. If Being cannot be grasped from a foundationalist standpoint, be it as fragile as *Dasein*, philosophy, as the self-elucidation of our facticity, can only reflect back on his historical thrownness and the possibilities open to it.

Such a philosophy of our historical finitude was developed by Gadamer, who thus linked Heidegger's later philosophy of the turn with its hermeneutical starting point. Chapter 6 will offer some insights on the genesis, composition and unity of *Truth and Method* by taking into account the first shorthand draft of the work written in 1956. Gadamer's book ends by raising a universality claim for hermeneutics, which stood at the center of the debates with Jürgen Habermas and Jacques Derrida. However, these discussions did not take into account the Platonic and Augustinian sources of this universality claim. Chapter 7 will thus focus on Gadamer's relation to Augustine and its bearing on the universality of hermeneutics.

If Gadamer's hermeneutics must be seen from the background of Heidegger's early hermeneutics of facticity and his later philosophy of the turn, it departs from Heidegger at some very crucial junctures, most notably on the question of humanism. Unlike Heidegger, who advocated a critical view of the humanistic tradition (which is, to a large extent, responsible for the widespread antihumanistic tendency in the humanities), Gadamer discovered in the very same stream of humanism a form of resistance to the exclusive claim of methodical truth. In this regard, Chapters 8 and 9 will investigate Gadamer's relationship to this forgotten humanistic tradition. Finally, Chapter 10 will draw the conclusions from the hermeneutical intelligence of language developed throughout all the studies. Central to them all is the concentration on the inner word, on the inner dialogue that we are. This notion of self-dialogue would thus like to be understood as a translation for Heidegger's notion of *Dasein*.

Acknowledgments

The text of Chapter 2 first appeared in the *Proceedings of the Boston Area Colloquium in Ancient Philosophy*, vol. VIII, 1992, 211–230.

Chapters 4, 6 and 7 appeared in German in the book *Der Sinn für Hermeneutik* (Darmstadt: Wissenschaftliche Buchgesellschaft, 1994). Chapter 8 was originally invited and written for the forthcoming Library of Living Philosophers volume, *The Philosophy of Hans-Georg Gadamer*, edited by Lewis Edwin Hahn and to be published by the Open Court Publishing Company, Peru, Illinois. Chapters 5 and 9 were first published by the *Graduate Faculty Philosophy Journal* (respectively in volumes 15, 1991, 85–108 and 16, 1993, 417–432). Chapter 7 also appeared in English translation in a volume edited by B. Wachterhauser, *Gadamer on Truth*, Northwestern University Press, 1994, 137–147. Chapter 3 was first published in French in the journal *Philosophiques*, 20, 1993, 383–398. Chapter 10 was first published in French in *L'horizon herméneutique de la pensée contemporaine*, Paris: Vrin, 1993, 253–269. All the texts were revised for the present book publication. Our thanks go to the original editors for permission to publish these pieces in this volume.

Very special thanks go to Gail Soffer for the translation of the "Prolegomena to an Understanding of Heidegger's Turn," to Lawrence K. Schmidt for the translation of "On the Sources of Truth and Method," to Brice Wachterhauser for his translation of "Gadamer and Augustine," to Gregory Byng for his translation of Chapters 3 and 10 as well as for his careful reading of the entire manuscript, and to Yvon Corbeil for making the indexes and his outstanding work as a research assistant.

Chapter 1

From Metaphysics to Hermeneutics

1. From Kant to Hermeneutics and Schleiermacher

There are very few things held in common in the fragmented field of contemporary philosophy, except perhaps for this very fact that we do live in a "fragmented field" of philosophical discourse, that is, one that is inescapably characterized by interpretation. The philosophy which tries to contend with this situation can safely be called "hermeneutics," since it has traditionally been understood as the theory of interpretation (*hermeneuein*). If interpretation is the only universal or common aspect characterizing philosophy, one could claim that hermeneutics functions as a *prima philosophia* of sorts. One is obliged to add "of sorts" here because the relationship of hermeneutics to the metaphysical heritage is an ambiguous one. Indeed, hermeneutics can be seen as both an overcoming and an accomplishment of traditional metaphysics. By stressing interpretation, it is mostly antifoundationalist and would seem to be anti- or post-metaphysical. Yet, by recognizing universal perspectivism, it is obviously raising a universality claim which is akin to traditional metaphysics (whether those who espouse such a hermeneutical conception acknowledge it or not). Indeed, many so-called "deconstructionists" seem to be blissfully unaware of the metaphysical nature of their own claim to truth. It is hence a much needed desideratum to reflect anew on the relation or tension between metaphysics and hermeneutics.

In order to do this, however, some historical recollection is called for. In what follows, I will try to reconstruct historically the transition from metaphysics to hermeneutics within the realm of philosophical thought, a shift that quietly took place over the last two centuries or so. The origins of this transition can be traced back in large part to the appearance of Kant's epoch-making *Critique of Pure Reason* (1781). And although Kant himself had no inkling that his destruction of dogmatic metaphysics would eventually usher in the age of hermeneutics, key elements in his philosophy do point to such a shift. The mere idea that two millenia of metaphysics had produced no real knowledge, but only illusions, is in itself a hermeneutical insight. Metaphysical reason doesn't only yield hard truths, it can also produce fictions, interpretations and even sophistry. What metaphysics took for rational truths could be nothing other than delusions which one becomes aware of only after a careful deconstruction of the capacities of cognition beyond the limited realm of experience. This suggests that reason could very well follow interpretations of reality which enjoy no other credence than the fact that they satisfy its impulses, an idea that Nietzsche, a hermeneutical thinker if ever there was one, would use against Kant, and most forcefully against his metaphysical understanding of practical reason.

The other important insight made by Kant that announces a shift towards hermeneutics is to be found in the simple distinction between things-in-themselves and phenomena or appearances (*Erscheinungen*). One can say that classical metaphysics or *prima philosophia*, defined by Aristotle as the science that pertains to Being as such, claimed to possess knowledge about the nature of things in themselves. According to Kant, however, this claim disregards the fact that the things we know are already schematized or conceptualized by our understanding. In this respect, Kant followed and perhaps radicalized Hume's idea that our cognition rests on the association of ideas accomplished under the authority of the subjective principles of our mind (*e.g.* causality), but whose objective reality cannot be ascertained. Our mind is not merely passive in the act of knowledge, it is active to the point of imposing on nature its own laws of logic. Kant's *Transcendental Logic* thus offers the guiding principles of physics, but also of nature itself, that is, nature as it is "produced" or "required" by the categories of our thought. The idea that the world we know is based upon a conceptual projection of such categories is a revolutionary notion which indicates a shift from the metaphysical to the hermeneutical, a realm where one no longer has access to the things-in-themselves, but only to interpretations of things which are produced in accordance with our conceptual apparatus. Kant, to be sure, never viewed his destruction of metaphysics as something that would lead to anything like a hermeneutical perspectivism. According to his system, the laws we impose on nature and the moral law that impels us to act according to the categorical imperative of reason are not mere interpretations or fictions that could vary from one culture or epoch to the next, nor from one individual to another. They testify to the unchallenged authority of reason where it is genuinely effective, *i.e.*, not in the area of theoretical and syllogistical metaphysics, which is doomed to sophistry, but in the realm of practical philosophy and the metaphysics of nature.

Yet, Kant's distinction between phenomena and things-in-themselves grew beyond its author's intentions, which is in itself a hermeneutical event. Kant's criticism of any knowledge that would claim to speak of things as they are in themselves had two somewhat contradictory offsprings. One actually paved the way for the notion of a general perspectivism, or for some kind of hermeneutics, whereas the other produced a new burst of metaphysical thinking in the form of transcendental idealism. This second progeny is well known. The idealists, Fichte, Schelling and Hegel, thought that Kant was too shy when he prudishly wanted to limit knowledge to the realm of the phenomenal. By showing in his *Transcendental Deduction* that our understanding produces out of itself the logic of the world, as it were, he clearly established, at least in the mind of the idealists, that it is our reason which dictates how things are in themselves. Kant's active notion of a genesis of the world out of the capacities of the transcendental *ego* thus opened up the possibility of a new metaphysics, a metaphysics of the absolute subject. This foray into idealism has been interpreted as the logical next step from Kant's alleged destruction of metaphysics to some new kind of metaphysics. Indeed, the very step that Kant's philosophical revolution secretly entailed, or so the idealists contended, but which it wasn't able to express fully. Others, however, have claimed that idealism was in fact a "step backward" from critical philosophy; indeed, a relapse into the type of metaphysics that Kant had been warning us against.

The silent transition from metaphysics to hermeneutics followed a somewhat different path and was carried out by authors who are less familiar in the history of philosophy, perhaps because Kant's destruction instilled in them some despair as to the possibility of developing any kind of philosophical or rational knowledge. It was the general "impact" of Kant's *Critique* which caused this sense of desperation regarding rationality. Of course, one has to distinguish Kant's impact on the times from his own intentions. Indeed, Kant aimed at a new foundation of metaphysics which he sought in both moral philosophy and the new metaphysics of nature.[1] Yet, most of his readers believed that Kant, in spite of his best intentions, had made this outcome totally impossible. This sentiment is expressed dramatically by Mendelssohn's famous phrase about the *"alles zermalmenden"* Kant, referring to him as one who destroys or crushes everything. According to Kant's argument, reason falls prey to a necessary metaphysical illusion when it seeks to go beyond the limited scope of experience and therefore it cannot be sure of anything it produces. With Kant, who would have followed Hume more than he would have answered his challenge to metaphysics, reason would become aware of its essential frailty. As it turns out, reason appears to be trapped in two ways: it cannot efficaciously go beyond the realm of phenomena, and even there, it is only dealing with its own projections and not with the things-in-themselves. Although Mendelssohn himself hoped that Kant would be able to build a new foundation of philosophy on the ruins of traditional metaphysics, many of his contemporaries, those who resisted the temptation to develop a new idealism of absolute subjectivity, were skeptical and, consequently, turned hermeneutical.

An important figure here was that of Jacobi who found a notorious contradiction in Kant's doctrine of the thing-in-itself. Kant appeared to exclude any notion of the thing-in-itself from his system, since it is essentially unknowable; yet he still needed an objective basis in reality in order to avoid any form of absolute idealism. Our knowledge, if it is to be more than a fictitious creation of the subject, has to find some objective corroboration in the things-in-themselves. However this is precisely what Kant's system prohibits. Most of the *idealist* readers of Jacobi, therefore, drew the conclusion that one could only resolve this contradiction by jettisoning the notion of the thing-in-itself as something extrinsic to subjectivity and by developing a coherent system of absolute idealism.[2] Jacobi, on the other hand, following indications he found in Kant (for instance, the famous passage of 1787 in which Kant confessed he had to limit knowledge to make way for faith), came to another conclusion: "fideism." If reason cannot bring us to reality, the only instance that can give us any sense of an objective and stable world is faith in an authority higher than that of our limited reason which can only lead us toward nihilism (a term, incidentally, which Jacobi himself coined).

It is by faith, and by faith alone, that we gain access to the true foundation of Being, one which the sisyphical projections of reason prevent us from reaching. This fideist reading had some appeal at the time and one can observe that it still manifests itself today. Many forms of religious fundamentalism clearly stem from the fear or anguish produced by the perspectivism which characterizes our knowledge. It is only through a leap of faith that some hope to become reacquainted with, and thus reassured about, hard reality.

Jacobi's radical rebuttal of reason in the name of fideism had a direct impact on the transition from metaphysics to hermeneutics. Through the mediation of the more radical skepticism of G.E. Schulze and S. Maimon, who wondered openly whether Kant's transcendental philosophy was more cogent than the classical forms of metaphysics it called into question, it reached the thought of Nietzsche's often forgotten mentor, Schopenhauer. For Schopenhauer, a pupil of Schulze, knowledge, being limited to a mere representation of reality, never goes beyond the illusory realm of phenomena. The things-in-themselves are seen to be dominated by forces of the "will," which remain impenetrable to our intellect. From here, it is but a small step to Nietzsche's universal perspectivism which views the world as the domain of the will to power and unmasks all truth claims as illusions fostered by hidden power structures. There is an historic path from Kant to Nietzsche, therefore, the road from Jacobi to Schopenhauer. And it is precisely this road that accounts for the passage from a metaphysical to a hermeneutical universe.

However, Jacobi's fideism also had a direct impact on the father of contemporary hermeneutics, Friedrich Schleiermacher. In his early *Discourses on Religion* (1799), Schleiermacher followed Jacobi in dismissing the claims of rational knowledge and characterized the religious sentiment as one of total dependence, a feeling of reliance on a reality that transcends our fragile understanding. This romantic promotion of the religious sentiment is a distant consequence of Kant's humiliation of reason in his first *Critique*.

It is also a notion which Schleiermacher took up in his own hermeneutical thinking, one which he never really brought to fruition in a satisfying or publishable form. In his manuscripts on hermeneutics, Schleiermacher distinguishes two ways of understanding the art of interpretation: a loose and a strict sense. In its loose or "relaxed" sense, understanding is something which happens naturally when one is reading a text. One only needs a doctrine of interpretation, or a hermeneutics, to deal with the limited problem of ambiguous or equivocal passages, where understanding is not arrived at immediately. By distinguishing two types of hermeneutics,

Schleiermacher is clearly taking aim at the hermeneutical attitude which prevailed before him, the notion that hermeneutics is nothing but an "auxiliary" science which one calls upon when one stumbles upon difficult passages, a science one can do without as long as understanding flows relatively well. Incidentally, most human beings do understand without the help of any hermeneutical technique. Against this loose understanding of the practice of interpretation, where understanding manifests itself naturally, Schleiermacher introduces a new conception of hermeneutical practice. According to the strict sense, a theory of understanding should follow the maxim that it is rather *misunderstanding* which proceeds naturally and that understanding must be sought after and grounded in every step of interpretation.[3] Hermeneutics, therefore, in its most stringent sense, presupposes the virtual pervasiveness of misunderstanding. In the absence of a sure and potentially methodical art of understanding, or *Kunstlehre des Verstehens*, there is no way one can be sure of one's own understanding.

Schleiermacher thus makes understanding dependent on hermeneutics. True understanding can only result from an interpretation which is grounded on the rules and canons of some *Kunstlehre*. This dramatic promotion of hermeneutics (where one does not understand *unless* one can provide a hermeneutical foundation) has to be viewed with the backdrop of Romanticism in mind and follows what was seen as Kant's humiliation of the capacities of human reason. According to this romantic conception, our knowledge dwells in the realm of phenomena, where it cannot be sure of anything. Finite reason cannot hope to grasp adequately the infinite reality which grounds it and that points to a higher subject (whether it be God, nature or some other superhuman reality) of which one can only have a presentiment through some form of "feeling" or *Ahndung*. This post-Kantian idea that the feeling of infinity takes up where reason lets us down was common to the first Romantics, most notably to Schlegel and Schleiermacher.[4]

Nevertheless, there is another motivation behind Schleiermacher's dramatization of the hermeneutical task. If understanding cannot be sure of itself unless it is grounded on a solid *Kunstlehre*, it is also because the prime objects of understanding are mostly works of genius, a tendency which is also evident in Schlegel's normative understanding of philology. How can one understand a piece of genius without misunderstanding it in a chronic way? Indeed, one can only misunderstand the products of genius if understanding means that one subsumes the *interpretandum* under what is already known. One understands an utterance when one can bring it back to something which is already familiar. Consequently, understanding is condemned to miss the originality that constitutes any work of genius. This is perhaps why geniuses are never properly understood in their own time. In a sense, this is tragic. For if one claims to understand geniality, one reduces it to something which is already familiar and common and therefore misunderstands it. The seduction exerted by the aesthetics of genius is certainly at work in Schleiermacher's own conception of hermeneutics. Confronted with originality and far-reaching geniality, the basis of hermeneutics has to be that one *doesn't* understand.

This is indeed a sound maxim of modesty. It can also apply to more common forms of understanding which do not deal with works of genius. In the most trivial forms of interpersonal communication, when can we be sure that we understand each other? It is normal to presuppose that we do and it would be psychotic to claim the opposite. But how can we be sure that we understand fully what others have to say? We seem to understand the utterances of others, but how can we grasp everything if we have not been through what they have experienced, nor been affected by the influences which have shaped their lives and so on? Because of this failure, misunderstanding frequently appears and can often seem to be the norm in interpersonal relations.

This insight is at the basis of Schleiermacher's hermeneutics and accounts for what one can call his universalization of the dimension of misunderstanding.[5] It is an insight which conveys a new dignity, and a new sense of urgency to hermeneutics. In the aftermath of metaphysics, where the pretension to know Being in itself has become ever more problematic, the rise of hermeneutics rests on this constant possibility of misunderstanding. In this regard, Schleiermacher is a very contemporary thinker. He derived from his premise of misunderstanding the notion that human knowledge is necessarily "dialectical" or, if one wishes to avoid the speculative connotations of Hegel's notion of Dialectic, "dialogical." Schleiermacher clearly understands dialectics in the Platonic sense as the art of dialogue. If all our perspectives on the world are limited, we can only but profit from the differing views, experiences and objections of others. Through dialogue, we can grow beyond our limited selves and achieve some kind of relative universality. We get to see things from different perspectives and enrich our limited understanding. This stress on the dialogical element of understanding is precious indeed. One can find traces of it in contemporary hermeneutics, in Gadamer's dialogical conception of the hermeneutic experience, but also in the project of an ethics of discussion (*Diskursethik*).

A less contemporary aspect of Schleiermacher's thought is perhaps his notion of a "technique of understanding" which seems to suggest a methodical conception of the hermeneutical endeavour. If one cannot be sure of one's own understanding, it would be very useful if one could rely on some *Kunstlehre* that would ensure the validity of our interpretations. But how can we be sure about the *Kunstlehre* itself or its application? In other words, isn't this technical conception of hermeneutics a scientistic ideal which in fact identifies a difficulty more than it actually solves it?

However, it should be noted that Schleiermacher himself had a keen sense of this problem. He often acknowledged that the task of understanding is a never-ending one if one follows the strict sense that he assigns to hermeneutics. He was also aware that one has to rely on divinatory methods in order to understand the individuality of the other. Nevertheless, is the appeal to methods and to a rigorous methodology not a misunderstanding of what hermeneutics is all about? Doesn't Schleiermacher's own universalization of misunderstanding and its consequent stress on dialectics point to the very limits of method?

As far as I can see, and the fragmentary character of his hermeneutics makes it most difficult to interpret, Schleiermacher constantly struggled with this daunting task. This struggle could also explain why he never published his work on hermeneutics. He had found no solution to the contradictory tensions of his hermeneutical thinking. There is indeed a deep tension in his philosophy between the cartesian and the more romantic motivation. His notion of a universal *Kunstlehre* of understanding alludes to a cartesian-like method that would precede actual comprehension and make it scientific. However, this cartesian aspect is undermined by his constant reliance on the dialectical, the divinatory element and the necessity of intuitive insight or sentiment. Schleiermacher, therefore, seems to have failed to reconcile the romantic background of his thought with the ambitious cartesian formulation he gave to his hermeneutics. And while it is clear that the cartesian dimension seeks to contain, as far as possible, the anguishing universality of misunderstanding, the total perspectivism which is looming here calls perhaps for a solution other than the one method alone can offer.

2. From Schleiermacher to Heidegger and Gadamer

The transition from metaphysics to hermeneutics takes on a new dimension when one leaps to the hermeneutics of the 20th century.

The pervasiveness of total misunderstanding has not disappeared. In fact, through authors like Nietzsche it has become an inescapable part of our intellectual universe. Hermeneutics, one could claim, is the philosophy that tries to come to terms with this radical situation which Schleiermacher was one of the first to confront.

Heidegger represents the crucial juncture in the philosophical transition from metaphysics to hermeneutics. One could say that he was the first to actually present the two as being directly opposed. There is no doubt that his early hermeneutics of facticity is intended as an alternative to classical metaphysics. The young Heidegger was perhaps not fully aware of this, since he seems to have entertained a "positive" understanding of metaphysics at least as late as 1929, in his last real book, *Kant and the Problem of Metaphysics*, where he alludes to the task of a "metaphysics of *Dasein*," thus claiming for himself the term metaphysics.

Nevertheless, from early on his hermeneutics takes the form of a destruction of the ontological tradition and, therefore, of metaphysics. It is in this context that one may again identify the dilemma that characterized Schleiermacher's hermeneutics, torn, as we have seen, between a cartesian and a more romantic or almost existentialist motivation. The possibility or even "peril" of total misunderstanding was the guiding force behind Schleiermacher's hermeneutics, but his cartesian instincts pointed to a methodical solution or some sort of *Kunstlehre*. Unlike Schleiermacher, Heidegger relegated the "methodical" solution to the age of metaphysics.

It is important to note that the notion of metaphysics encountered with Heidegger is slightly different from the notion present in Kant. For Kant, metaphysics was the type of thinking that aimed at *a priori* knowledge of what lies beyond our experience (for example, in rational psychology or theology). For Heidegger, metaphysics stems from a more basic urge, namely, man's tendency to secure his fragile position in the world by understanding the totality of Being out of an onto-theological framework. In this regard, Heidegger claims that onto-theology sums up the general constitution of metaphysics. This "constitution" rests on a threefold axis, alluded to in the three Greek terms that make up the notion of onto-theo-logy. Metaphysical thinking is:

1. *Ontological*, in that it aims at a universal, comprehensive and totalizing grasp of Being (insisted upon by Aristotle's definition (*Met.* IV, 1) of *prima philosophia* as a discipline which does not deal with a specific province of Being, but with Being in its universality).

2. *Theological*, in so far as it unfolds this universal perspective on Being out of a general principle, an *archè*; it is this basic principle which makes the totality of Being understandable and derivable (this principle need not be "theological" in the divine sense; wherever one seeks a principle of Being, in the form of a common denominator to which Being can be reduced, even if it is a materialistic or a sensible principle, one is still thinking "theologically" or in a foundationalist way, that is, metaphysically).

3. *Logical*, in that metaphysics reads its universal and principled understanding of Being through the lenses of a specific logic, that of propositional and syllogistical discourse; it is through the basic categories of logic, or even grammar (the subject being viewed as substance; the predicate with the notion of property or accident; the "if-then" language game with ontological causality, etc.), that one hopes to get a secure grasp on Being. By transposing its own logic onto the world, metaphysics tacitly secures its onto-theo-logical hold on what is.

It is obvious enough that the basic impulse of Heidegger's step back from metaphysical thinking is the fact that metaphysics leads man away from his own finitude. The notion of a science, or outlook, that would provide a universal, causal and logical account of Being, and of ourselves, masks the sheer uncertainty and facticity of our Being-in-this-world. Metaphysics is thus to be understood as a flight from one's own temporality and mortality. It is because we are mortal that we seek to ground Being on something like eternal permanence, whose model is provided by divinity or reason.

One can see to what extent methodical thinking can appear to be a by-product of metaphysics for Heidegger. In face of the utter insecurity of our knowledge, it is alluring indeed to appeal to a method of certainty (for example, to a *Kunstlehre*, to take Schleiermacher's term), that would eradicate, as it were, our essential finitude by imparting certain knowledge to us. But for Heidegger, this is nothing but an illusion, a self-delusion of *Dasein*, comparable in a way to Kant's notion of a transcendental *Schein* or illusion. *Dasein* flees from itself, from its own insecurity when it falls into onto-theology (a "fall," a *Verfallen*, which one can oppose to an authentic mode of *Dasein* which, in resolute lucidity, would stand up to its inescapable finitude).

It is against this metaphysical outlook that Heidegger proposed his own hermeneutics of *Dasein*, *i.e.*, his philosophy of human finitude as that which metaphysical thought consistently and constitutively erases, and thus necessarily presupposes. All of metaphysical thinking, from Parmenides' notion of monolithic Being and Plato's theory of the Ideas up to Descartes' *Discours de la méthode*, Schleiermacher's *Kunstlehre*, Hegel's Logic and the merely logical conception of knowledge in Logical positivism, is based upon this shying away from man's radical finitude. Heidegger's hermeneutics promises to open the door to a more lucid account of our finitude. This is how the general shift "from metaphysics to hermeneutics," that began with Kant's *Transcendental Dialectic*, aquires a new radicality with Heidegger.

Heidegger's claim is that metaphysical thinking is vitiated in its inception by its option for "infinity," in whatever shape or form it happens to take and that one also encounters in some of the more "materialist" philosophies (to the extent that they are reductive or foundational). According to Heidegger's conception, metaphysics stands under the domination of a specific understanding of Being as permanent presence. What "is" or deserves the dignity of "Being," is that which is permanently there. Something that passes away cannot count as Being in the full sense of the word. It only enjoys a derivative ontological status as a predicate or attribute of some permanent Being. Permanence in the present erases again the shrieking finitude of our future. What is primordial for Heidegger is always this mortal finitude—the fact of our limited being in time. It is out of a negation of this finite facticity that the metaphysical reading of Being as permanent presence comes to the fore.

Heidegger sees this reading of Being in terms of "presence" at work in propositional logic. For this logic of accountable presence, all that can be said of something can be put in propositional form, following the schema "S is P": this subject has this predicate, a statement whose "truth claim" can be verified by the means of method and logical analysis. For Heidegger, however, human language cannot be reduced to the logical content of our propositions. The essential can never be said or put in propositional form, since there is always more to what is being said than can be grasped from a logical proposition. This is why Heidegger urges a "hermeneutical" understanding of language, one that is attentive to all that isn't said in a statement. In this regard, his early lectures presents "hermeneutical" understanding in opposition to the "apophantical" sphere which remains exclusively on the level of the proposition, without taking into account what lies behind language and cannot be seen by logic.

Heidegger gives a now classic example of this in the sentence: "the hammer is heavy," a sentence that is thought of as a gasp which may come to the lips of a suffering carpenter in her workshop. Now, what the statement "states" is merely that the object "hammer" is endowed with the property of "heaviness." It seems, therefore, to be a theoretical statement about an independent object in the world. According to this logical reading, one that metaphysically concentrates on what is presently at hand in the statement, what is neglected is the hermeneutical dimension of the suffering carpenter. In the theoretical, "apophantical" understanding of the statement as a claim regarding a subsistent object, no mention is made of *Dasein*. But if the statement is to be understood properly, that is, hermeneutically, one has to develop an ear for *Dasein*. The statement could then mean something like: "I can't take it anymore," "please, help me out," "please, take over," "let's have a break," etc. The essential dimension in language is not the logico-semantical content of our statements, on which logic focuses, but the relation of *Dasein* to that which strives to be understood in language. Heidegger will even go as far in *Sein und Zeit* as to claim that the proposition is a "derivative" mode of understanding (SZ § 33).

Throughout his philosophical itinerary, Heidegger will constantly struggle with this propositional conception of language. It is a view which is cemented by logic and, ultimately, by metaphysics with its stress on Being as that which is readily at hand, presently observable and thus susceptible of mastery. He will even characterize his own philosophical concepts as mere "formal indications" (*Formalanzeigen*) which are not to be taken literally in their semantic context, but as invitations for us to fill them with content by applying them to our existence. This is also the idea behind his appropriation of the Augustinian distinction between the *actus signatus* and the *actus exercitus*. If one remains exclusively on the level of the *actus signatus*, or the level of what the proposition states or "signifies," one will necessarily miss its intent and purview. True understanding occurs only if one goes "into" language, or into the "exercise" (loosely playing on the notion of an *actus exercitus*) of what is happening in this *logos*.

According to Heidegger, this hermeneutical interpretation or "hearing" of *logos* has been obliterated in the metaphysical tradition through the dominance bestowed on logical thinking. Again, this domination can be seen as an erasing away of finitude, as the masking of the finiteness of our language, and an avoidance of the fact that the words we use cannot be literally taken as manipulable bits of information that exhaust all there is to say about something. In terms of logic, the presence of meaning occurs fully in propositional language. However, Heidegger's hermeneutics proposes that this metaphysical logic misses what really happens in language, *i.e.*, the unending struggle to find words for all that should be said in order to understand ourselves. The transition "from metaphysics to hermeneutics" thus alludes to a shift in our relation to language, one that would take adequate distance from the propositional or "presential" conception of our linguistical dwelling in this world.

This hermeneutical understanding of language, which is leveled against the domination of propositional logic, has been taken up in Gadamer's hermeneutics. Gadamer follows Heidegger when he writes at the end of *Truth and Method* that "the concept of the statement (. . .) stands *in the greatest possible contrast* to the essence of the hermeneutical experience and to the linguisticality of our experience of the world in general,"[6] He correctly uses the word "contrast," because what we seek to understand is always what propositions *mean*, what they have to say, why they say it, and that, no proposition on earth can state it fully. It is an abstraction or a fiction to concentrate simply on what is said in our statements. The "said" can only be adequately understood if one takes into consideration the unsaid side of our statements, what hopes to be heard in our utterances even if it cannot be said. This hermeneutical relation of the said to the unsaid corresponds to what Gadamer calls the "speculative" dimension of language. "Speculative" comes from the Latin word *speculum*, which means "mirror." Our statements are always the mirroring of a meaning that is never entirely uttered. Proper understanding must go beyond the uttered words themselves in order to reach this motivating dimension of the unsaid.

To illustrate his critique of strictly logical interpretation, Gadamer compares the logical fixation on statements with what happens in police or judicial "interrogations" where statements that are made, and recorded, can easily be used in a context very different from the one that was intended. In this fixation on the "stated facts," the notion that language can only be understood according to its original intent, context and motivation, is lost. All this, of course, cannot be spelled out in the statements we come to utter and this is why they receive very different interpretations (as is evident in the case of police interrogations). To further explain this notion, it is helpful to quote at some length Gadamer's subtle analysis: "Language itself, however, has something speculative about it, (. . .) as the realization of meaning, as the event of speech, of mediation, of coming to an understanding. Such a realization is speculative in that the finite possibilities of the word are oriented toward the sense intended as toward the infinite. A person who has something to say seeks and finds the words to make himself intelligible to the other

person. This does not mean that he makes 'statements.' Anyone who
has experienced an interrogation—even if only as a witness—knows
what it is to make a statement and how little it is a statement of
what one means. In a statement the horizon of meaning of what is
to be said is concealed by methodical exactness; what remains is the
'pure' sense of the statement. That is what goes on record. But meaning thus reduced to what is stated is always distorted meaning."[7]

Gadamer expresses this speculative element of language, the
fact that our words refer to the hermeneutical dimension of the unsaid which begs for understanding, in what he terms the logic of
"question and answer." An utterance or a sentence can only be understood properly if one seeks to understand the question to which
it is the answer. A proposition hardly ever says it itself. One has to
go into the proposition to get at it, engaging into the dialogue out of
which the statement "emerges," in the literal sense of the word.
To understand is to know or to have an idea of the question to
which the statement may be read as an answer. It is in this specific
logic of question and answer, developed in contradistinction to the
propositional logic which reduces our words to their "visible" logico-
semantic content, that one finds the basic hermeneutical experience.
In his essay of 1966 on "The Universality of the Hermeneutical Problem" (which incidentally sparked the debate with Habermas),
Gadamer writes that it is the "hermeneutically primordial phenomenon," that "there is no possible assertion that cannot be understood
as an answer to a question and that it can only be so understood."[8]
Adequate understanding can only be achieved if one ventures into
this realm of questioning. A questioning which is not always stated,
or cannot be fully articulated, but which is nevertheless essential
to the penetration of what is being said.

This hermeneutical intelligence of language stands in direct
opposition to the logical understanding of language which focuses
solely on what is said and the logical connections of our propositions,
as if our struggle with language always obeyed some form of propositional logic. For Gadamer, therefore, the transition "from metaphysics to hermeneutics" can be understood as a passage from a
restrictive, logical conception of language to a more dialogical understanding, one which is attentive to the speculative dimension of
linguisticity. In this respect, Gadamer would appear to be following
the lead of his teacher Martin Heidegger.

Yet, Gadamer somehow refuses to drive a wedge between metaphysics and hermeneutics. The two need not be seen as a rigid alternative, as Heidegger might have suggested. In the important
chapter on the speculative dimension of language, Gadamer even

writes that his "hermeneutics of the human sciences—which at first appears to be of secondary and derivative concern, a modest chapter from the heritage of German idealism—leads us back into the problems of classical metaphysics."[9] This enigmatic passage invites us to think that there might be some form of reconciliation between metaphysics and hermeneutics.

If hermeneutics leads us back into the problems of metaphysics, it is in part because it is attentive to elements in this tradition which divert from the mainstream "onto-theological" trend that became dominant and which celebrated the virtues of the logical, technical and methodical, as that which enables us to have a secure grasp on things. This is true about the understanding of language. The third part of *Truth and Method* argues that the bulk of the metaphysical tradition has stood under the aegis of a technical, instrumental view of language, according to which words are there to express our thoughts and the connections between them. Yet, Gadamer points to a few exceptions, most notably those of Augustine and Plato. In his insistence on the gap between the external word we utter, the *logos prophorikos*, and the internal word of the soul, the *logos endiathetos*, which we can never adequately express, Augustine was well aware that there is more to language than what is and can adequately be said.[10] The words that we pronounce are nothing but the contingent signs that come to our mind, signs which never exhaust everything that we might wish to say or we need to say if we were to be understood properly. Plato was also attuned to this element of contingency, even if he espoused a rather instrumental understanding of language in his theoretical reflections on linguisticality, as in the *Cratylus* for instance. However, in his *Seventh Letter* as well as in the *Phaedrus*, he took into account the steep indigence of the words we happen to utter. This is especially true of written discourse, because written words can receive the most ludicrous of meanings if the author is not there to defend his or her intentions. Some logicians would fault Plato with being auto-contradictory because he himself *wrote* about this. In this regard, we have here a prime example of how statements can lead to false readings if they are not understood hermeneutically. Plato does not condemn language in itself, but only the way in which it can be misused (by the sophists, for instance, who keep playing with sentences without regard for the truth of our statements). Words, written or oral, should only be employed as means of rememoration (*hypomnemata*) of the truths they wish to express. What is to be understood is not what is or can be said in words, but the whole of meaning they wish to convey to the capable ear. So, there are

indeed luminous elements in our metaphysical tradition for
hermeneutical understanding. Hermeneutics, therefore, cannot dismiss the whole tradition of metaphysics. Such a dismissal, stemming
from an attitude not unlike the one sometimes found in Heidegger,
would in itself perhaps be something "metaphysical." It is only if we
pretend to stand on a firm, universal, principled and logical ground
that we can discard an entire tradition. Heidegger's massive shift
"from metaphysics to hermeneutics," if one can sum it up that way,
would remain tacitly metaphysical in nature. Some elements of
metaphysics need to be saved against hermeneutical thinkers who
are too sure of themselves.

If metaphysics contains some resources which point beyond the
logical, methodical and technical, one can also ask whether there
really is such a thing as a closed "language of metaphysics." This is
a point Gadamer made against Heidegger in his study of 1968 on
"Heidegger and the Language of Metaphysics," which seems to have
been a matter of direct debate between Gadamer and Heidegger.[11]
Can two millenia of metaphysics be reduced to a simple formula, to
that of "onto-theo-logy"? Again, isn't such a reduction "metaphysical" in the sense it is criticizing?[12] It is Gadamer's contention that
the language of metaphysics is not one that can be put at a distance.
It is still part of the way we think and we cannot but use it in our
effort to make sense of ourselves. Moreover, the alleged "language
of metaphysics" is not some kind of confinement, or prison. It is a
genuine avenue of humanity's self-understanding, an avenue which
cannot be dismissed without, at the same time, unsettling the ground
upon which our own thinking is articulated. Furthermore, if language is our way of becoming at home in language,[13] one which
remains open to new experiences, there is no such thing as a preor-
dained language of metaphysics that would fatally limit our avenues
of understanding.

So far, we have seen that the transition "from metaphysics to
hermeneutics" is far less dichotomous than one would have thought
in the wake of Kant, Schleiermacher, Nietzsche and Heidegger. This
is true despite the fact that most of modern philosophies have tried
to situate themselves outside or beyond what had been done before
them. There is perhaps no common denominator which has characterized the philosophy of the last two centuries more than its urge
to surpass metaphysics. Kant, Schleiermacher, Marx, Freud,
Nietzsche, Dilthey, Husserl, Heidegger, Habermas (who published
a collection of essays in 1988 under the title "Postmetaphysical
Thinking"[14]), Wittgenstein, Carnap, Foucault, Derrida, etc. all heralded their thinking as one which would finally bring us beyond

metaphysics or tell us the final truth about what metaphysics was all about. It is perhaps odd to note in a chapter which considers this very transition "from metaphysics to hermeneutics," but the philosophical hermeneutics of Gadamer is perhaps the only philosophy in the 20th century that did not recommend itself as an overcoming of metaphysics. Hermeneutical thinking disbelieves the notion that there could be something like a completely new era in philosophy. We are too finite, too dependent on tradition and the work of history (*Wirkungsgeschichte*) to entertain the utopian and perhaps dangerous hope of a new beginning in the realm of thought. Indeed such a rupture would disregard the achievements of the past out of which contemporary thought continues to nourish itself.

With regard to our metaphysical heritage, the only thing that is required is that one become aware of this debt. This is why Gadamer urges the elaboration of a consciousness of our being worked upon by history (*wirkunsgsgeschichtliches Bewußtsein*). Through an explicit consciousness of the presence of metaphysical thinking in us, we can perhaps come to a reflective awareness of our debt to this tradition, an awareness both of what cannot be discarded and also of that which cannot compel us anymore. Through hermeneutics, a differentiated, more subtle, and more dialogical understanding of metaphysics can be brought about. So long as we continue believing in philosophy, metaphysics can help us become aware of the truth-claim we are raising and the type of questions we wish to answer in doing so. One of the elements of the metaphysical tradition that has to be kept alive is the universal scope it attributes to philosophy. Gadamer's hermeneutics is fully aware of this when it raises a claim to universality. However, hermeneutical thinking does not necessarily renew the onto-theo-logical framework of metaphysics exposed by Heidegger. It reactualizes its universal (or "ontological") scope, while realizing that the notion of an ultimate "grounding" goes well beyond the capacities of our finitude. As Heidegger has credibly argued, this quest for an ultimate ground may well stem from the self-concealment of finitude.

As is already evident in the Aristotelian texts that make up his *Metaphysics*, metaphysical thinking has always been torn between its option for universality and its quest for the theological. The onto-theo-logical constitution of metaphysics presented a solution to this problem, but it always remained problematical whether a theological answer could lay claim to universality, but also whether a universal or philosophical investigation had to end up in the security of theology. Nevertheless, with hermeneutics, we encounter a new form of metaphysics. The metaphysical claim of Gadamer's

hermeneutics only renews the universal or ontological claim of philosophy, while shunning its theological (or ultimately grounding)
foundation. The truly universal character of hermeneutics is indeed
this dimension of finitude.

Chapter 2

The Task of Hermeneutics in
Ancient Philosophy

In this chapter, I would like to identify the sources of hermeneutic thinking in ancient philosophy. Nevertheless, one might justifiably question whether there was such a thing as "hermeneutics" in the ancient world? Indeed, the latin word *hermeneutica* did not emerge until the 17th century when it was first introduced by a theologian from Strasbourg, Johann Dannhauer, as a necessary requirement of all the sciences that rely on the interpretation of texts—an understandable demand in light of the fact that the Renaissance sought fresh avenues of wisdom in returning to the classical texts.[1] When Dannhauer created the word *hermeneutica*, he openly drew his inspiration from Aristotle's treatise *Peri hermeneias* (*De interpretatione*), claiming that the new science of interpretation was in effect nothing but a complement to the Aristotelian Organon.[2] However, the first real historian of the hermeneutic tradition, Wilhelm Dilthey, proclaimed that hermeneutics was in fact created a century earlier by Protestantism[3] in the wake of Luther's principle of the *sola scriptura*. This principle, which had been used to undermine the authority of tradition advocated by the Catholic Church, was to be the one and only norm of Biblical exegesis. Following Dilthey's lead, many prominent historians of hermeneutics, such as Bultmann, Ebeling and Gadamer have paid great attention to Luther's hermeneutic revolution. However, even if Luther launched a hermeneutic revolution in the history of the Church, one would

be hard-pressed to find in his own writings anything like a hermeneutics (i.e. a theoretical reflection on interpretation). Luther,
who, as is well known, shunned theoretical and philosophical reflection, equating them with "dead scholasticism," concentrated entirely
on exegesis. For instance, as a university professor, he only gave exegetical lessons, which involved concrete interpretation of texts.[4]
However, even if Luther's exegesis cannot properly be thought of as
a "hermeneutics" or a theoretical reflection on this practice, his exegetical interpretation of texts and the Catholic reaction to it are
not without significance in regard to the emergence of hermeneutics.
The Catholic counterreformation's response to Luther was that it had
no difficulty with his scriptural principle of *sola scriptura*, since its
own authority also derived from the Bible. The only problem resided
in the interpretation of ambiguous passages. Despite Luther's ac-
claimed principle, the Catholic Church contended that it was far
from certain that the Bible is always clear and consistently serves
as its *sui ipsius interpres* (its own interpreter). Indeed, the striking
divergences among the Protestants themselves on very important
matters of Biblical interpretation confirmed this suspicion. Thus, the
Catholics concluded that it was necessary to rely on tradition and
the authority of the magisterium to establish the correct interpretation of ambiguous texts. And, it was precisely in the Lutheran response to this Catholic counterreaction that one can pin-point the
emergence of a hermeneutics in the Protestant tradition. The first
to offer such a hermeneutics were followers of Luther, Philipp
Melanchton (1497–1560), in his treatises on rhetoric of 1519 and
1531,[5] and Matthias Flacius Illyricus (1520–1575), who delivered his
hermeneutics in his *Clavis scripturae sacrae* in 1567. The task of
Flacius was to develop a specific hermeneutics which would serve
as a "key" for understanding difficult passages of Scripture while
still relying on the Lutheran principle of the *sola scriptura*. Flacius
took on this challenge by insisting on the prerequisite of grammati-
cal or, as one would say today, linguistic knowledge. He also offered
rules for the elucidation of ambiguous passages, borrowing most of
them from the rhetorical tradition, following the example of
Melanchton, but also from the Fathers of the Church and especially
from Augustine's hermeneutic treatise *De doctrina christiana*. By
doing this, Flacius ably wanted to underscore that Luther's revolution was in perfect accord with the scriptural convictions of the Fathers, and thus less revolutionary or subversive than the Catholic
Church had portrayed it. And while the theological implications of
Flacius' hermeneutics cannot occupy us here, it is still important
to note that the first hermeneutics of the modern age, those of

Melanchton, Flacius and Dannhauer, drew heavily on an earlier hermeneutic tradition. This is true despite the fact that the name *hermeneutica* itself was not employed until the 17th entury. It is also obvious that the first hermeneutic treatises of the patristic age depended on the achievements of Greek philosophy. It is, therefore, tempting to look to the Greek tradition for the roots of what may be called "hermeneutics" (i.e., a theoretical reflection on understanding and its difficulties).

Indeed, ancient philosophy offers some well-threaded paths for the elaboration of the classical sources of hermeneutics. First and foremost among them is the allegoric tradition which was established as a means of giving a rational account of the Homeric tradition. A second path would be to consider the role of interpretation and divination in the broad realm of Greek religion. A third approach would be to look for something like hermeneutics in a classical text like Aristotle's *De interpretatione*, even though it hardly deals with "interpretation" as we understand it, but with the basic elements that constitute a sentence[6]. These three perspectives on Greek "hermeneutics"—that one can call the allegorical, the religious and the logical—are the object of a wide range of scholarly and specialized studies. However, their interconnection, if there is any, has seldom been analyzed in itself. In this Chapter, I would like to seek a common ground for this entire hermeneutical endeavour by starting with an elucidation of the word ἑρμηνευτική as it appears in ancient texts. Although, this would seem to be a natural starting-point for an analysis of Greek hermeneutics, strangely enough, the notion of ἑρμηνευτική has seldom been studied on its own. To the best of my knowledge, there are no systematic studies of this notion in the available literature, with the notable exception of a short, but too general and unfocused study by Karl Kerényi.[7] In addition, while the word is obviously related to the more commonly used terms ἑρμηνεία, ἑρμηνεύς, etc., its etymological origin remains quite unclear.[8]

In the absence of a definite etymological source and of related specialized studies, therefore, one has no choice but to confront, if not the things, at least the texts themselves. The notion of ἑρμηνευτική first appears in the Platonic corpus where one finds three occurrences (*Politicus* 260 d 11, *Epinomis* 975 c 6, *Definitions* 414 d 4). Of course, one also finds many others incidences of words like ἑρμηνεία or ἑρμηνεύς. Unfortunately, none of the three occurrences of ἑρμηνευτική give a precise indication about the exact meaning of this notion, and two of them are found in works that were not written by Plato himself (i.e., the *Epinomis* and the academic book of *Definitions*). In the *Definitiones*, ἑρμηνευτική is used as an adjective in the definition of the noun, characterized as "an uncompounded utterance meaning (ἑρμηνευτικὴ) what is attributed to some existing thing and all that is said of its substance." The adjective ἑρμηνευτικὴ thus signifies "to mean something," to "point toward something," in the way a noun "means" or "stands for" a certain thing. One may call this the semantic understanding of ἑρμηνευτικὴ (an understanding which is in itself important since it echoes the notion of ἑρμηνεία, understood as the transposition or the translation of thought into language). In the two other contexts, the *Epinomis* and the *Politicus*, the word is also used as an adjective. However, in these instances, it characterizes a specific skill or art, a τεχνὴ. Unfortunately, in these two cases, the nature of this specific type of skill or art is presupposed rather than named. Indeed, ἑρμηνευτικὴ is simply listed among a series of other sciences, and consequently its precise meaning is far from clear. Nonetheless, it should be noted that in both cases, ἑρμηνευτικὴ appears next to the art of divination, μαντικὴ. Let us focus on the passage in the *Epinomis*, which is the least unspecific of the two, and which is at least more "Platonic" in spirit than the *Definitiones*. The author of the *Epinomis* is considering which forms of knowledge can lead to wisdom. After jokingly excluding such sciences as the art of cooking, hunting and the like, divination and ἑρμηνευτικὴ also have to be excluded, so we are told, because they can only know what is said (τὸ λεγόμενον), but not whether it is true (ἀληθὲς). Although a certain τεχνὴ is obviously implied, it is difficult to figure out what it is, or how it differs from divination itself, μαντικὴ.

Most translators of the *Epinomis* and the *Politicus* have tried to twist their way around this difficulty by inventing an equivalent for ἑρμηνευτικὴ; and although nobody really knows what it is, the word they chose usually tends to assimilate it to the art of μαντικὴ. Thus, Léon Robin translates μαντικὴ by "divination" and ἑρμηνευτικὴ by the "interpretation of oracles."[9] In similar fashion, Lamb translates ἑρμηνευτικὴ by "interpretation," specifying in a footnote that what is meant is the "interpretation of omens, heavenly signs, etc."[10] Nonetheless, how do we know that ἑρμηνευτικὴ was ever used to characterize the interpretation of oracles? Indeed, the art of interpreting oracles, as is well known, also fell within the competence of μαντικὴ (divination). Numerous scholarly studies since A. Bouché-Leclerq, W. Halliday, A.W. Persson, J. H. Oliver have informed us of the multifarious functions of divination and the art of the seer (μαντίς) in Greek religion.[11] And although it is not our task to study in detail the religious function of the μαντίς in the present context, it is striking to note that the word ἑρμηνευτικὴ remained conspicuously absent, until Plato at least, from earlier accounts of μαντική. Moreover, no textual evidence appears to suggest that ἑρμηνευτική ever had any meaningful significance in Greek religion.

Since Plato was the first author to use the word, both in the *Politicus* and at least "in spirit" in the *Epinomis*, one could perhaps attempt to understand the original meaning of ἑρμηνευτική from its immediate Platonic context. Given this hypothesis, one would have to recognize that while ἑρμηνευτική is different from μαντική, it is still closely related to it. However, if the two terms were synoymous, as some translators imply, there would be no sense in using two different concepts. Yet, if they were totally different, it would not make sense to place them in such close proximity, as is the case in the *Epinomis*. In order to differentiate the two, one has to start with the more familiar term, μαντική. Plato's view on divination is well documented.[12] He accepts the traditional notion that the art of μαντική is related to a certain μανία or frenzy. One might perhaps expect a rational philosopher like Plato to dismiss this frenzy as nothing but crazy folly, unsuited for the philosophical pursuit of truth. It is certainly on account of this suspicion that he passes such a severe judgment on the claims of poetical inspiration. Nevertheless, if Plato is suspicious of the poets, he seems to have more sympathy for the more specific art of divination as practiced by the seers. In a well-known passage of the *Phaedrus* he praises, for example, the priestess of Delphi for having bestowed so many benefits on Greece, this despite the fact that she was subject to manic frenzy (although this eulogy on the alleged "benefits" of the Delphi priestess might also be ironic, since the Delphic oracle fell in some disrepute after having erroneously predicted a Greek defeat in the Persian wars, having even recommended surrender before the Greek victory![13]). Madness, however, can be a genuine indication of divine presence. The priestess or seer (μαντίς) ceases to be merely human when she is befallen by divine revelation. Her utterances in such a state of ecstasy are so strange for human ears that they require interpretation. According to the *Timaeus* (71–72), it is the task of the προφητής to provide a rational account of the, at first, incomprehensible meaning of what is uttered in a state of trance by the seer. Possessed by a higher force, the seer cannot pronounce a sound judgment on the meaning of what she is herself experiencing (72a). The *prophetes* therefore functions as an instance of sobriety that sheds light on the proper meaning of what is being uttered by the seer. As L. Tarán rightly points out, the author of the *Epinomis* surely had this passage from the *Timaeus* "very much in mind" when he spoke of the art of divination and ἑρμηνευτική.[14] In this regard, I

would like to suggest, again as a hypothesis, that this distinction
between divination and the *prophetes* in the *Timaeus* be paralleled
with the distinction between divination and ἑρμηνευτικὴ in the
Epinomis. The "hermeneutical" skill would thus consist in explaining the meaning of what is uttered through the art of μαντική. The
hermeneut acts, therefore, so to speak, as an intermediary between
the seer and the rest of the community, in like manner to the seer
who is an intermediary between the gods and mortals. Furthermore,
the passage from the *Epinomis* states that while the interpreter can
ascertain what is said, he cannot determine if it is true. In other
words, the interpreter can translate the meaning of a revelation, but
cannot say if its prediction will turn out to be true. The task of
hermeneutics thus consists in explaining "what something means,"
and the truth of this meaning, being a separate matter altogether,
is to be determined by a higher science, such as philosophy. It is interesting to note that this function corresponds exactly to the definition that hermeneutics would later receive from Dannhauer in the
17th century. According to Dannhauer, there are two basic sciences:
logic and hermeneutics.[15] The role of logic is to determine the truth
claim of our knowledge by showing how it derives from higher rational principles. However, in order to understand what an author
actually means, another science is required. This science, the science of interpretation or hermeneutics, sorts out the signification
that the author attached to the signs he used, regardless of the validity of what was conceived on the level of thinking. Dannhauer thus
distinguishes two kinds of truth: hermeneutical truth, which strives
to discover what is meant; and logical truth, which seeks to find out
if what was meant is true or not. This distinction, which also corresponds to the medieval distinction of *sententia* and *sensus*, that gave
rise and legitimacy to the modern science of hermeneutics represents
a distant, yet direct echo to the *Epinomis*.

 Understood in this semantical fashion, hermeneutics, as we can
now call it, can be separated from the context of religious divination. Everywhere where there is some meaning to be sorted out, a
hermeneutical effort will be called for. In an often quoted passage
from the *Ion*, Plato contends that the poets are ἑρμηνῆς τῶν θεῶν
(534 e), intermediaries for the gods, and those who recite the works
of the poets (i.e., the rhapsodes) will in turn have to be called intermediaries of those intermediaries, that is interpreters of the interpreters themselves, ἑρμηνέων ἑρμηνῆς (535 a). Therefore, wherever
the meaning of an utterance needs to be determined and mediated,
a hermeneut is required.[16] Ultimately, as contemporary hermeneutics
has rediscovered, this hermeneutical effort is rooted in language it-

self. Indeed, one may recall that in the *Definitiones* of the platonician corpus, the term ἑρμηνευτικὴ generally signified "to mean something." This general definition of the spirit of ancient "hermeneutics" can help us understand the meanings associated with the terms ἑρμηνεία and ἑρμηνεύς. ἑρμήμνεία, an uttered sentence, is the transposition into the linguistic medium of "what is meant" at the level of thinking. Uttered language is nothing but uttered thinking, the translation, or "interpretation," of thought into language. In fact, this was so evident for the ancients that the Latins immediately translated ἑρμηνεία by the latin word *interpretatio*. However, ἑρμηνεία can also mean "style."[17] Aristotle was not the only one in antiquity to write a Περὶ ἑρμηνείας. Demetrius, himself a Peripatetic, also wrote one. However, his dealt exclusively with what one might call stylistics. Again, the Latins displayed remarkable flexibitlity in translating the title by *De elocutione* (in English: *On Style*).[18] The fact that the Greeks used the same word to characterize the linguistic utterance, the statement and style is itself revealing. For style is nothing but a way of meaning something, of expressing something, and of transmitting it to others. Language itself is a "style," a means of both putting things and of being properly understood by others. The unitary function of ἑρμηνεία consists in meaning something through language, of translating thought into expression, of making oneself understood. The Greeks also used the word ἑρμηνεία to describe what we would call translation, and the ἑρμηνεύς also functioned as a "translator," that we, in Greek fashion, continue to call an "interpreter."

One should not, however, put too much stress on the task of "translation" for the Greeks, since it was never a major preoccupation for them. They even lacked a specific word for translation, using more often than not the term ἑρμηνεία or the verb ἑρμηνεύειν, usually reserved for language and style (but they could also invoke very graphic notions such as μεταφράζω and ἀναλαμβάνω εἰς τὴν φωνήν). In fact, to say that the Greeks had little interest in translation is hardly an understatement. Not only did they not reflect on the theoretical problems of translation, they did not translate foreign works (with the exception of one) and did not bother to learn foreign languages.[19] The only relevant language for the Greeks was their own; and although we have no real way of knowing, they probably felt that "barbaric" languages (barbaric was not meant pejoratively: foreign idioms just sounded like a repetitious "bar-bar"[20]) served only to express their particular thinking and did not deserve any special attention. The Latins, on the other hand, displayed great interest in the problem of translation, and indeed, they had little choice since most of their culture derived from Greek translations. It was they who coined the word *translatio*, which literally means: "to carry over on the other side" (which was also to be understood geographically: to carry a body of culture across the Adriatic[21]). The Greeks themselves had developped an homogeneous culture and consequently did not burden themselves with translations. As a matter of fact, they seemed much more interested in the problems raised by the translation of *proper names* into Greek. In this regard, they usually solved the problem by remoulding foreign names into Greek-sounding words. For example, Nabu-Kudurri-Ussur became Nabouchodonossor, and Khshaiarsha, Xerxes.[22]

According to the Greek understanding of language, the linguistic element does not appear to enjoy any respectable autonomy of its own. It is but a means of expressing something, a thought process that lies "behind" the graphic or phonetic expression itself. The unitary task of hermeneutics in antiquity seems to have consisted in going back from what was said to what was meant, to the *vouloir-dire* beneath language. This understanding of hermeneutics tacitly assumes that language is invested with a meaning that precedes or goes beyond the uttered word itself. There is something like a transcendence or excess of meaning in regard to what is uttered. An utterance can even carry a different meaning than the one it appears to have (as exemplified by irony, and, say, radicalized in the practice of allegory). However, if the Greeks showed no interest in translation, they still seemed to have been startled by this bizarre, yet undeniable fact of language that words can mean something different from what they immediately express. This is genuinely puzzling. If one considers that words are the very expression of thinking, how is it possible to use words in a manner that conveys a meaning other than the one which is immediately uttered? This discrepancy might appear trite to us, accustomed as we are at looking up the different meanings of the words we use in dictionaries. But dictionaries appeared very late in the history of civilization and were unknown to classical Greek philosophers. In fact, dictionaries are based on the abstract view of language that words have in themselves different "levels" of meaning, levels which happen to find application in the varied, but somewhat "extrinsic" contexts of linguistic use. It is much more natural, or so it was for the Greeks, to suppose that each word has a specific meaning and serves as an instrument or accessory to make something present by using its sign. Any meaningful word can only have but one specific meaning, and, in spite of dictionaries, this remains a contrafactual presupposition of the everyday speaker: every word has but one meaning. To this end, Plato teaches in the

Phaedrus that one should find new words to alleviate the ambiguities of polysemy and to eradicate synonymous words that redundantly refer to the same thing.

But how did the Greeks become aware of this chasm between the word and what it really means? In the light of new research in the field of classical philology, it seems appropriate to trace back this insight to the propagation of writing that occurred around the end of the 8th century. In this regard, I am alluding mostly to the pioneer work of the Yale classicist Eric Havelock on the "literate revolution."[23] Before the invention of the written alphabet, and long after its appearance, the survival of Greek culture depended solely on oral transmission. The entire body of knowledge, culture and statutes necessary in order to maintain the coherence of the Greek community was preserved in an oral mode, through memorization, and more specifically through the memorization of the poetic verses that made up the epic tradition, and that were repeatedly recited and sung at the festivals and public ceremonies which were a constitutive part of the Greek community. The invention of writing made memorization and its dependence on the poetic medium less important and, ultimately, dispensable. From that point on, one no longer had to rely exclusively on the immediacy of oral transmission. As Havelock has demonstrated, the oral medium is a more holistic medium of communication. It alludes to a whole yet undifferentiated sphere of meaning when it speaks. The tone of a voice in a conversation for instance can induce a whole atmosphere of sense and evocation that is specific to the oral medium. Written language, on the contrary, is more linear, more easily retraced. For example, one says A, because of B, that precedes it, and that derives from C, etc. One can thus readily understand how the spread of writing made the appearence of linear, rational thinking possible. To think rationally is to be able to retrace the ground of something and to understand its presuppositions, which are constructed in such a manner that they can be traced back by any mind that can think properly, *i.e.,* that can read and follow a linear argument.

In spite of the irreversible nature of the invention of writing, Greek philosophers retained for a long period of time a nostalgia for the oral medium. Early philosophers such as Xenophanes, Parmenides and Heraclitus wrote in verse, in hexameters. Evidently, such works were meant to be recited and not to be read (as we know, the Greeks always read aloud, such was their fascination for the oral medium). In addition, one might also recall the fact that one of the most influential philosophers of antiquity, Socrates, did not even write a single word. Plato, his pupil, tried to remain faithful to the spirit of his oral teaching by placing his ideas in dialogue or conversational form.

Given that in a pre-literate context it was clearly impossible to distinguish a word from its meaning, there was thus no room (if one allows the anachronism) for hermeneutics or any hermeneutic reflection on the estrangement of meaning. There is an immediacy to oral transmission; the spoken word immediatedly means what it says; the context is immediately present at hand to the listener or to the hearer, and the tone of the voice already gives an indication on how the "utterance" is to be understood. Moreover, should misunderstanding occur, the speaker would always be present to elucidate what is said by evoking a wide range of what we would call "synonyms" to re-establish the immediate flow of understanding and shared meaning. In fact, one may argue that language (i.e., a distinct body of signs with transcendent meanings) does not really exist in a a purely oral context. In other words, given that in a purely oral context the linguistic medium is never separated from the person using it, there is no such thing as a language that would exist independently from the speaker and the context of the utterance.[24]

Furthermore, when written language finally began to exist, it manifested itself as just that, "written orality," as it were. In this regard, when Plato reflects on literary discourse in the *Phaedrus*, he underscores that the best written discourse can only have a function of "rememoration" (276 d, 278 a). The written word is only there to help us recall the immediacy and fullness of meaning that belongs to orality, which in turn, ultimately echoes discourses written in the soul itself. Words are nothing but "mnemotechnic" devices to help us recreate a density of meaning, a density which remains foreign to the written medium as such. For Plato, thinking is nothing but "the dialogue of the soul with itself"[25]—that is, in essence, an oral means of self-communication which is so immediate and pure as to be thought almost "wordless." In like manner Aristotle states in his *De interpretatione* that written signs are merely symbols for oral utterances.[26] Thus, we see that both Plato and Aristotle refer the written medium back to the spoken word, which is itself a symbol for the "word" of the soul, the "inner Word," as the Stoics and Augustine will aptly call it.[27]

Nonetheless, there is a small, yet important difference between Plato and Aristotle in their explanation of the relationship between the written word, the spoken word and the soul. Aristotle seems to assume that nothing is really lost in this chain of transmission from the soul to speech and from speech to writing. The written sign functions as a "mark" that conveniently stands for the voice and the "affections of the soul."[28] This suggests that such signs and affections are, in principle, the same for everybody. Plato, however, seems to put more stress on the gap between the written and the spoken word. Just as for Aristotle, the written is a means to indicate or rememorate the spoken word of the soul, but there is no assurance that the written medium will be understood properly.

The "peril" of the written is that it is fixed and is therefore subject to a double alienation. It can first be alienated from the intention of the speaker and even outlive him, thus making it impossible for the speaker, the immediate utterer of the word, to specify what he or she meant. It can also become alienated from its meaning and context and receive the most superficial and ludicrous interpretations. Only the wise will be able to apprehend the truth of the statement, by relating the words back to the spirit that animates them.[29]

The full significance of the word, or its "truth," is not something that merely lies "beyond" the word, as if the word was simply an exterior manifestation of an intellectual meaning that is beyond language. Indeed from the perspective of contemporary hermeneutics, this full sense of the word is what is already at work in language itself. This is true provided we are attentive to it in a hermeneutical way, i.e., understanding the spoken word as an answer to a question, a quest, or a query. According to hermeneutics, the essential logic of language is not to be found in a propositional logic that would take predicative judgments for being self-sufficient semantic entities. For hermeneutics, there is no such thing as a self-sufficient judgment nor a "pure proposition" that would exhaust all there is to say about what is being said. Propositional logic, which has dominated our philosophical tradition ever since Aristotle, proposes that all knowledge can be expressed in predicative statements (i.e., S is P). Furthermore, this logical requirement happens to "copy" (or dictate) the substance-accident relation in the things themselves, an ontological structure which is in itself a logical construction of Aristotle's "hermeneutics." However, according to Gadamer's more Platonically motivated hermeneutics, this "construction of logic on the proposition" was "one of the most fatal decisions of Western culture."[30] For hermeneutics, for Gadamer, and for Plato, there is no such thing as a pure statement, i. e., an utterance which one could fully understand without taking into account its motivation, its intent, its addressee, its context, in a word, its soul. The privilege of the proposition in the Western logical-metaphysical tradition is, to be sure, something all too understandable. If all that is said can be put into propositional form, then all knowledge can be verified, reiterated, repeated, and controlled. This presupposes an understanding of truth as something that we can dispose of, that we can master, verify, and control. And while control and verification are useful in certain areas of our knowledge, do they really render justice to the life of language, to the dependence of language on all that is not and cannot be said? Do we understand language only to the extent that we can master and dominate it? For hermeneutics, we only understand to the extent that we are willing to engage in the dialogue opened by what is said and venture into all that isn't said, but remains essential to understanding. Understanding is less a domination of a state of affairs than a participation in shared meaning.

This is why Gadamer retreats back from Aristotle's propositional logic to the spirit[31] of Plato's dialogical hermeneutics. One can only understand language, both the written and the spoken, if one goes back to the soul of what is said. Language is never self-sufficient. In order to understand an utterance, we must always ask ourselves: To what question or to what provocation was it the answer? Was the statement ironic? To whom was it addressed? Without taking into account this motivational context, which makes the understanding of the written more perilous than that of the spoken word, there is no way one can hope to understand. This is the heart of both Plato's dialectic and of contemporary hermeneutics. As we saw earlier, this inner dimension of the spoken discourse is not to be thought of as something beyond the utterance. It lies within it or even "around" it, so to speak, circumscribing the meaning which wishes to be grasped in language. The Greeks had a nice word to express what is meant here: ὑπόνοια, which was regularly used by authors such as Plato and Xenophon. The word literally means: what is thought under, the thought at the root of what is said. It was first used at Plato's time to characterize the "hidden meanings"[32] in the work of Homer and later as a technical concept by the Stoics who popularized it in order to present their allegoric interpretations. In fact, ὑπόνοια was the forerunner of the word ἀλληγορία which appeared much later, not before the first century A.D., so that the first Stoics were not acquainted with it.[33] It is somewhat misleading to translate ὑπόνοια by "hidden meaning," even if this is perhaps accurate for the allegorical interpretations the Stoics were so found of. For what is "thought underneath" is not necessarily "hidden," it is only that which is presupposed, that which precedes the utterance and makes it understandable. In addition, this interpretation of the word ὑπόνοια as the "thought underneath" also helps us comprehend the original meaning of "allegorical" interpretation as it was practiced by the Greeks. As J. Tate convincingly demonstrates in an

article that goes back to 1934,[34] the first motivation of allegory was
not defensive or apologetical. Its purpose was not to defend Homer
and Hesiod against accusations of immorality but to expound, in-
trinsically, what the first poets really *meant*. The motivation of allegory, as it was first practiced, before and during the time of Plato,
was therefore positive and strictly exegetical. What did the poets
actually mean when they said what they said? The preoccupation
of the first allegorists was not with the moral impunity of the poets
but with the inner truth of their sometimes less than transparent
doctrines.[35] It is this notion of inner truth and that the truth of the
statement lies behind or "under" what is said, as suggested by the
word ὑπόνοια, which is the soul of hermeneutics.

   This notion of an "inner word" might appear naive, even bizarre, and it is indeed meant here as somewhat of a provocation. To
be sure, no physician or linguist has ever found anything like an
"inner word" under their scalpel. Contemporary philosophy has no
use and no patience whatsoever for anything resembling a world of
"ideas" or "representations" that would precede the linguistic medium. It is often argued that the stress on the precedence of "representations" has functioned as a smoke-screen that prevented
philosophers from Plato to Frege from actually seeing the phenomenon of language as it has come to impose itself so massively on the
philosophy of the last century. In short, a strong case can be made
against the mere notion of an "inner word" or its actuality.

   Nevertheless, I would still like to argue that the notion of an
"inner word" is what hermeneutics justifiably aims at when it seeks
to understand. This inner word is not so much "beyond" language,
in a sort of "stratospheric representational sphere," it is rather "in"
language itself, in what is said or conveyed "with" language.
The Greeks knew all too well that the written medium is not self-
sufficient and that it has to be supplemented by an understanding
of what lies before, better still, beneath or in language itself. In this
regard, when the Stoic philosophers expounded this notion of an inner "logos," they recognized in it precisely what distinguishes the
human species. Unlike other animals such as crows and parrots who
are also quite able to utter meaningful sounds, what characterizes
the human species is the fact that their speech is preceded by something like an inner reflection, an interior capacity of reasoning
(λόγος) that is not to be found in other animals.[36] Whereas animals
are bound by the sounds they utter, the human species is able to
take a distance from what has been uttered, to reflect on its meaning, to put it in context and, in short, it is able to think when it
speaks.

Nevertheless, this does not mean that thinking could occur in a wordless fashion in some kind of nonlinguistic medium, as Greek philosophers such as Plato and the Stoics would seem to suggest. In this regard, our attention should not be placed so much upon the "wordless" nature of thinking (which is an impossibility for human beings anyway), but on the insufficiency and indigence of the "outside" word, of the word that alone is read and heard if one fails to take into account the context, the "soul," the motivation and the overall thrust of what is being said. This is what one can call the "dialogical" nature of language, the fact that one can only understand what is said if one also understands to what question it is an answer, the motivation and situation from which it springs. In short, one can only understand human language, that is language in its irreducible humanity, if one also hears through the outside word the inner word which is present.

What the hermeneutical distinction between the inner and outside word means is that there is, and always is, a tension between what we happen to say and all that wants to be said and heard. Language can never be reduced to what is uttered in propositional statements. There are always presuppositions, motivations, and conditions that remain unsaid, but which nevertheless have to be heard if we wish to understand the outside word properly. To understand language hermeneutically is to trace back what is said to what wishes to be said. However, this inner word is not something that "pre-"exists in some way "before" language (e.g., in a representational realm, or in the "purity" of the human heart) nor is it something (some "thing") or some discrete sphere of meaning one could astutely distinguish from that which is said. Rather, it is the soul or "spirit" which never ceases to nourish every human utterance and constitutes its human depth. It is, to be sure, not something that one could reach once and for all, but an endless source of questioning and dialogue.

The focus on language that has dominated philosophy in recent decades was less a focus on language than it has been a focus on its alleged propositional nature. It could very well be that propositions and statements are more abstract entities than is usually believed. And despite the fact that one may believe statements and propositions to be self-sufficient entities ("S is P, x is a function of y, and that's that"), perhaps, it is never just "that." Indeed, there is more to say than one can encounter in a single proposition, or even in the explanations it can receive. The proposition is always embedded in a situation. It emerges from a context, answering a question, a query, or a provocation. In short, language cannot be understood without taking into account what language means, what carries it, and what makes it human (i.e., the inner word). The terms we stammer out are just that, eloquent stammering. The words we use are the ones that happen to come to our lips, or from our fingers when we write. We are not the authors of these words. They come to us. This is why no psychological sphere whatsoever, no neatly circumscribed *"mens auctoris,"*[37] is implied by the idea of the inner word as being the constant goal of the hermeneutical quest. Moreover, others can find better, or less indigent words for what we have to say. It is often in dialogue with others, or with ourselves (i.e., the self-dialogue Plato called "thinking"), that we find expressions for all there is to say, for the toil of the inner word that hopes to be heard behind any spoken word.

The task of hermeneutics, from Plato to our times, is to preserve this true meaning of the word, the written or spoken word, by relating it back to its intent, original meaning, scope, and context. Insofar as Plato was attuned to this task, which is central to his dialogical, Socratic endeavor, he can rightly stand as the father of hermeneutics as we know it. It is perhaps no coincidence that he was probably the first to use the notion of ἑρμηνευτική. If it is true, as Whitehead wrote, that the "safest characterization of the European philosophical tradition is that it consists of footnotes to Plato,"[38] then perhaps another footnote should be added: the development of hermeneutics—concerned as it is with the living and tragic discrepancy between the outside and the inner word—is also a footnote to Plato's insight into the logos.

Chapter 3

Husserl's Silent Contribution
to Hermeneutics

If Husserl contributed to hermeneutics, it was certainly in spite of his best intentions. Indeed, Husserl had a twofold "allergy" to the thinking which one might qualify as "hermeneutics." First, as his confrontation with Dilthey in the *Logos* essay (1911) testifies, he rejected its historicist bent, a disdain which is also confirmed by his more secret and hence bitter debate with Heidegger's hermeneutics. Furthermore, Husserl did not ascribe such a fundamental importance to the idea of interpretation. In simple terms, what interested Husserl was not the interpretation of phenomena, but the phenomena themselves. However, in a landmark study,[1] Paul Ricoeur calls attention to Husserl's employment of terms such as *Deutung* and *Auslegung* (interpretation), which would demonstrate that Husserl's hermeneutic allergy was perhaps not complete. Yet, for Husserl, if it is necessary to interpret certain phenomena and to take into account the interpretative variations (*Abschattungen*) of things, it is precisely so that one may better arrive at their essence. In this regard, it should be noted that the intuition of essences does not have a "magical" meaning for Husserl. Across intentional interpretations, one always finishes by seeing what is essential to the phenomenon. Returning to the "things themselves" means that it is necessary to know how to detach oneself from the deforming hold of theories and unilateral interpretations of phenomena in order to come to the essential or that which maintains itself across interpretations. One

35

sees, therefore, the utility of multiplying the number of "interpretations" so as to make sure that the essential has been discerned.

It is somewhat ironic to note that a philosopher who sought to liberate philosophy from interpretations, theories and books gave birth to a "continental" philosophy which is characterized by such a historical and bookish orientation. As Gadamer aptly notes: "Every phenomenologist had his own opinion about what phenomenology was. Only one thing was certain: that one could not learn the phenomenological approach from books."[2] It is well known that Husserl himself published rather little. By his own admission, he was less interested in publishing than philosophical research. Indeed, he only published one of the three volumes of his *Ideen*, a work that originally appeared in the form of an article in the first volume of his *Annals for Philosophy and Phenomenological Research*. And this volume proposed only "some" ideas concerning "a" (*Ideen zu einer. . .*) pure phenomenology and a philosophical phenomenology. Nothing indicates therefore that for Husserl it was a definitive foundation or the sole which was possible. Afterward, Husserl hardly published at all. Moreover, he believed that his students, instructed by the almost geometric evidence of phenomenology, were as capable of accomplishing the technical work of writing and publication as he was. This explains, for example, why it took so much time for him to become aware of the differences which separated his work from Heidegger's. Persuaded that Heidegger had been won over to the cause of phenomenology, he did not at first bother to become acquainted with his writings; he even published *Being and Time* in his own *Annals* without having read a single line.[3]

Husserl's students also inherited his Platonic reserve with regard to publication. As Gadamer notes, Husserl's literary production as well as that of the first generation of phenomenologists remained rather modest; eleven volumes of the *Jahrbuch* which appeared over two decades and almost nothing in other sorts of publications.[4] It is well known that it was only following administrative pressure that Heidegger resolved to publish his only real book, which was itself only programmatic: *Being and Time* (which also appeared in a volume of the *Jahrbuch*). With regard to Gadamer, it was his students who pushed him, at 60 years of age, to publish *Truth and Method* (1960), his first book since his university dissertation of 1929.

Given that the essential was to think from the standpoint of the things themselves, Husserl demonstrated a great amount of liberality in leaving to his students, undoubtedly at their instigation, the care for the publishing of several of his courses. Martin Heidegger edited the *Lessons on the Intimate Consciousness of Time*

and Ludwig Landgrebe assembled a collection of several courses and
manuscripts which served as the basis for the editing of *Formal and
Trancendental Logic* (which appeared in the *Jahrbuch* in 1929).[5]
Some years later, Langrebe, following the authorization (*Vollmacht*)
of Husserl, relied as much on courses and manuscripts as his con-
versations with his mentor when he assumed the entire responsibility for the editing of *Experience and Judgement* (1939).[6] In
addition, Husserl entrusted to his young student Eugen Fink the
task of editing a "sixth" Cartesian meditation which would be added
to the five conferences that he had delivered in Paris. Fink's ("and"
Husserl's) Sixth meditation was only published in 1988 in the
Husserliana collection.[7]

Husserl's last publications, the *Cartesian Meditations* and the
Krisis were both born out of lectures; and even if it was necessary
to wait for the posthumous edition in the *Husserliana* to obtain integral texts, Husserl, for once, appears to have devoted special attention to their publication. Confronted with the success of *Sein und
Zeit*, Husserl was jarred into realizing the effectiveness of the written word in philosophy. Wishing to reverse the "harmful" influence
that, according to him, Heidegger's work had wrought, Husserl
hoped that new writings from him would be able to confer a new
voice and a new weight to what he viewed to be authentically phenomenological thought.[8] The return to writing became necessary in
order to reiterate the rigor of returning to the things themselves.
However, the political tragedy of Germany shattered the projects and
hopes of Husserl. Indeed, it is not in Germany but in Belgrade that
the *Krisis* appeared in 1936; and for many decades the voice of
Husserl remained sorrowfully inaudible in phenomenology.

Nevertheless, it still remains possible to discern the properly
hermeneutic meaning of the call to return to the things themselves,
beyond writing, formulas and theories: *von den blossen Worten (. . .)
zu den Sachen selbst*—"from simple words (. . .) to the things themselves."[9] It has again become current in philosophy, as it already was
during Husserl's time, to almost exclusively discuss philosophical
matters in terms of theories, arguments or propositions which one
attempts to derive from propositions that one claims to be yet more
fundamental. Of course, no philosophy escapes the cycle of argumentation, theorization, and historical contextualization. However, beyond the deluge of propositions, there is always a meaning to
understand and things that it is necessary to see if one wishes to speak
about them. The most hermeneutic students of Husserl, Heidegger
and Gadamer, naturally conceived the phenomenon of understanding according to the model that Husserl had proposed to them. To

understand is to return from the spoken word to the meaning that
animates it. In other words, understanding involves discerning the
question that motivates the exterior word. Heidegger's entire polemic
against the jargon of the "one" (*das Man*) is, in fact, only a
hermeneutic application of the phenomenological injunction of the return to the things themselves. Indeed, the "conventional widsom" of
the "one" discharges us of a direct vision of things, a vision that we
are however able to acquire by ourselves, if it is true that we are, in
principle, "*Da-sein*," beings susceptible of being "there," that is to say,
directly by the things when the fundamental decisions concerning our
existence fall. The call to the authenticity which constitutes our *Dasein*
is that of a return to things, of a direct confrontation with oneself.

The entire critique of propositional discourse in *Sein und Zeit*
presents itself under the imperative of a hermeneutic return to the
anti-predicative order which gives body to the real discourse.[10] What
are the things that wish to make themselves heard behind or "in"
discourse? Gadamer is inspired at the same time by Husserl and
Heidegger when he seeks to understand language starting from dialogue and following the guideline of a "logic" of question and answer.
One only understands the discourse (of others or of a text) if one
knows the question to which it seeks to be an answer. Yet, if one
wishes to enter into the horizon of the question (and the notion of
horizon, which is so important for hermeneutics, comes directly from
Husserl), there is no choice but to return to the things themselves
which are at play in discourse. Thus, Paul Ricoeur had perfect reason to perceive in the thesis of the "secondary" character of the linguistic order "the most important phenomenological presupposition
of hermeneutics."[11] Propositional discourse never says everything
that is essential for its penetration. In order to seize its meaning, it
is necessary to return to the things themselves and to introduce oneself into the dialogue from which the statement proceeds. Indeed,
there is always a gap between the thing which is seen and the language that expresses it, between the singular thing and the plurality of words that attempt to stutter it out. As we have seen in the
last section, this abyss which exists between the exterior discourse
and the interiority that one attempts to understand is eminently
hermeneutical. If phenomenology remains an urgency for philosophy, it is because it is often convenient to remain solely at the level
of theory and discourse without concerning oneself with the things
themselves. In the autonomous system of theories that which is important is often the internal coherence of formulas rather than the
adequacy of the discourse itself. For phenomenology, truth remains
a matter of adequation. It is thus essential to fight against what

Heidegger, in his 1924 course on the *Sophist*,[12] superbly named "the forfeiture in the *logoi*," the propensity of *Dasein* to abandon itself to the assurance of received opinions.

The "return" to the things itself also obeys the logic of question and answer. It does not fall from the sky. It has not always been well-noted, but the *zurück zu den Sachen selbst*, the "re-turn" to the things turns its back (literally: the *Rücken*) to something. The return presupposes a detour or, in other words, a diversion from the things in favor of the reign of discourse. On this point, the solidarity of Husserl and Heidegger is complete, even if their point of departure appears a little different. When Husserl proclaims his return to the things themselves, he wants above all else to turn his back on the falsely autonomous kingdom of scientific "theorization." From the *Logical Investigations* to the *Krisis*, this critique of abstraction in the name of the evidence of the things themselves, characterizes all of Husserl's work. Stemming from a science as apodictic as geometry, where the vision of essences remains "essential," he never understood why his philosophical colleagues relied on, with as much steadfastness as blindness, preliminary theories, either the theories themselves, of which philosophy claimed to be the "meta-theory," or the "classics" in the practice of the history of philosophical problems. Against epistemology, but also against the history of philosophy posed as an end in itself, Husserl hammered the necessity of a debate which was directed toward the issues themselves. One is wrong therefore to criticize the lack of philosophical or historical erudition of a thinker like Husserl. Naïvely or courageously, Husserl thought that the essential was not there. To speak about the things themselves is what really counts. This demands, however, a total conversion of philosophical outlook, a putting into parentheses of one's "natural" attitude, or, simply put, a phenomenological "reduction." We will return later to this notion.

Heidegger imprinted a more existential meaning on the order to return to the things themselves. His *"zurück zu den Sachen selbst"* does not limit itself to the phenomenon of "abstract theory" which had so irritated a thinker like Husserl. With Heidegger, the return to the things is first of all directed by the phenomenon of "inauthenticity" or of chattering. A phenomenon which concerns, according to Heidegger, an essential absence of *Dasein* from itself. To be a *Dasein*, as we have already noted, is precisely to be capable of being "there," that is to say, capable of opening one's eyes and of seeing for oneself. Yet, most often, Heidegger argues, *Dasein* chooses rather not to see for itself and to leave the matter of truth to the omnipotent authority of chattering (*Gerede*). The Heideggerian

return to the things themselves challenges this hegemony of discourses which have no other credit than of having been repeated or
commonly accepted (herein lies, by the way, one of the limits of the
ethics of discussion). All the problematic of the hermeneutic circle remains dominated by this phenomenological urgence, even if one has
often thought that Heidegger distanced himself from the phenomenology of his master by imparting a hermeneutic turn upon it. For
Heidegger, "the constant and ultimate task of interpretation (. . .) remains not to let oneself pre-give the fore-acquisition, the fore-sight
and the preconception by "intuitions" or popular concepts (*Volks-
begriffe*), but, in elaborating them, to always assure its scientific theme
starting from the things themselves."[13] The Heideggerian return to
the things themselves turns its back therefore to the inauthenticity
which befalls *Dasein* when it cedes (*Verfallen*) to the facility of common opinions and evidences of the "one" instead of opening one's eyes
and assuming for itself the fundamental decisions which concern its
existential orientation. First conceived with Husserl as a response to
the primacy of poorly assured theories, the return to the things themselves became with Heidegger a response to the inauthenticity of
Dasein. But from one phenomenology to the other, the continuity is
evident since the demand for authenticity was itself already inscribed
in Husserl's call for a return to the things themselves, which presupposed that abstract theories overlooked or omitted the essential.[14]

The cardinal injunction of phenomenology rests upon this requirement of vision, beyond signs and writing. The mastery of a language or of a jargon never signifies that the thing itself has been
mastered. Intelligence, in all things, is mesured by what there is
behind speech, by what has been seen behind the words which are
offered up. This is what fascinated Heidegger in his first appropriation of phenomenology.[15] But Husserl had been the first to recognize
in this the "principle of all principles" in his *Ideen*: "all originally-
given intuition functions as an original source of knowledge. . . ."
However, one does not always cite the five little words which precede the principle of principles in the *Ideen* in the beginning of
§ 24: "But enough of these far-fetched theories! *Doch genug der
verkehrten Theorien.*"[16] The *doch* at the very beginning of a chapter
is a true parataxis. Yet, its audacity founds all phenomenology. The
remarkable thing about the principle of principles, is that it explains
nothing. Nothing flows logically from this principle. It does not imply corollaries, nor scholiae. If it explains nothing, it justifies everything. All that is brought to speech must be capable of being brought
back to an intuition. The essential is to see what one is speaking of.

It is this hermeneutic exigence of probity which, according to
Husserl, commands the exercise of philosophical thought understood

as the first science. Most simply put, philosophy must start from the things as they present themselves intuitively. Thus, the urgent need to abandon theories which run on without having been founded directly in a phenomenality which allows itself to be seen and thus shared. It no longer suffices for a phenomenologist to link together arguments or formulas. At each step of its "research" (and the term *Forschung* implies here its full sense, that of a penetrating exploration of phenomena), phenomenology must assure itself of a direct legitimation on the level of the things themselves. In a call which would become more revolutionary than he would have dared himself imagine, since it finished by coming back to haunt certain admissions of his phenomenology, Husserl invited rigorous philosophical thought to avoid all metaphysical constructions in order to stick to that which the intuition "gives." To the extent that it looked to rid itself of that which does not give itself directly through intuition, phenomenology prepared the overcoming of metaphysics undertaken by more recent hermeneutics.[17]

However, the order to return to the things themselves often finds itself charged with naïveté and triviality. Indeed, what theory does not claim to speak in terms of phenomena? Yet, Husserl's order or injunction is coupled with a critique, or, more precisely, a suspension of the naïveté which characterizes the natural attitude. Husserl invites us to practice a phenomenological reduction which consists of remitting oneself of the evidence of the "transcendent" world. The term "reduction" comprises an essential ambiguity. First of all, it appears to possess a somewhat positivist significance. Thus, one sometimes speaks of a "reductionary" interpretation when it simplifies the real or when it reduces the real to just one of its aspects: "this reduces itself to that." Yet, Husserl's "reduction" implies rather a "re-direction" of regard, following the etymology of *re-ductio*, that one would be able to render as a "re-duction." For Husserl, the essential accomplishment of reduction resides in a conversion of vision. Again, it concerns detaching one's regard from the hold of worldly evidences which circulate around us in order that one may re-conduct (*re-ductio*) it to the primary evidence, that is, according to Husserl, to the world as it presents itself. Yet, this world, as is well-known and one recognizes here one of the great acquisitions of phenomenology, is first of all given as an intentional phenomenon, so much so that the phenomenological *re-ductio* will call for a *Forschung* or exploration of intentionality.

Two hermeneutic moments merit being underlined in this idea of a *re-ductio*. First of all, one must emphasize the idea that the access to the essential things proceeds from a re-conduction of our view or regard. Hermeneutic intelligence must start from the given signs, but it must also know how to free itself from them in order to direct itself toward the intention which animates that which is said. To understand is to perform a "reduction" of regard, to know how to take a distance from the stories that are told, in order to gain access to the meaning of what strives to be understood. However, the reduction also discovers the infinity of the hermeneutic task. If the meaning toward which hermeneutic intelligence directs itself stems from an intentionality, or from an "intention of meaning," it is this intention that one must penetrate if one wants to practice phenomenology. However, one measures the difficulty of the enterprise. It concerns intending at an intention or of intentionally engaging oneself in intentionality. Certainly, the intentionality appears to constitute an ultimate given for phenomenology (in its scholarly versions at least), but this fundamental "thing"—i.e., more fundamental than all the givens that present themselves (the world, the things, etc.), is beset by a centrifugal motion. Intentionality is by definition a movement beyond its own starting point, toward intended meaning. It is precisely here that the union of phenomenology and hermeneutics is consummated. The return to the thing itself, which is the intentionality, finds itself in front of a given which is itself intention of meaning. That which one must "see" here has in itself the character of a vision or an intention. It is necessary to see the vision itself, to practice a type of *noesis noeseos* (an analogy which attests, of course, to the lexicon of the *noesis* with Husserl himself). However, one would be wrong to assimilate this vision of vision to a pure "egology," even if Husserl was at times re-duced to it, because the intent of meaning in fact aims at that which is beyond the *ego*. In apparently technical terms, but ones that we hope will be nonetheless intelligible: The *noese* of the *ego* in the intentionality is from the outset, as an intention, an opening to the other; it is not aimed at oneself. There is of course a "correlation" between the aiming intention and that which is aimed at, but the *noema* does not reduce itself to the *noesis*. There is always tension between that which the consciousness aims at and the meaning aimed at itself, which goes beyond egological consciousness. This tension between the aspired meaning and the meaning itself merits being called hermeneutical.

The Husserlian reduction, whatever precise form it might happen to take in given contexts (and the *Husserliana* continue to reveal to us new ones),[18] institutes itself each time as a *reductio* with regard to the constitution of meaning, the *Sinnkonstitution*. Like that of reduction, the term "constitution" has often lent itself to misunderstanding. Indeed, one often believed that the transcendental subject was somewhat the creator of meaning.[19] However, such a transcendental genealogy is foreign to phenomenology, although Husserl's terminology sometimes does remind one of idealism. The phenomenological idea of "constitution" only wishes to underline the fact that the "subject" of the intention always co-constitutes meaning since it is always "there" when meaning occurs, as Heidegger underscored through his concept of *"Da-sein."*

One of the great hermeneutic merits of Husserl is to never have reduced meaning to the intentional aim of the subject. The subject only co-constitutes meaning, it is born with it (following Péguy's allusion to the etymology of "con-naître," i.e., to be born with): the ego remains in constant dialogue with a meaning that it never fully masters. Thus, one notes the importance for Husserl's phenomenology of an exploration of the "layers" of intentionality or of the different steps in the constitution of meaning which escape the immediate and natural consciousness. Gadamer has retained such a preoccupation: "Constitution is nothing but the movement of reconstruction that follows the accomplished reduction. (. . .) The process of building up out of the accomplishments of subjectivity is not the real engendering of anything, but rather the way of understanding everything that is to have meaning."[20] For Husserl, the problem of constitution pertains only to the reconstitution of the horizon of meaning which overcomes intentional consciousness.

By orienting phenomenology toward the phenomenon of the constitution (or giving) of meaning, Husserl opened the path to hermeneutics, but also, more surreptitiously, to a calling into question by hermeneutics of certain non-phenomenological presuppositions of phenomenology.[21] However, this deconstruction was also rendered possible by Husserl himself. Indeed, he had been the first to instruct his students to distrust theories who had no intuitive basis in the things themselves. Thus, by inviting them to permanently criticize all nonphenomenological constructions, he oriented them more toward the task of a destruction of metaphysics than towards a prolonging of the avenues opened up by his own research.

The hermeneutic turn of phenomenology (i.e., Heidegger, Gadamer) procedes itself from tensions and openings which already characterize Husserl's project. These tensions have to do with the conception of the *ego* and the transcendental or foundational conception of philosophy. If the *ego* which interests phenomenology is from the start intentional, *i.e.,* an *ego* dispersed throughout horizons of meaning which exceed it, one can ask oneself if the *ego* can still be maintained as the starting point. Heidegger came to the conclusion that the *ego* was so little present to itself that it was first and foremost "being-in-the-world." In his 1927 course of the "Fundamental problems of phenomenology," he expressly presented his conception of the being-in-the-world as a radicalization of Husserl's notion of intentionality (which he did not do in *Being and Time*).[22] However, the understanding of intentionality starting from the horizon of the world, which Husserl also helped to prepare, goes hand in hand with an "ethical" metamorphosis of this *ego*. Falling "into" the world, the subject is not in the beginning with himself, rather has to become it. From the start, the presence to oneself of the *ego*, which is now "*Dasein*," becomes to a certain extent a practical imperative for Heidegger. Swallowed up in intentionalities which disperse it to the four corners of the world, the *ego* lacks itself. Thus, Heidegger breaks the theoretical conception of the *ego* which continued to govern the phenomenology of his mentor. The *ego* is first and foremost a being of care or anxiety of which the first concern must be that of its authentic being-in-the-world. This rehabilitation of the *ego* as a being of care, as a practical project, is not foreign to the renaissance of practical philosophy which came out of the heart of the phenomenological movement, among such authors as H. Arendt, L. Strauss, J.-P. Sartre, J. Patocka, E. Levinas, H. Jonas, G. Krüger, H.-G. Gadamer, and H. Marcuse. The *ego* which becomes conscious of itself as an existential project, as a care of itself also knows itself as projected into horizons of meaning which precede it. The hermeneutic idea of *Dasein* as a thrown project echoes Husserl's conception of the world of life (*Lebenswelt*) as the source of all constitution of meaning. Thus, Husserl had recognized that the *ego* was not the source of all its projects of comprehension, already reconducting the horizons of the *ego* to the anonymity—and more and more, to the "intersubjectivity"—of a *Lebenswelt*. For a long time one had thought that the theme of *Lebenswelt* and intersubjectivity only appeared late in Husserl's preoccupations and that they perhaps revealed Heidegger's influence. Indeed, in his published works, intersubjectivity only appeared in the *Cartesian Meditations* and *Lebenswelt* in the *Krisis*. However, such an interpretation overestimates the importance of publications for Husserl. The posthumous publication of the *Husserliana* demonstrates that the theme of intersubjectivity appeared much earlier (cf. notably volumes XIII–XIV) than was believed. The above is also true for the concept of *Lebenswelt*, which the young Heidegger employed profusely, for instance, in a 1919 course without taking the time to explain whether it was a term original to him.[23] Most probably, he had simply adopted a term which he had shared with or heard from Husserl. Even the very idea of intentionality calls for a concept of a life-world which precedes the consciousness of the self. Indeed, this already amounted to a recognition of the finitude of the *ego*.

However, one must ask if this consciousness of finitude does not itself render problematical the very enterprise of a philosophy understood as apodictic and foundational. It appears that Husserl maintained this Cartesian conception of philosophy until the end, even if he never claimed to have himself brought it to completion. Assuredly, his personal claim was more modest, as the postface to the *Ideen* shows. He held himself to simply recalling his concern for the absolute integrity which the idea of philosophy represents for humanity. However, one must ask if a philosophy which has become aware of the dispersion of the *ego* in its various intentionalities and of the embeddedness of the experience of meaning in a previous life-world, can still aspire to an "ultimate foundation" (*Letztbegründung*), to a *fundamentum inconcussum* which transcends history?

It is in this respect that the hermeneutical orientation Heidegger imparted on phenomenology appears insuperable and more conforming to the things themselves than Husserl's dream of an ultimate foundation. The famous sentence in the *Krisis*, "philosophy as science, as serious, strict and even apodictic science—this dream is truly finished"[24] is without doubt more suitable for his contemporaries than for Husserl himself, but it was nonetheless him who spoke of a dream (*Traum*). Indeed, what if it was nothing but a dream which is incompatible with human finitude? Heidegger's contribution to phenomenology was to have discovered the ontological presuppositions of the Cartesian notion of an ultimate foundation. The first given for a hermeneutical phenomenology which radicalizes the idea of intentionality, to the point of depriving the *ego* of its role as subject altogether, is that of a finite *Dasein*, vowed to projects of meaning of which the last foundation will always escape it. Looking to flee from its temporality, *Dasein* "dreams," to use Husserl's own words, of a *fundamentum inconcussum*, but this dream especially betrays to what extent it is itself "*concussum*," temporal and finite.[25]

In the hermeneutic turn which Heidegger stamped on phenomenology, it is the idea itself of a transcendental foundation (that is to say, one which entirely escapes time) that in the end was put into question.[26] It is clear that this distancing from the notion of foundation, which announces the leap "outside of reason" (the *Satz vom Grund* of 1957), stupefies the classical conception of philosophy and that it is not without its problems. However, it is also liberating in that it ceases to orient philosophical consciousness toward an ideal which it can never fulfill. Thus, this phenomenology which has become resolutely hermeneutical remains faithful to the things themselves, that is to say to the original questions (or intentions) of our being. As a hermeneutics of facticity, it strived, with Heidegger, to render the *Dasein* transparent to itself in order to remind *Dasein* that it was a thrown project which is capable of becoming conscious of its real possibilities in the order of history. With Gadamer, hermeneutical phenomenology constituted itself in terms of the logic of question and answer whereby all statements must be understood in function of a dialogue which is more original or "primitive" than the one which is immediately at hand. Once again, the Husserlian ideal of an absolute beginning was put into question by a dialogue according to which there can never be a "point zero." Finitude, or the insertion of our being within intentionalities of meaning which exceed it, thus becomes the first given of phenomenology. Since it concerns us all, it is also universal. Thus, hermeneutics maintains the claim to universality which was so important for Husserl's understanding of philosophy. Yet, it is precisely in its renouncement of a final foundation that its universality is attested. In so doing, hermeneutics will always identify itself with Husserl's heritage and will only depart from its unphenomenological expectations on behalf of the things themselves.

Chapter 4

The Ethical and Young Hegelian Sources
of Heidegger's Hermeneutics of Facticity

The absence of an ethics has almost routinely been singled out as one of the most glaring lacunae of Heidegger's philosophical endeavor. In France, Emmanuel Levinas was the first and foremost philosopher to criticize this absence of the ethical dimension. His protest was directed mainly against the alleged primacy of ontology and the question of being. According to Levinas, the pre-eminent question of our existence and, thus, of philosophy is not being, but the ethical imperative represented by the other. The irreducible "alterity" of the other challenges my own being and thus reveals its essential "secundarity" or its peripheral status in the face of the other. Through his forceful insistence on the question of being, Heidegger, in spite of his self-proclaimed critical ambitions, would fall back into classical ontology and renew its totality claim which engulfs whatever form of alterity. The reduction of individual beings to the sameness of Being, that is alleged to be constitutive of ontology, would make the ontological question blind to the defiance of being and sameness that proceeds from the plea of the other. Although Levinas' critique, which was set forth as early as 1951, received little attention at the beginning, it rapidly acquired a new urgency in the wake of the widespread discussions and suspicions raised by Heidegger's entanglement with National Socialism. The events of 1933 led some to believe that the political error had something to do with a certain blindness typical of ontology towards the ethical dimension. Seen from an outside perspective (i.e., irrespective of the precise circumstances and the specific context of Heidegger's own Janus-like involvement), there is something to the suggestion, reinstated by Adorno among others, that the totality claim of philosophy can translate into a tendency for some form or other of political totalitarianism. In this blindness, that one could date back at least to Plato, Heidegger would be just one of the more recent links in a long chain of philosophers. Indeed this chain also includes many of his contemporaries, like Lukács or Sartre who were known to have celebrated Stalinism as a progress in the consciousness of freedom. Intuitively, one could actually think that philosophy, with its inner drive toward clear, ultimate and certain principles always had a hard time reconciling itself with such a gray element as democracy, that rests on the wavering ground of public opinion and its seductiveness. In this regard it is well known that philosophers, whose science Plato once described as being of a "kingly nature," have never been outstanding democrats.[1]

It would certainly be hazardous to dispute any relationship between Heidegger's philosophy and his political error. Heidegger, for one, was the first to recognize it. His political proclamations drew all their authority and substance from his philosophy. It was as if he had wanted to stamp on the political events of his time the seal of a "philosophical spirit," as Jacques Derrida recently pointed out.[2] However, regardless of the intensity of the philosophical as well as of the political involvement, it appears doubtful whether this engagement has to be attributed to any absence of an ethics in Heidegger, as is customarily believed in large parts of the literature. Indeed most ethical philosophers of the time found their peace with National Socialism (that to most did not yet appear in 1933 to be clearly totalitarian—in this regard, the Röhm putsch of June 30, 1934, opened the eyes of everyone, including Jaspers and Heidegger). It is clear that Heidegger possessed a brazen ethical awareness. When Jean Beaufret asked him just after the war, "When are you going to write an ethics?" he responded immediately, thus demonstrating his sensitivity on this matter, with a long letter on humanism, which became the first public testimony of his newly accentuated thinking in the footsteps of the *Kehre*. To this day, it has remained one of the most representative, evocative and readable texts of the later Heidegger. Insofar as an ethics has to reflect on the ἦθος or the dwelling of humankind on this earth, replied Heidegger, this thinking was already under way in the ontology of *Being and Time*. The ontology of *Dasein*, he provokingly stated, was in itself an "originary ethics" (*ursprüngliche Ethik*).³ By stating this, Heidegger anticipated Levinas' accusation: ontology is not outside ethics, it offers rather its most radical realization.

However, in what sense can ontology claim to be the original form of ethics? Was this ethics really to be found in the fundamental ontology of 1927? This claim is far from obvious since, if it were, nobody would have dreamed of incriminating the absence of an ethics in Heidegger's main work. In order to sort out this important question, we can now fortunately go beyond, or behind, *Sein und Zeit* and take into account the earlier lectures. Given that *Sein und Zeit* is so cryptic, so formal in a way, it is at times hard to take it at face value. For instance, did Heidegger really intend to set forth the pure idea of Being and to deduce its generic variations? Furthermore, to what extent did he understand himself as a phenomenologist after exposing his anti-phenomenological notion of *phainomenon*? Why did he outline such an ambitious table of contents if he had no certainty of bringing it to its conclusion? Why did he question the whole project of the book on its last page? Was existential, or even theological self-understanding more important to him than ontological, phenomenological inquiry? What or who were his true inspirations—Luther or Husserl, Augustine or Kant, Kierkegaard or Dilthey? Then came the numerous reinterpretations after *Being and Time*, that in the meantime have been discovered to be just that, reinterpretations.

For a long time, readers who did not have the privilege to follow Heidegger's notorious lectures were left in the dark as to the ultimate intentions of *Sein und Zeit*. However, the publication of texts from the early Heidegger could offer a key to the understanding of his whole philosophy. In a sense, Heidegger appears more "honest" in his earlier lectures, philosophizing ingenuously on the issues that preoccupied him, without a philosophical system in his back pocket or, despite his obvious self-awareness, wanting to make a name for himself (otherwise he would have published some of his work). When pressed by his students to be more specific on certain theoretical issues, such as his relation to Husserl's phenomenology, he bluntly told them that he was "not a philosopher" and even went as far as to say that he might even be something like a "christian theologian."⁴

Wherever Heidegger speaks of ontology in his earlier lectures, he always associates it with the general task of an ontology of *Dasein* that would spring from the "self-preoccupation" that characterizes every human being. The strongest indication of this can be seen in the title of his 1923 summer semester lecture (a relatively late stage for the "early" Heidegger): "Ontology" with the subtitle in brackets

"Hermeneutics of Facticity," as if the terms were equivalent.[5] Facticity means our own specific being inasmuch as it is something that we have to "be," that is, to assume or to take into our care. This idea of a *Zu-sein*, that we have "to be" this specific being that we are, will enter into the concept of "existence" in *Being and Time*. It suggests, simply put, that our being, our *Dasein*, is a task for itself, for ourselves. Whether it realizes it or not (and not to, is to flee from oneself according to Heidegger), our *Dasein* is characterized by the fact (thus, the facticity) that it is open to its own being. In classical terms, which Heidegger is trying to avoid, one could say that our *Dasein* is distinguished by a capacity of self-reflection concerning its own possibilities of existing, a self-reflection that is of an utterly ethical character, since it deals with a decision we have to assume concerning our "Being-in-this-world." To be a *Dasein*, to be "there," means that this "there," that we are, can be elevated to consciousness and, yes, our conscience, as something that each one of us has to take up according to the possibilities that are at the time specifically (*"jeweils"*) available to us, and only to us.

I would like to expound on this point by saying that, for Heidegger, our *Dasein* is constituted by something like an "inner dialogue," a dialogue with itself because it knows or can always know how things are standing about its own self (i.e., what possibilities of existence are being offered to ourselves). Our "self" is nothing but this ongoing tacit discussion on what we should, could or must be. The fact that we are confronted by such a "choice" or "resolution" can be confirmed by the negative experience we may have of ourselves when we realize that we could have done things differently or that we missed this or that possibility. Without any doubt, the early Heidegger could find this idea of an inner dialogue in the work of Saint Augustine. Indeed Augustine was one of the most notable mentors during this early period, even though Heidegger did not write or speak much about him. Beyond this historical link to Augustine, which forthcoming publications of the earlier Heidegger will document more extensively, it is more important to see the issue itself, the fact that *Dasein* is a self-dialogue, that is in a state of permanent confrontation with its own self and thus with others (that can very well dwell within us).

Sein und Zeit retained this idea of an inner dialogue of facticity by defining *Dasein* as the being whose own being is constantly at stake. In the same breath, Heidegger was able to write that *Dasein* is singled out as a being of *Sorge*, of care, and, more specifically (lest we be indulged by the later Heidegger into thinking that care only concerns Being in itself!), care of oneself (*Selbstbekümmerung*). In this way, the "ontology" of *Dasein* was unmistakenly directed towards ethics; indeed, it was in itself an ethical enterprise. Humanity is not characterized by its purely theoretical, intellectual or rational grasp of the world, which follows from an understanding of man as *animal rationale*, a notion that dominated the rationalist tradition of philosophy from Plato to Husserl. Rather, it is circumscribed by the task that it is for its own self, by its dialogical existence as something it has to take in its care. This task can be described in Kantian terms as a *Sollen*, an imperative "to be" that is inscribed in every one of us, whether we want to follow it or not. Therefore, it is not surprising that Heidegger relied on Kant's practical philosophy in a lecture course of 1930 on the essence of human liberty, a course that was conceived as nothing less than an introduction to philosophy.[6] To be "free" means that we are not fixed in reality, but that we have to assume ourselves as a project, a future we can open up for ourselves. Even where man appears to be preoccupied by theoretical pursuits, he remains governed by the fundamental imperative of the "care" of *Dasein*. There is no knowledge that is not an answer to a specific quest worth caring for. The primary mode of our relationship to the world is thus for Heidegger "intoned understanding" (*befindliches Verstehen*). Furthermore, understanding does not primarily signal here a form of "knowledge," as it was, say, for Schleiermacher or Dilthey who saw in this knowledge the specific avenue of the human sciences. Originally, Heidegger claims, understanding is not to be thought of as a mode of cognition. Rather, it alludes to a "possible being" (*Seinkönnen*), more something that we can do than something that we can know. Heidegger relies on the German locution *sich auf etwas verstehen* (to be able, to be up to the task, to "know-how," etc.) to suggest that understanding is more something like a "competence," an ability to run things, to "know one's way around," than it is a specific form of theoretical insight. To "understand" something, is to be able, to be up to it, to cope with it. It is thus according to such a mode of "understanding" that *Dasein* muddles through existence and sorts out how it can manage its affairs. One could say that this understanding is thought of as a mode of self-orientation for *Dasein* that is not so much a means to know as it is to know-how. Some interpreters have pertinently suggested that this analysis brought Heidegger in the vicinity of pragmatism.[7]

According to Heidegger, *Dasein* already finds itself immersed in possibilities of understanding, that is, more or less conscious projects whose function it is to forestall a potentially threatening course of events. In order to stay afloat in this world in which we are and feel "thrown into," our understanding clings to different

possibilities of being and behaving that represent as many interpretative, caring or "fore-caring" (*"vor-sorgende"*) anticipations on the
world. Before we become aware of it, we find ourselves entangled in
historical perspectives and ways of understanding the world (and
thus ourselves since we are essentially, following Heidegger, "beings-
in-the-world"). Heidegger states: "Those perspectives, which stand
at our disposal more often than not in an implicit manner and in
which factual life enters into much more through custom than
through any explicit appropriation, open up the avenues for the mo-
bility of care."[8] However, as *Dasein*, or, better still, as potential
Dasein, we do not remain inexorably captive of these interpretative
possibilities. We have the opportunity to elaborate and to raise them
to consciousness. This unfolding of our specific situation of understanding is what Heidegger terms *Auslegung*, a concept that ordi-
narily means "interpretation," but that here amounts to a "rendering
explicit" of what guides our understanding. This possibility of
Auslegung, which we can call one of "explicitation," necessarily belongs, as a possibility, to a being that is already characterized by
self-care, by self-awareness, even if this self-elucidation is always
limited. This (self-)interpretation is not a process that is added to
understanding. Rather, it is nothing but understanding carried
through to its own end. We understand in order to keep abreast and
to sort our way out in our world. Consequently, we are also capable
of sorting our way out in *Verstehen* itself and to shed light on the
anticipations of understanding. Interpretation, hence, merely brings
understanding to itself, as, so to speak, a "self-understanding of understanding." Heidegger writes: "The development of understanding
is what we call interpretation (*Auslegung*). In it understanding becomes aware of what it has comprehensively understood. In interpretation, understanding does not become something else, but itself."[9]

    The philosophy that reflects on this self-interpretation accom-
plished in the name of a practically oriented understanding necessarily carries the name "hermeneutics." "Hermeneutics," specifies
Heidegger, is hereby understood "in the original meaning of the word,
in which it signifies the task of interpretation."[10] Interpretation, in
turn, has to be taken in its Heideggerian sense, where it signalizes
the development of the anticipations of understanding. As a philosophical project, hermeneutics will thus carry to its end a reflective
task of interpretation that *Dasein* naturally performs out of itself.
The hermeneutics of facticity will thus offer an interpretation of the
interpretation of *Dasein*, a self-interpretation of facticity.[11]

    Its intent is eminently critical and in accord with the tradition
of the Enlightenment. This self-interpretation wants to pave the way

to a level of self-transparency (*Selbstdurchsichtigkeit*) that has to be conquered by every *Dasein*.[12] Heidegger's hermeneutics promises to announce to *Dasein* the fundamentally open ground-structures of its own being so that the particular *Dasein* can take hold of them. This specific "announcement," *Kundtun*, says Heidegger, is called for since, more often than not, these structures and this openness are missed by factual *Dasein*. It misses its own self because it recoils from the task of defining and developing its own avenues of understanding through a process of reflective interpretation or appropriation. Instead, *Dasein* lazily takes over the prevailing and public view of things, which alleviates it from the burden of self-determination. Of course, no one can avoid stumbling into the "proven" interpretations that are already there before us. No single *Dasein* can take it upon itself to create its own modes of understanding out of the blue. We all depend on the per-formance of tradition. However, if we do so without self-awareness, without acknowledging what we are doing by repeating what has been transmitted to us, we succumb to a certain "fall" or forfeiture (*Verfallen*). One could easily single out the "theological" origins of this notion of fall, but again it is more urgent to see why it is so appropriate for a being labeled "*Dasein*." For, in this fall from the possibility of self-determination, we can no longer be said to be a *Dasein*, to be "there" when and where the determining decisions concerning ourselves take place. The earlier Heidegger spoke of an essential "ruin," a *Ruinanz,* to evoke this self-abolition of *Dasein* In lectures posterior to *Being and Time* and in his recently published *Beiträge zur Philosophie* of 1937–39, Heidegger coined the notion of "*Wegsein*" to describe this venue of a *Dasein* that "is not there."[13] It is not there (*da*), but away(*weg*), away from itself, by letting someone else (the "we," *das Man*) conduct the self-dialogue of *Dasein*. It has to be stressed that this fall or ruin is in a sense unavoidable. Indeed, Heidegger singled it out as an existential or as a foremost category or predicament of our existence. Nevertheless, the notion of *Dasein* is constituted as a possible, perhaps Sisyphical counter-instance against this fall from oneself; and the reflective unfolding or elucidating interpretation of our hermeneutical situation is the means through which we can become aware of ourselves as *Dasein* and control our tendency to fall into anything but this debate with ourselves, to which we are invited or compelled as *Dasein*.

As a self-interpretation of our self-interpretation, the philosophical hermeneutics of factual existence takes up this declaration of war against the falling tendency of *Dasein* in the name of a more authentic, more *Dasein*-like way of comprehending ourselves. In so doing, one has to acknowledge that its point of departure is thoroughly ethical. It aims at combatting the cover-up of facticity that holds sway wherever *Dasein* gathers its self-determination "from the world" instead of obtaining it from its inner dialogue, as it is incribed, as a possibility we all have before our eyes, in the fundamental structure of *Dasein*. This self-definition of *Dasein* out of the world (the "we," etc.) is qualified by Heidegger, in the strong terminology of the young Hegelians, as nothing less than "self-alienation" (*Selbstentfremdung*). The expression is rigorously justified since *Dasein* is not itself anymore. Rather than being the virtual agent of its own self-determination, it is the mere exponent of an unquestioned interpretation that stems from elsewhere. It is "away" from itself, literally "self-alienated." The avowed program of the hermeneutics of facticity will be to fight against this self-alienation in the hope of reminding *Dasein* of its virtual possibility of liberty or self-determination, regardless of how limited it may be according to the perpetually different situations we are in, or that we are. In this regard, Heidegger states: "It is the task of hermeneutics to enable the specific *Dasein* to gain access to its own character of being as *Dasein*, to proclaim it and to trace back the self-alienation that is plaguing *Dasein*."[14] What is envisioned, to remain in the vocabulary of the young Hegelians, is something like an autonomous self-consciousness of man, that Heidegger identifies as an "awokenness" that needs to be conquered: "The theme of hermeneutical inquiry is the always particular *Dasein*, more specifically questioned as to its character of being with a view of developing a radical awokenness of its own self."[15]

Those potent formulations carry a tone that is reminiscent of the critique of ideologies. In reality, the enterprise of the early Heidegger is not so distant from the concerns of the young Hegelians. The prime objective of this generation of students, who were disillusioned by Hegel's system, was to do away with the merely theoretical and idealistic perspective of classical philosophy to make way for a more practically oriented form of critical reflection. This motive found its expression in the famous 11th thesis of Marx on Feuerbach: "Philosophers have only interpreted the world in different ways; what is important is to change it." It is not surprising to see Heidegger, in spite of his well-documented aversion for communism, express his sympathy for Marx's notion of alienation and his understanding of it as an essential dimension of our historical destiny in as late a text as the *Letter on humanism*.[16] It corresponded all too well to his earlier motivations, at a time when he was certainly unable to read anything from Marx or even Freud.

While Marx is surely not the most fashionable of authors nowa-days,[17] it should be recognized that a form of critique of ideologies is at work wherever one attempts to unmask a doctrine that aims to hamper the exercise of human freedom. This is true whether it be propagated by the metaphysical understanding of man, the capitalist ideology, the politically correct movement, self-proclaimed liberators, or, in short, by any form of prevailing wisdom that does not question its own foundations. What Heidegger espouses is not a determined form of a critique of ideology, such as those found in the young Hegelians (i.e., a socio-political version or a critique of religion). And although one can encounter some traces of these in his work, Heidegger merely teaches that the ethical motive for a critique of ideology or false consciousness is already inscribed in the fundamental structure of a being potentially understood as *Dasein*. Heidegger reminds us that this "authentic" structure of *Dasein* always has to be conquered anew by each and every one of us, and that it has to be saved from any dogmatic claim that attempts to exhaust the promise of liberty. *Dasein* is inhabited by a fall, by a being-away-from-itself, in Kantian terms, by a "self-inflicted minority." Out of this universal philosophical horizon it becomes possible to differenciate and to hail different forms or applications of a critique of ideology. The Marxist version, which is but one of the possible realizations, has to accept other forms besides itself.

One of the opportunities the hermeneutics of facticity offers philosophy today could be to help put into perspective the prevailing and unquestioned opposition of schools and traditions, most prominently the opposition of hermeneutics and critique of ideologies that has dominated the scene ever since Lukacs' and Adorno's attacks against Heidegger and up to the more recent debates between Habermas, Gadamer, and Derrida. It is not surprising that students of Heidegger, like Marcuse, Löwith or even Apel, could start off with Heidegger and then feel completely at home in the critique of ideologies of the Marxist tradition. Through Heidegger they had learned that the primary impetus of philosophy lies in a fundamental critique of the flattening or leveling effect of prevailing dogmaticisms that restrain the possibilities of human freedom and self-awareness.

Heidegger certainly shares the unsatisfactory feeling of the young Hegelians concerning the philosophical concept that remains strictly theoretical. The theoretical ambition of traditional philosophy has been to grasp the totality of the world, and more often than not its results have appeared irrelevant to the practical concerns of our *Dasein*. What the concept can never encompass, because it is,

in principle, open, is the particular and specific realization of the
possibility of existence that each one represents. Besides Augustine,
it was Kierkegaard who imparted to Heidegger this "young Hegelian"
suspicion regarding self-sufficient speculation; and this suspicion
awoke in him a sensitivity for the higher urgency of the ethical.

Nevertheless, Heidegger knew that his philosophical endeavor
could not entirely forfeit the theoretical medium. This is why he took
good care to propose his own conceptual framework (which he, sig-
nificantly, never ceased to modify before and after *Being and Time*
and to protect with more or less success from any scholastical rigidity) under the provision that he was just offering "formal-indicative"
(*formalanzeigende*) orientation. The notion of "formal indication"
means that the terms used to describe existence require a specific
and unprescribable process of appropriation on the part of the reader
or listener. This process, which is not contained in the concept itself, can only be awakened, encouraged, admonished by it. The formal indication is not to be misunderstood as the description of an
objective state of affairs. As an exhortation to self-awareness on the
terrain of every specific *Dasein*, it wants to be "filled" with concrete
content according to our different situations. Therefore, the formal
indicative can only suggest or "indicate" the possibility of *Dasein* or
the openness of self-determination. Heidegger stresses this point
clearly: "All the propositions on the being of *Dasein* (. . .) have, as
uttered sentences, the character of an indication: they only indicate
Dasein, whereas, as uttered sentences, they at first look mean something that is readily perceptible; (. . .) but they indicate a possible
understanding and the conceptuality of the structures of *Dasein* that
lies in such an understanding. (As sentences indicating such an
ἑρμηνεύειν, they have the character of a hermeneutical indication)."[18]

Such formal indications are what the Jaspers' review of 1921
alluded to under the heading of "hermeneutical concepts," that is,
notions that "we can only gain access to in the always renewed attempt to accomplish the task of interpretation."[19] While the formal
indication introduces us to a situation of decision, its concrete realization must remain open[20] since is has to be "performed" by every
specific *Dasein* and according to its own unique way. The admonished awokennness has to happen as a free accomplishment against
the stream of self-alienation. This self-illumination of existence is
what Heidegger's hermeneutics of facticity is all about.

This appellative, exhortatory dimension of the urged awokenness will go on to command the entire problematic of conscience
(*Gewissen*) in *Being and Time*. As an existential, this conscience only
takes the form of a "call" (*Ruf*), which is a call "to-want-to-have-a-

conscience"(*Gewissen-haben-wollen*). Therefore, this call remains formal in nature, and critics were quick to incriminate here yet another lacuna of Heidegger's analysis. However, according to
Heidegger, it does not fall in the immediate competence of philosophy to recommend any concrete models for our edification. His existential hermeneutics is content with the task of "recalling" this call
of conscience which has to be filled by everyone of us, and in our
way, and whose structure is strictly identical to that of *Dasein*. For
man is as a potential "*da*," or "awokenness" regarding its existential decisions, distinguished as a being of conscience, aware of a
"debt" (*Schuldigsein*) to his or her own self. *Dasein* is "in debt" insofar as it has the tendency, in falling from its possibilities, to have
someone else take those decisions for it instead of confronting them
resolutely and with full responsibility. Here again, one can perceive
in Heidegger's analysis of *Gewissen* an echo to Kant's ethics of *Sollen*.
Kant also only wanted to recall the appellative character of moral
duty which stems from every human reason—and stands against the
primacy of theoretical, syllogistical metaphysics. Although we cannot avoid being touched, perhaps even shattered by a compelling
moral law, its application can only occur at the level of our own specific maxims and judgment. For the application of the moral law,
there are in turn no rules nor edificatory examples. Every *Dasein*
must take full responsibility for its own self. Similarily, moral
awokenness also retains for Heidegger the status of a "task" that
lies before everyone and from which we can never recoil so long as
we exist and feel summoned by the call "to be" our own *Dasein*. Each
human being as *Dasein* is thus characterized from the outset as a
Being of possibility (*Seinkönnen*) and of "having-to-be" (*Sollen*).

Through this understanding of humanness from the vantage
point of an existence approached in purely ethical and practical
terms, through the vocabulary of care (*Sorge*), Heidegger certainly
contributed immensely to the rehabilitation of practical philosophy
in our century. It has to be noted that Heidegger's earliest lectures
were followed by students like H.-G. Gadamer, L. Strauss, H. Arendt
and H. Jonas, all of whom were later credited with a revival of practical philosophy.[21] One could also evoke later students like J. Patocka
or E. Tugendhat who clearly perceived the ethical implication of
Heidegger's ontology of facticity. Even if this rehabilitation of practical philosophy took on many different forms, some of which are
clearly at odds with Heidegger's own intentions, it is more than likely
that, in terms of its own possibility, it must be traced back to
Heidegger and, more specifically to his rediscovery of man as an
essentially caring and ethical being that was carried through by his

hermeneutics of facticity. This rediscovery of our situated and ethical humanity was outlined as a counter-model against the strong
epistemological bent of neo-Kantianism and the methodological perspective that was dominating the course of philosophy in the twenties and also prevailing in some sections of phenomenology. The
methodological perspective was grounded in a mainly theoretical,
contemplative understanding of human subjectivity. Consequently,
humanity was defined through its primarily intellectual competence
or through an attitude of theoretical perception of the world. The
issue of the cognitive relationship between the subject and its object thus became the central concern of philosophers. In his early
lectures, Heidegger discovered that this academic question was not
up to the urgencies of his time, that he found in a state of moral
disarray, manifest in the all-prevading nihilism, a crisis of the val-
ues of modernity and its scientificity. A new beginning was therefore called for. Under the "young Hegelian" influence of Kierkegaard,
Heidegger called into question the entire epistemological background
of his contemporaries and attempted to reconquer a more radical
and, consequently, a more *ethical* understanding of our being-in-this-
world. The fact that this momentous step was followed by a multifarious rehabilitation of practical philosophy was nothing but the
natural outcome of his ambitious hermeneutics of facticity.

    If Heidegger did not develop any specific "ethics," it is only be-
cause his entire project, founded as it is on the self-preoccupation
of *Dasein*, which is also "there" collectively, was ethical from the
ground up. For a hermeneutics of facticity, the clear-cut division of
philosophy into disciplines like logic, aesthetics, epistemology, and
then, besides the others, ethics, corresponded to a false reification
and fragmentation[22] of philosophical inquiry that is always directed
at the whole of our experience (*"das aufs Ganze geht"*)—a reification
against which all young Hegelians are immuned. This ethical
motive remained predominant in Heidegger's later work, even
though the high-flown discourse of conscience, indebtedness and authenticity seemed to fade in order to make room for a more prudent,
more serene approach of our dwelling on this earth. The thinking
of the destiny of being that we encounter in the later Heidegger
clearly results from a radicalization of the experience of human
"thrownness" (*Geworfenheit*). In view of its being-thrown-unto-the-
world, human *Dasein* ceases in a way to emerge as the sole archi-
tect of its projects of existence, as appeared to be the case in the
early lectures as well as in *Being and Time*. It now receives its possibilities from the history of being that has already decided, before
us, how being is to be seized. The somewhat peripheral character of

humanness in respect to this seemingly overbearing history of being does not have to lead to resignation in front of the *fatum* that
we always come too late and thus have to renounce any attempt at
enlightenment. On the contrary, historical enlightenment has now
become the main task of philosophy. Out of its throwness, *Dasein*
comes to reflect upon the projections and paths of intelligibility that
have constituted its history. With respect to his interpretative praxis,
Heidegger's thinking remained thoroughly hermeneutical. The ethical motivation that distinguishes his hermeneutics did not cease to
command Heidegger's attempt to clarify the history of being. The
"destruction" of this history of being still aimed "to prepare a meta-
morphosed dwelling of man in this world," as Heidegger reinstated
in a text of April 1976, which could have been his last philosophical
pronouncement.[23] This quest which directs Heidegger's entire work
is obviously ethical both from the outset and in its consequences.

What one could find questionable is thus not the absence of an
ethics in Heidegger, but perhaps the somewhat utopian character
of this idea of a whole new type of dwelling on this earth. This revolutionary zeal also goes back to the young Hegelians. It could very
well be that such a utopianism might also have been a determinating
factor in Heidegger's political engagement. He wrote explicitly that
Hitler's "revolution" implied an entire metamorphosis of our own
Dasein,[24] as if National Socialism would provide the opportunity to
finally carry out the revolution sought for by the young Hegelians!

It would be erroneous to abscribe the political error of 1933,
an error that one has to learn to differenciate from what later became manifest as the reality of National Socialism, to an "absence"
of an ethical consciousness. While we hope not to be misunderstood
on a issue so sensitive as this, one could also see in Heidegger's political errancy the consequence of an exacerbated moral consciousness. There is no doubt that the hermeneutics of facticity was
characterized by an ethical motive. One will also not call into question the fact that Heidegger jumped into the fray in 1933 *because*
he felt he could not remain indifferent to the requirements of his
time, thus putting into praxis his own idea of resolute existence.[25]
Although events proved him humiliatingly wrong, Heidegger was not
lacking any principle of responsibility. On the contrary, since *Dasein*
must bear the responsibility for its situatedness and thus its community, Heidegger (with great risk to his personal reputation)
entered into the political arena with the hope of orienting what he
took to be a promising revolution in the appropriate direction. If
Heidegger had any right to see some promising possibilities in the
"revolutionary" outburst of 1933, born out of many motives, is a moot

point. To be sure, there were at the time more lucid and much braver estimations of what the "awakening," the "*Aufbruch*," was all about. However, the mistake that is relevant for philosophers could lie in the expectation that a *fundamental* and *ethical* revolution of *Dasein* could be brought about through political means. It is the illusion that concrete politics could some day satisfy the requirements of the ideal state. My point is that the sense of the ethical dimension is possibly overburdened in this respect. It could very well be that the radicality of human finitude and the limits it sets on any dream of a total revolution are not heeded in such an expectation.

In conclusion, one will have to recognize that the revolutionary point of departure of Heidegger's early hermeneutics of facticity had the often overlooked merit of calling to attention the primacy and the urgency of the issue of ethicity for a being such as *Dasein*. Against the backdrop of an epistemological and methodological self-reduction of philosophy that he saw in neo-Kantianism, in the epistemological orientation of Dilthey's hermeneutics and even in phenomenology itself, Heidegger contributed greatly, by re-appropriating some tenets of young Hegelianism, to the reawakening of an original ethical consciousness. Furthermore, this ethical consciousness in turn led to a rehabilitation of practical philosophy. However, we could also learn from this new sensitivity to the ethical sphere that there are also limits to the possibilities of a philosophical ethics, such that they can underscore the problematic nature of any messianism that would promise to revolutionize *Dasein* by finally bringing it back to its forgotten essence. Is the young Hegelian hope for a total and political revolution not the expression of an overexcited moral conscience and a seduction that surpasses the realm of what is possible for our finitude? Indeed, a practical philosophy that would take into account this finitude of moral conscience would have many lessons to learn from Heidegger's example.

Chapter 5

Prolegomena to an Understanding of Heidegger's Turn

"People are still waiting for the second part of *Being and Time*. That's because they don't know the book on Kant."

Martin Heidegger[1]

In his work on what he terms "the philosophical discourse of modernity," Jürgen Habermas argues that Heidegger's philosophical turn is a consequence of his political engagement.[2] It is alleged that in order to justify his involvement with the Nazis, Heidegger developed a bizarre philosophy, one destitute of argumentative rigor and which frees the subject from all responsibility, imputing all agency to an autonomous and anonymous history of being. It is a philosophy which could easily be located at the antipodes of the activist and resolute conception of human existence elaborated in *Being and Time*. The details of the Habermasian interpretation are not our central concern here. We wish only to dispute the premise upon which his entire reading of Heidegger rests, i.e., that the thinking of the turn appears only after 1935. The present analysis is essentially a condensed version of one I presented in 1987,[3] but I will here also take into account the most recent publications on and by Heidegger.

Translated by Gail Soffer.

A philosophical interpretation of Heidegger's turn must respect four general principles. First, it must give a privileged position to the relatively rare texts in which Heidegger himself expressly speaks of the *Kehre*. In addition to the "Letter on Humanism" of 1946, the Bremen lectures of 1949, and the letter to William Richardson in 1962, it must take into account the winter semester course of 1937–38, and the *Beiträge zur Philosophie (Contributions to Philosophy)*. Further, it must also consider the texts contemporaneous with *Being and Time* in which something like a turn is manifest, especially the summer semesters courses of 1927 and 1928, *Kant and the Problem of Metaphysics* (1929), and the lecture "On the Essence of Truth" (1930). An examination of the ensemble of these texts makes it possible to discern the properly philosophical problematic surrounding the concept of the *'Kehre'*—a concept which is all the more important for its rarity in the Heideggerian corpus. In this manner, the philosophical question of the *Kehre* can be *dissociated* from the question (still only very superficially debated) of the *evolution* or shift in perspective of Heidegger's philosophy. In the absence of this heuristic dissociation, one runs the risk of mistaking every change in the thought of Heidegger for the turn itself. It is certain that the "later" Heidegger is concerned with questions such as that of art, poetry, and the history of being, and that he thoroughly revised certain aspects of his fundamental ontology, e.g., the concept of spatiality called into question in *Zur Sache des Denkens*.[4] However, these metamorphoses must not be confused with the turn itself, for (following Heidegger in his letter to Richardson) this turn is not primarily a sudden alteration in the itinerary of a thinker, but rather a *thing* or *cause (Sache)* which has to be thought for itself. What may be termed the "biographical turn" of Heidegger will be more comprehensible the more clearly it is distinguished from the philosophical turn—the *Kehre* which appears in the writings of Heidegger without denoting, for the most part, an inflection or a rupture in the intellectual itinerary of the thinker. When this is done, it will be found that the philosophical question of the *Kehre* remains connected to the evolution of Heidegger's thought, but in a relation of consequence, not one of equivalence. This is because the so-called biographical turn results from the taking into account or discovery, at a precise moment of Heidegger's itinerary, of that which demanded the thinking of the primary *Kehre*, the "thing" which is not as such the affair of a particular philosopher.

The second requirement which an interpretation of the *Kehre* must satisfy is to present a philosophical or argumentative reconstruction which brings out the rigor and necessity of the thinking of the turn. This principle has recently been criticized on the grounds that Heidegger could never have been able to subscribe to it, insofar as "the vocation of the turn is to turn thought away from the horizon of intelligibility of metaphysics in order to guide it towards a region which is radically *other*."[5] It is clear that for the later Heidegger, or better, the *last* Heidegger, the overcoming of metaphysics is equivalent to the *end* of philosophy. This perspective, which definitively dismisses philosophy and relegates it to another age (the one which extends, roughly, from Plato to Hegel or Nietzsche), is certainly that of Heidegger's final public lectures, "Time and Being" (1962) and the lecture on "The End of Philosophy and the Task of Thinking" (1964), read at UNESCO. Unquestionably, the hidden consistency which led the last Heidegger to renounce philosophical intelligibility (the intelligibility of metaphysics) represents a distant consequence of the thinking of the turn. However, Heidegger was still convinced that he was doing philosophy when the turn first appeared on the scene, at the end of the twenties and in the mid-thirties. Indeed, his major work of this period is the *Contributions to Philosophy*, and it speaks explicitly of a *"Begreifen der Kehre"* (a conceiving of the turn).[6] Thus a philosophical interpretation of the turn must be carried out in the name of this kind of effort of conceiving and of seeking to understand the necessity of the turn *in statu nascendi*, well before the avatars that would be embraced in the sixties.

Third, any reconstruction of the turn must begin with what remains the key text: the passage from the "Letter on Humanism" in which Heidegger chooses to speak of the *Kehre* publicly for the first time (or rather in a published form, since the term itself had appeared earlier in his courses). There is reason to believe that Heidegger had patiently allowed the ideas of this text to mature, a text which is often misunderstood, because the signposts of the philosopher were so extraordinary and unheard of. This passage contains a response to Sartre and to the metaphysics of subjectivity, the misinterpretation of which would like to make the "projection (*Entwurf*) of being" into a representational positing (*vorstellendes Setzen*), or even an accomplishment of subjectivity (*Leistung der Subjektivität*). No, says Heidegger, the understanding of being must rather be grasped as the "ecstatic relation to the lighting of being (*der ekstatische Bezug zur Lichtung des Seins*)."[7] But this thought, whose first fruits (and this is completely correct) are located by Heidegger in *Being and Time*, could not be properly grasped on the basis of the transcendental and apparently subjectivist horizon which still overlay the work in 1927. Thus, Heidegger states in the "Letter on Humanism":

The adequate execution and completion of this other thinking that is *on the way* to abandoning subjectivity is surely made more difficult by the fact that in the publication of *Being and Time* the third part of the first division was held back (see *Being and Time*, p. 64). Here everything is reversed. The section in question was held back because thinking *failed* in the adequate saying of this turn and did not succeed with the help of the language of metaphysics. The lecture "On the Essence of Truth," *thought out* and *delivered* in 1930, but not printed until 1943, provides a certain insight into the thinking of the *turn* from "Being and Time" to "Time and Being." This turn is not a modification of the point of view of *Being and Time*, but in it the thinking that was sought first arrives at the location of that dimension out of which *Being and Time* is experienced, that is to say, experienced from the fundamental experience of the forgetfulness of being. (*LH*, 207–208; my emphasis)

In a way which has rarely been noticed, this text brings together the question of the turn and the transition from the second to the third part ("Time and Being") of the first division of *Being and Time*. To speak *here* of a *Kehre* has something perfectly luminous about it, since the title of this third unpublished part is precisely the inversion (*die Umkehrung*) of the title of the work. A "turn" is indeed to come about, even if the published portion of *Being and Time* never speaks of a *Kehre* as such. What the "Letter on Humanism" teaches or confirms is that *Being and Time* fails to say this *Kehre*, remaining in a certain respect prisoner of the horizon of the intelligibility of metaphysics (even if not completely, since the thinking of 1927 was already *on the way* to overcoming subjectivity). The horizon of metaphysics brings everything back to an autonomous, completely self-transparent subjectivity; in short, to the rationality of a sovereign subject. We thus come to the fourth and final requirement: a rigorous interpretation of the *Kehre* must show, if this can be demonstrated, what type of turn was presaged by the architecture of *Being and Time*—and more particularly, what type was foreseen for "Time and Being"—and attempt to explain why it miscarried, giving place instead to something else.

This reading of the 1946 letter could give the impression that it too addresses only the question of the "biographical reversal" of Heidegger's perspective. This is not the case. One should not take lightly Heidegger's assurance that the turn is not simplistically equivalent to a "modification of the point of view of *Being and Time*." One should also keep in mind the warning in the letter to

Richardson, stating that the turn does not concern the thinker or the thought of Heidegger alone, but rather a *Sachverhalt*, the thing or the relation to the thing.[8] When one treats the *Kehre* within the architectonic of *Being and Time*, it can only be a matter of the philosophical problem which the turn opens to reflection. According to the text of 1946, the failure to say this *Kehre* arises from the chronic inadequacy of metaphysics. But when Heidegger takes cognizance of this inadequacy, a new *Kehre* imposes itself on his thought, reflecting a turn of the thing itself which forces his own philosophy to readjust its bearings. In what does this turn itself consist, the turn which Heidegger invites us to understand out of the miscarriage of "Time and Being"?

It is reasonable to suppose that the most fundamental turn occurs when Heidegger becomes aware of the impossibility of bringing to completion the turn foreseen in the third part of the first division of *Being and Time*. This could be established on the basis of the texts in which Heidegger endeavored to say this turn in 1927. But did the third part not remain unpublished? We know that this section was effectively drafted. But Heidegger was so dissatisfied with the text, he not only did not publish it, he burned it,[9] something he did not always do with the numerous manuscripts he chose not to make public. If not contemporaneous with *Being and Time* (completed in 1926), the *first* draft of "Time and Being" must have been from the beginning of 1927, because a *second* version was offered at the end of the summer semester course of 1927 (in *The Basic Problems of Phenomenology*). This is evidenced by a signpost found at the beginning of this course, expressly presenting it as a "*new* elaboration of the third part of the first division of *Being and Time*."[10] This signpost confers upon the 1927 course a significance of the first order within Heidegger's work as a whole, already highlighted by the fact that this course was included in the *first* volume to appear in the *Gesamtausgabe* edition in 1975. Heidegger was responsible for the decision to open the *Gesamtausgabe* with this volume (number 24).[11] He seems to have wished to indicate by this that an integral understanding of *Being and Time* and the philosophy which followed, that of the completed *Kehre*, must first pass by way of the problematic (or the *Holzweg*) of "Time and Being," as it was thought, and, no less importantly, as it miscarried in 1927 (and here we must speak of a "miscarriage," since otherwise the section would have been published). In the absence of the original version of "Time and Being," the course represents the most comprehensive document of what was to have been the first turn, its miscarriage, and what this latter allowed to dawn on the horizon of Heidegger's thought.

Another hint for understanding the aim of "Time and Being" is provided by the Introduction to *Being and Time*, especially § 5, where Heidegger sets out the task assigned to the first division of the work and to be brought to completion in the third part. The first division is to offer an analytic of *Dasein*, in order to free a horizon for an interpretation of the meaning of being in general (according to the title of § 5). It is in this first division, or its conclusion, that an answer to the central question of the book is to be found (the question of the meaning of being), promising to reveal the horizon on the basis of which being has always been understood. Of course, this horizon will turn out to be time. The first division is to make evident the sense in which time constitutes the transcendental horizon for any understanding of being,[12] hence the title of the first division (whose realization was deferred by the failure of "Time and Being" to be published): "The Interpretation of *Dasein* according to Temporality (*Zeitlichkeit*) and the Explication of Time as the Transcendental Horizon of the Question of Being."

Here Heidegger employs the term '*Zeitlichkeit*' to refer to the temporality of *Dasein*, an analytic of which is presented in the second, and in fact the last, part of the work ("*Dasein und Zeitlichkeit*"). He reserves the Latinism, "*Temporalität*' (which we render, in the absence of a better alternative, by the Latin '*temporalitas*'), to designate the problematic, more properly ontological than '*daseinological*,' of understanding being itself in its temporal aspect. Yet despite the insistence on the question of being, the analysis of the *temporalitas* of being itself is hardly treated at all in *Being and Time*. This analysis was to have been carried out in the third part of the work, the section in which, according to the Introduction of 1927, there was to have been a "concrete" response to the question of the meaning of being,[13] a response which would have given a sense to the work and even to the entirety of Heidegger's philosophy. Since this section was never published, Heidegger's central work remains de facto a book without an answer—a path, if not to nowhere, at least to no "concrete" response, but rather only to new questions.

To obtain a clear view of the 'turn' as anticipated in 1927, one needs only to notice that the second part was to treat the temporality (*Zeitlichkeit*) of *Dasein*, while the third, unpublished part was to address the question of the *temporalitas* of being. To put it banally: the third part was to mark a passage (that is, a turn) from the question which had been the preoccupation of the first two sections of the published work, the question of *Dasein*, to the question of being itself. The priority of being over *Dasein* is not only the leitmotif of the "later" or the "last" philosophy of Heidegger. Rather, it is clearly outlined in the third part of *Being and Time*. In this sense, Heidegger had good reason to write in 1946 that the turn from "Being and Time" to "Time and Being" arose from a thinking which had been *on the way* to leaving subjectivity behind since 1927. This desertion was already presaged by the concept of the 'thrownness' (*Geworfenheit*) of *Dasein* and by the idea of an interpretation of *Dasein* in terms of its radical temporality—radical to the point of stripping *Dasein* of the title of 'subject' bestowed upon it by modernity. All of this was effectively under way at the time of *Being and Time*, but the architectonic of the work had not drawn all the consequences.

Indeed, the treatment of the *temporalitas* of being was to spell out the temporal characteristics of being itself, and this treatment was to *result* from the transcendental horizons opened up by the temporality of *Dasein*. The latter still represented the *a priori* (or necessary and universal) condition for the appearance, or giving, of being according to its temporal structures. In fact, this attempt to derive the *temporalitas* of being from the horizonal and transcendental structures of *Dasein* occupies the entire section at the end of the 1927 course, entitled *The Basic Problems of Phenomenology*, a section in which Heidegger tries to carry through the distinction between the temporality of *Dasein* and that of being (in accordance with the spirit and program of "Time and Being"). These analyses borrow heavily from the terminology of Kant and Husserl, certainly the authors who most influenced Heidegger's thinking from 1925 to 1929. However, the rather technical details of these analyses are beyond the scope of the present study.[14]

One cannot fail to be struck by Heidegger's extraordinarily tentative manner of proceeding in this final attempt to "save" the third part of *Being and Time*. Already evident in the developments connected with *Being and Time*, these hesitations finally led him to suspend its publication in 1926, 1927, and 1928. Heidegger thus put his finger on a sore point central to his approach, rather than trying to hide it from his students. These students must have found it very difficult to follow their teacher as he brought the questioning of fundamental ontology back to the workshop. At the end of the course, Heidegger self-critically affirms that a "fundamental untruth" is hidden in "the temporal interpretation of being as such" (*GA 24*, 459/322). He continues:

The history of philosophy bears witness to how, with regard to the horizon essentially necessary for them and to the assurance of that horizon, all ontological interpretations are more

like a groping about than a methodical or univocal questioning. Even the basic act of the constitution of ontology, that is,
of philosophy, the objectification of being, *the projection of being upon the horizon of its understandability*, and precisely this
basic act, is delivered up to uncertainty and stands continually exposed to the danger of being reversed, because this objectification of being must necessarily move in a projective
direction that runs counter to everyday comportment toward
beings. For this reason the projection of being itself necessarily becomes something ontical. . . . (*GA 24*, 459/322–323)

The crucial weak spot seems to lie in the temerity of the projection of being upon the horizon of its intelligibility, a projection carried out in the third part. Put otherwise, the danger consists in
reifying being and proceeding as though being allowed itself to be
embraced in a project of subjectivity. It is here, as well as in numerous related passages of the course and writings of this period, that
one should locate the discovery or onset of an explicit thinking of
the turn.[15] (This period is an eminently critical one, since it forced
Heidegger to renounce the publication of "Time and Being" and, consequently, the systematic conclusion of *Being and Time*). The thinking of the turn was already suggested by the plethora of critical and
self-critical questions with which *Being and Time* ends. To cite only
the final two: "Is there a path which leads from originary *time* to
the meaning of *being*? Does time manifest itself as the horizon of
being?" (*SZ*, 437/488).

These question marks dramatically signal the breaking off of
the question of *Being and Time* and present a challenge to nothing
less than its essential project. They will resound again at the end
of the 1927 course, when the "un-truth" of the schematico-horizonal
approach to the question of being is openly proclaimed. In what does
this untruth consist? In the audacity of a *Dasein*, projected into
being for a time, to submit 'something' (a deliciously inadequate
expression) such as being to an ultimate project of comprehension
or intelligibility (where by 'being' we must understand the totality
of that to which our existence exposes us). Being is that in which
(or rather, *by which*, since we have nothing to do with it) we are
projected into this world and to which we could never claim to possess the key. This thinking of *Geworfenheit* is certainly already
present in *Being and Time*, and, in this respect, the work was already on the way to leaving the horizon of intelligibility of subjectivity behind. This same thinking will eventually present an obstacle
to a project which is rigorously conceptual (or, if we may risk the

term, strictly *rational*), a project which seeks to attain being from the horizon of *Dasein*. For *Dasein* proves to be too finite and too historically situated to obtain a perspective on being which would enable it to derive *sub specie aeternitatis* the transcendental structures of its most fundamental being.

A marginal note from Heidegger's personal copy of *Being and Time* clearly indicates the radical experience which gave rise to this new thinking. This note occurs in § 8, next to the title "Time and Being," that part of the text which was the first site of the turn: "the overcoming of the horizon as such"—the concept of 'horizon' was indeed the key transcendental and metaphysical concept of the third part of *Being and Time*, as can be reconstructed on the basis of the 1927 course—"the return (*Umkehr*) to the origin," "thinking out of this origin." To our knowledge, this note cannot be dated with certainty,[16] but it corresponds perfectly to the movement of thought that comes to light in the work done on the subject matter of "Time and Being," where *Being and Time* is again put into question.

It should again be emphasized that the *Kehre* to be thought is not primarily a radical shift in Heidegger's thinking, *his* inability to bring the program of fundamental ontology to a successful conclusion. This is because this inability is not in the first instance an inability of a particular philosopher, but of being itself. It is being itself which *refuses* itself to a purely metaphysical understanding. To say this is not to revert to attributing some animistic or anthropological character to a hypostacized being. On the contrary, to say that being refuses itself to, or turns away from, a thinking which attempts to set it within a metaphysical totality is simply to recognize that man, as a finite being dedicated to historical interpretations, can never claim to have put his finger on the common denominator of the real, or to have established an ultimate foundation for or truth about his being-in-world. The refusal or turnaway which constitutes the *Kehre*[17] is nothing other than this impossibility or this finitude, itself the condition for the search for truth and dialogue. The Bremen lecture entitled "Die Kehre" will address *this* turn, somewhat cryptically evoking "a self-denying of the truth of being."[18] This latter is opposed by Heidegger to the "standing-reserve" to which the totality of the entity reduces for metaphysics, which seeks to dominate the entity by delimiting its totality, principle, and logic (a threefold plan which Heidegger subsumes under the appropriate title of an "ontotheological constitution" of metaphysics).[19] However, that which metaphysics "forgets" is the little nothing that is being, Heidegger interjects somewhat ironically (since metaphysics has always constituted itself as ontology), or rather, the inexorable temporality of being. This temporality threatens the entire enterprise of establishing domination over the entity and must be taken into account by all human endeavor. What the *Kehre* discovers and names is the essential refusal with which being opposes an unilateral enterprise of domination.

Being's "refusal" is in itself benevolent, since it has a better appreciation of the self of *Dasein* in view. It would not be mistaken to understand this refusal as a philosophical radicalization of finitude. It has not been sufficiently noted that finitude occupies a rather secondary place in the architecture of *Being and Time*, at least explicitly and thematically, especially in view of the preponderant role it takes on in a book such as *Kant and the Problem of Metaphysics*, where finitude appears as the keystone of what will be called "fundamental ontology" for the last time. Although omnipresent in this work on Kant, finitude is still completely absent from the Introduction to *Being and Time*, where, as is well-known, Heidegger sets out the fundamental concepts of his project in 1927. However, a very close reading of the text reveals that the term 'finitude' does, indeed, appear in *Being and Time*, although always within a framework strictly limited to each of the four occurrences (*SZ*, 264/308; 329–331/377–380; 384–386/435–438; 424–426/476–478). In each case, the terms 'finite being' and 'finitude' designate the *authentic* mode of being-toward-death—a being-toward-death which takes charge of itself. The only *Dasein* which is authentic and existing in a finite manner is precisely the *Dasein* who, instead of fleeing its mortality, runs on ahead of its death, no matter what the exact or concrete direction of such a running might be.[20] Admittedly, 'unauthentic' *Dasein* is no less finite, in the usual sense of the term, than is authentic *Dasein*. However, on the terminological and thematic level, only authentic *Dasein*, the one open to its mortality, is to be called "finite," since this is the one able to understand its temporality in a finite manner. Here we are far from the finitude of the Kant book, which is *identified* with the understanding of being.[21] In the lecture course given in 1929–30 which followed the Kant book, this finitude becomes one of the three fundamental concepts of metaphysics.[22]

To read the fourth part of *Kant and the Problem of Metaphysics*, one would believe that finitude represents the alpha and the omega of fundamental ontology. Yet, the Introduction to *Being and Time* fails to mention it a single time. Pure coincidence? Unless it is supposed that Heidegger was not fully aware of the essential concepts of his project in 1927, it must be concluded that his thinking came upon a fundamental discovery after and because of *Being and*

Time. What showed itself was nothing less than the turn, the turn away or the refusal inflicted by being upon any attempt which aspires to exhaust its intelligibility, to reify it, as though being were first of all a "ground" or a "thing" at our disposal, and whose principle, totality, and logic allowed itself to be established once and for all. However, this finitude did not appear after *Being and Time* from out of the blue. It is clearly the result of the radicalization of the idea of *Geworfenheit,* an idea which ultimately undermines from within the architecture of *Being and Time,* by rendering problematic its projection of being along its horizon of intelligibility (i.e., time), a projection to be carried out by *Dasein.* This radicalization means that what was once merely peripheral, one property of *Dasein* among others, will henceforth be located at the root. How could one fail to perceive that finitude finds itself located at the root of fundamental ontology in the Kant book when previously, in 1927, it was no more than an existential modality of the being-toward-death of *Dasein?*

We do not mean here to exclude the possibility that finitude might have constituted an essential motivation of Heidegger's philosophy well before *Being and Time.* Indeed, although Heidegger generally does not employ the *term* 'finitude' in his lectures spanning the period from 1919 to 1926,[23] one finds here a clear consciousness of the hermeneutical facticity of existence and hence already the germs of a critique of metaphysical intelligibility. This anti-metaphysical or hermeneutical tendency has not failed to prompt authors such as Gadamer to speak of a *"Kehre* before the *Kehre."*[24] Formulations such as *"es gibt"* and *"es weltet"* are to be found well before *Being and Time,* and these manifest a thinking of the brute facticity of the *Ereignis* which projects us into being. The idea of a *Kehre* prior to 1927 has the notable merit of shaking the confidence of those who would make the turn a cause of Heidegger's last philosophy. Indeed, the thinking of the turn (that is to say, of the refusal of being and of the necessary overcoming of metaphysics indicated by it) is a matter of Heidegger's entire philosophy, that toward which his entire effort of thinking tends. Perhaps, it was Heidegger himself who took some time to realize this. Certainly, it was necessary for him first to sink into a metaphysical or transcendental perspective of the sort still shared by *Being and Time* in order better to be able to withdraw before metaphysics and to take the full measure of the turn, which, from the start, his philosophy sought to bring to words. Thus, far from dividing the thought of Heidegger, the *Kehre* could enable us to reconquer its unity. This could be one of the tasks of Heidegger research to come.

However, it remains the case that it was Heidegger himself who associated the disputed matter of the *Kehre* with the passage from "Being and Time" to "Time and Being." Thus, he situated the essential discovery after *Being and Time* and was perhaps the first to forget or to repress the intentions of his youth. An interpretation of the turn which is philosophical rather than genetic must seek to understand it as the consequence of a problematic which appeared after and because of *Being and Time*, but which permitted a better articulation of this work's first intuitions.

The first known occurrence of the term '*Kehre*' in the Heideggerian corpus to date is indeed *after Being and Time*. The term appears in the summer semester course of 1928, halfway between Heidegger's two most important books: *Being and Time* and the *Kant and the Problem of Metaphysics* (in fact, the only ones he published that are not collections or lecture courses). The idea of the *Kehre* is related to a completely new problematic, one called '*metontology*' by Heidegger. This "discipline" is to be established *after* fundamental ontology (already interrupted) and is to take the form of a metaphysics of existence within which it will be possible to raise the question of ethics.[25] Heidegger here "recalls" that fundamental ontology is to contain two major parts: the analytic of *Dasein*, and the analytic of the *temporalitas* of being. This dichotomy does not really correspond to the double task and double division of *Being and Time*, which is divided into the analytic of *Dasein* (Division I), and the destruction of the history of ontology (Division II). Rather, that which in the summer semester course of 1928 Heidegger terms the 'analytic of *Dasein*' relates to the two first published sections of *Being and Time*. The idea of an analytic of the *temporalitas* of being corresponds quite precisely to what the third, unpublished part, "Time and Being." was supposed to accomplish. The tripartite division of the first part gave way to a binary separation, with the first half now equivalent to the first two published parts, and the second to "Time and Being." This binary division remained the order of the day in 1928 (with everything proceeding as though the second division of *Being and Time*, the destruction, no longer was one). Heidegger informs us that the temporal analytic of "Time and Being" is at the same time the turn (*die Kehre*). Through it, ontology expressly returns to the ontical metaphysics in which it was already implicitly located. Ontology thus finds itself constrained to execute a reversal (*Umschlag*) which was latent within it and which must occur as a partial transformation into a "metontology" (*GA 26*, 201; compare *GA 22*, 106). Together, fundamental ontology and metontology are to constitute the integral concept of metaphysics—the one concept which, writes

Heidegger in a surprising manner, was already indicated by the double concept of philosophy as πρώτη φιλοσοφία and θεολογία (*GA 26*, 202).

Where is the turn to be located in all of this? It is difficult to say, since the text of the summer semester course of 1928 remains allusive, hopefully relying upon an earlier, unpublished discussion of the idea of metontology.[26] It appears faithful to the spirit of *Being and Time* in its assimilation of the idea of the *Kehre* to the temporal analytic of being that was to be elaborated by the third part and which here has become the second part of fundamental ontology. However, there is no trace of the horizontal-transcendental schematism which had characterized "Time and Being" a year earlier in the summer semester of 1927. A new problematic has grafted itself onto this first turn, the turn toward *temporalitas*. This new problematic is the turn towards a metontology, the realization of which is to take place *after* fundamental ontology, thus after or on the basis of the temporal analytic of being. We know nothing more about it. However, at least this much can be gathered from the very brief passages on metontology: the *Kehre* which it sets forth is to make good the *deficiencies* of a fundamental ontology which has remained too formal or schematic. Thus, the function of the turn toward a metontology is to bring back within the fold of philosophy everything which the ontological or transcendental problematic (largely equivalent terms in *Being and Time*) had to leave outside. The idea of a metontology therefore contains a hint of self-criticism, something new, because hardly anything would have allowed one to foresee it in 1927. Soon, the entire edifice of transcendentalism will be put into question by the turn, the radicalization of finitude. Its destruction will also sweep away that somewhat factical appendage of fundamental ontology which metontology apparently was supposed to have been in 1928.

Finitude is propelled to the center of what remains of fundamental ontology in the final section of *Kant and the Problem of Metaphysics*, which is not completed by any metontology. The radicalization of finitude also asserts itself in smaller works, such as "What Is Metaphysics?" and "On the Essence of Truth." The inaugural lecture of 1929 will identify the philosophical predicament par excellence as the anxiety which plunges us into the nothingness (i.e., finitude) of our being-in-the-world, and this will be the most 'inaugural' revelation of 'being'.[27] Here, all philosophical effort will be directed to liberating man from the dominion of ontical reification, so as to expose him to his essential insignificance in the face of being. Where are the transcendental schemes? What remains of the temporal horizon of *Dasein*? Nothing more. "On the Essence of Truth" will develop the idea of an original belonging-together of truth and untruth or error.[28] This belonging-together contains *in nuce* a very precise conception for Heidegger (a conception which can still be called "ontological"): the uncovering of the entity as it is may, of course, be called "truth," but this uncovering is accompanied by a partial concealing, due to the fact that the uncovering remains centered upon the entity from a particular point of view. What is "concealed" by this view (which remains the most natural thing in the world) is the being of this entity, or being as such. This fairly simple Heideggerian thesis lends itself to a phenomenological illustration: so long as the entity is revealed by a truth-intention (also called a "truth-*pretension*," or "truth-claim"), the uncovering necessarily remains on the ontical level of its immediate aim, concealing the being which makes such an uncovering of an entity possible. Insofar as all metaphysics is oriented toward the uncovering only of the entity according to a project of universal intelligibility or rationality, metaphysics "defines" itself (literally) by a constitutive error, that is, by forgetfulness of the free giving of being, prior to all concepts and explanation. Metaphysics is "in-sistence" on the entity and, thus, is characterized by a sleight of hand with being, a forgetfulness of the being or the finitude of *Dasein*, if one does not want to accuse it of never having been an ontology at all. Thus, any history of metaphysics becomes for Heidegger a narrative of the various guises with which the entity has presented itself, while being held itself back, withdrawing from the obsession with the ontical. Thus, the forgetfulness of being means being's avoidance of the totalizing and unifying nets set out for it by metaphysical understanding.

Following the indications of the "Letter on Humanism," Heidegger's meditation thinks the turn out of the crucial experience of the forgetfulness of being. As such, it may well appear impotent in the eyes of those who expect philosophy to deliver the concrete directives of an immediately practical philosophy, thus confusing the tasks of thinking with that of a board of directors or a committee on ethics. The realization articulated by this meditation demonstrates that all metaphysics proceeds from a forgetfulness of time. This realization is to be able to accompany all exercise of thought and all human activity. Finitude does not oppose an aim of non-acceptance to any theory of rationality or any "practical" philosophy, although this is what some would like us to believe today (as though there were a generally accepted conception of 'rationality'). Rather, the point is only that so-called "enlightened" rationality or practice should take note of the hypothetical character and limited scope of its projections of being. To relativize the metaphysical hegemony over being in the name of the refusal of being to human existence (which will never have done with being) is to make it understood that other perspectives are always possible and that certain ones prevail in part because of the injustice that these are the ones that have imposed themselves.

It is therefore not by chance that the "Letter on Humanism" makes reference to the lecture, "On the Essence of Truth," in order to comprehend the turn. The heart of this lecture is the idea of a forgetting, a turn away, a refusal of being, or an error inherent in all truth. Of course, one could be overly fastidious about scholarly details and emphasize that this lecture, although first delivered in 1930, was published only in 1943, and this occurred only after having been retouched. Perhaps we should take Heidegger at his word (why would he have wanted to mislead us on precisely this secondary point?) when he writes in 1946 that the lecture on truth was "*thought* and spoken in 1930" and, therefore, that the changes made after 1930 were only minor ones. An unpublished but circulating transcription of the lecture on the essence of truth, held in Marburg on December 5, 1930, confirms that although the term '*Kehre*' does not yet figure in it, no more than in the 1943 text, still, the idea of an essential error or untruth tied to the "in-sistence" on the entity or the forgetfulness of being had already been attained by 1930. This error would be situated within the history of metaphysics and applied to Plato's myth of the cave from 1931 onwards, in the course in the winter semester of 1931–32, entitled *On the Essence of Truth*.[29] Hence, it is to be concluded that the seeds of the idea of an historical, Platonizing distortion of the meaning of ἀ-λήθεια — a central theme for what has been termed the "last philosophy" of Heidegger, the thinking of the history of being (*das seinsgeschichtliche Denken*) — had already appeared at the beginning of the thirties.

All of this demonstrates that it is rash to locate the thinking of the turn around 1935–36, as remains common in Heidegger research. This hypothesis was based essentially upon the absence of philosophical publications by Heidegger between 1929 (*Kant and the Problem of Metaphysics* and "What Is Metaphysics?") and 1935 (*Introduction to Metaphysics* and "The Origin of the Work of Art"), but it can no longer be maintained now that certain lecture courses from this period have appeared in print. Undeniably, Heidegger found a new point of departure in the middle of the thirties. However, it was in fact no more than a *renewal* of the philosophy of the turn which had been set in motion after *Being and Time* and then left dormant during the relatively brief episode of Heidegger's political rectorate.

We in no way wish to lessen the gravity of this episode, whose tragic dimension remains to be reflected upon. However, given the present state of the documentation (which remains very unsatisfactory), in our estimation the political engagement of the philosopher was no more than an "intermission"[30] based upon his misapprehensions of the realities of National Socialism. It is evident that this episode coincided with a certain interruption of Heidegger's *philosophical* publications.[31] When the gestures made and positions proclaimed by Heidegger the rector are evaluated, one must indeed admit that his political adventure corresponds, according to the words of Heidegger himself, "to a *renunciation of the task of thinking* in favor of action as an administrator."[32] There was a great deal of illusion (*Realitätsferne*), hardly suitable to philosophers, in Heidegger's political intervention, which resulted in his adhering to a coalition government led by Hitler and aiming at a National Socialist revolution. Heidegger's hope was to effect a reform of the German university in the wake of this revolution, as though National Socialism and science were not mutually exclusive.

Even if Heidegger retained his National Socialist convictions for some time, he rather quickly realized his mistake, which was indeed enormous, although shared by the majority of the non-Communist intellectuals of the period. In 1934, he withdrew from the rectorate, refusing to work within the bosom of a party whose intentions were becoming clearer and clearer each day. Heidegger then devoted himself once again to philosophical questions, proceeding systematically with his thinking of the *Kehre*, left in the workshop at the outset of the thirties.[33] The lectures on the origin of the work of art of 1935 and 1936 were the first *visible* testimony to this manifest return to philosophy and to the questions of the late twenties and early thirties. There can be no doubt that from 1935 onwards, Heidegger no longer associated his philosophy and its concepts with the Nazi movement, as indubitably he had done, due to blindness, in his rectorial proclamations. From 1936 to 1938 he composed the voluminous manuscript, *Contributions to Philosophy*, in which this dissociation appears as univocally as could be desired. Published in 1989, some go so far as to consider the *Contributions* Heidegger's second *chef-d'oeuvre* after *Being and Time*. Alexander Schwan, a commentator who is usually very and openly critical of Heidegger's "political philosophy," has recently argued that the *Contributions* constitutes a radical and systematic repudiation of Nazi ideology.[34] Here, Heidegger sees the totalitarianism and gigantism of National Socialism as the most evident sign of the forgetfulness of being (*GA 65*, 30, 98ff., 122, and passim).

The *Contributions* contains remarks on the *Kehre* which are very important for our immediate purposes. Yet here, as elsewhere, the *Kehre* is *never* associated with the representation of a turn in Heidegger's own philosophy or in his "second" thinking, even though the *Contributions* constitutes one of the most massive testimonies to this latter perspective. What we can say is that the *Kehre* becomes the theme of his philosophy and that his taking cognizance of it will give rise to a new point of departure. This new departure is to bring to a conclusion the overcoming of the intelligibility of metaphysics initiated after *Being and Time*, but this only by way of a radicalization of the ideas of *Geworfenheit* and finitude at the root of that work. The fundamental experience of the *Contributions* is clearly that of the refusal of being, its essential *Verweigerung*. Being proves to be inaccessible and refractory in relation to a metaphysical intelligibility designed for the domination of the entity and for it alone. The *contribution* of the *Contributions* to *philosophy* consists in thinking the manner in which this 'refusal' (*Verweigerung*) belongs to the essence of being (*GA 65*, 175). This knowledge of being, this "essential nothingness of being," which Heidegger also terms '*Kehre*',[35] is not nihilism. To the contrary, its aim is to indicate the authentic overcoming of nihilism (*die eigentliche Überwindung des Nihilismus; GA 65*, 175). Why? Because nihilism remains the insurmountable and paralyzing horizon of thinking so far and so long as one maintains the idea of a metaphysical παρουσία or of the absolute, in view of which the refusal of being is no more than a negative experience or a vulgar nihilism. According to Heidegger, this nothingness of being or of finitude—its *Kehre*—is not merely something negative, but rather an extraordinary and unheard of chance for the *Dasein* of man. Once the attempt to attain a metaphysical transparency has been abandoned, man is called upon to think his finitude as the unsurpassable site and possibility of his freedom. Man will then be able, says Heidegger, to dwell in the *Ereignis*. What is this *Ereignis*? We will not tax ourselves with an attempt to answer this question here, since, as Heidegger cautions, any elucidation of the *Ereignis*, of the mystery of the "*es gibt*," necessarily bypasses its essence. It is Heidegger himself who struggles throughout the *Contributions* with the difficulty, if not the impossibility, of saying the *Ereignis*, or finitude, without falling back into metaphysics. This difficulty is not unrelated to the miscarriage of the attempt to say the turn in "Time and Being," a miscarriage mentioned by the "Letter on Humanism" and evidenced by the 1927 lecture course. But the renunciation (*Verzicht* or *Verhaltenheit*, 'reservedness') of the idea of metaphysical comprehensibility is certainly one of its fundamental components. It is true that the reign of intelligibility is one of meta-physics. Because of its project of explicating the entity so as to place it at the disposal of the subject, metaphysics "forgets" being in its original inexplicability, that is, in its free giving. Heidegger goes so far as to write that "comprehensibility is already equivalent to a de-struction of thinking" (*GA 65*, 435). Without a doubt, this "philoso-phy" (a title which Heidegger has not yet renounced) is the result of a radicalization of the finitude or *Geworfenheit* of *Dasein*, who will no longer attempt to understand itself as the master and owner of the entity, but rather will experience itself as projected by being. As such, this "being," this irrecoverable ground of its existence, escapes any explanation. Being will therefore be the failure of all explainability (*die Versagung jeder Erklärbarkeit; GA 65*, 477).

This refusal of being (which at first glance might be confused with a cheap mysticism) aims first and foremost at demobilizing metaphysics, at imbuing thought with a sense of the limits assigned to any enterprise of thinking. The "reservedness" of being is to serve as a reminder of that which always escapes the unmeasured effort of rationalization which swells the head of metaphysics and its lat-est modality, contemporary techno-science.[36] The *Contributions* seek to develop a thinking of the absence of being, in contradistinction to metaphysics, and to bring out that which could be liberating in this thinking. If nihilism can be overcome, asserts Heidegger, it is perhaps thanks to this experience of the cosmic refusal of being. The most troubling thing is that the silence of being, its flight, is not even experienced as such. Nothing is more urgent, Heidegger concludes, than to convey man into the urgency of the absence of urgency, that is, to sensitize him to the question of being and its essential oblivion.

We see that this thinking of being in its negativity, or its "oblivion," calls for a response from *Dasein*. It beckons it to dwell in a manner in keeping with the veiling of being, or as we translate, to comprehend its being-in-the-world with an explicit consciousness of finitude. In the *Contributions*, the term '*Kehre*' refers precisely to the relation which establishes itself between the upsurge of being as refusal and the response or type of foundation which this being can call forth out of the earth of *Dasein*. To the question, "What is the *Kehre* to the *Ereignis*?" the *Contributions* respond: "only the upsurge of being as the event of the *there* brings *Da*-sein to itself and so to the accomplishment (safekeeping) of the truth patiently founded on the entity, which finds its abode in the lighted conceal-ment of the there."[37] Admittedly Sybilline, this passage illuminates the innumerable texts in which being offers itself as the refusal which gives, as that which resists all finite projections. This pas-

sage exhorts us to think the new site of *Dasein* (to be explored by
the *Kehre*) in the direction of a radical realization of finitude, as
"lighted concealment of the there." The philosophy or thinking of the
Kehre would thus culminate in a thinking of the upsurge of being
on the earth (the *there*) of *Dasein* in a manner which reminds one
of one's finitude.

Does this *Kehre* of *being* still have something to do with the
rather technical problematic of the *temporalitas* of being, which was
to have been laid out in the third part of *Being and Time*? *Prima
facie*, not very much. However, a more careful examination reveals
that the *Contributions* retain and develop only too well the lesson
which results from the undertaking and miscarriage of "Time and
Being." The *Contributions* precisely invoke more than once the danger risked by the third part of *Being and Time*, that of a reification
of being or that of its projection along the preliminary horizon of an
intelligibility without remainder.

We have seen that this was the theme invoked by the 1927 lecture course in order to point a finger at the cardinal untruth of
fundamental ontology. The same leitmotif reappears in the *Contributions*. To think time as the transcendental horizon of being,
Heidegger reminds us, was seemingly to reduce being to something
ontical or dominable. "Through this procedure, being itself took on
the appearance of an object, thus attaining the most decisive opposite of what the setting into motion of the question of being had already opened up." Now, *Being and Time* is indeed designed to seek
to demonstrate that time constitutes the horizon for the projection
of being (*GA 65*, 451; in § 262, "The 'Project' of Being and Being as
Project"). To bring being back to a phenomenon which appears only
within a temporal horizon belonging to *Dasein*, to proceed as though
being were only the project or object of *Dasein*, is to deprive oneself
of the chance offered by the setting in motion of a questioning in
the direction of being (*GA 65*, 250), a questioning which discovers
in being the tribunal that rejects the claims of metaphysics. This crisis, the text of the *Contributions* continues, leads to the interruption
of the project of *Being and Time* at a precise moment, i.e., when it is
suddenly confronted with the resistance to reification of a rebellious
being—hence, the failure of "Time and Being" to be published:

> In order to surmount, at a decisive moment, the crisis of the
> question of being (a question which must necessarily be set into
> motion in this manner); above all, in order to *avoid a reification
> of being* (*vor allem* eine Vergegenständlichung des Seyns zu
> vermeiden), we must, on the one hand, retain the '*temporal*'

interpretation of being, and, on the other, attempt to render
the truth of being 'visible' independently of this perspective. . . .
The crisis cannot be mastered by simply thinking further in
the direction of questioning already initiated. We must attempt
a multiple leap into the essence of being itself, which will at
the same time necessitate a most original penetration into history. (*GA 65*, 451)

This new thinking of the *Kehre* opens itself to the refusal of
being, that is, to *its Kehre*, to the admonition that in withdrawing,
being is prodigal with its reminder to us of our finitude. This new
thinking is the result of the miscarriage of "Time and Being." The
Contributions strengthen the argumentation elaborated from the
time of the summer semester course of 1927, reaffirming that the
essential flaw of the *project* of *Being and Time* (independent of the
realization of this project found in the published sections of the work)
consists in the danger of a reification of being according to a purely
metaphysical horizon of intelligibility, something which goes counter
to the originary impulse which presided over the launching of an
unprecedented questioning toward being.

It is now that Heidegger "holds back" (*zurückhalten*, in the
words of the *Contributions*, which strictly echo the "Letter on Humanism") the third part of *Being and Time*. The 1927 course offers
the final version of this part, which is at the same time its most incisive critique: to reify being by inscribing it into the transcendental horizon of a temporality decreed by a *Dasein* elevated to the
dignity of a subject is to miss the truth of being and what being has
to say to us by manifesting its irreducible inaccessibility. The turn
is not a modification of the perspective of *Being and Time* which concerns merely the person or the philosophy of Martin Heidegger. First
and foremost, it designates itself as the *Kehre* into the *Ereignis*, following the *Contributions*, or as the *Kehre* into being, following the
1949 Bremen lecture. It is this discovery of the refusal, of the turn
of being itself, which gives rise to what is called the "second" philosophy of being, its transformation into a thinking of the history of
being.[38] The thinking of the *Kehre* began at the end of the twenties.
Thus, if one wishes to respect the texts and itinerary of a thinker,
one should cease to see in it, as does Habermas, a "consequence" of
Heidegger's 1933 political engagement (as though he had rapidly invented a passivist philosophy so as to settle his accounts with National Socialism and to exculpate himself from all responsibility). On
the contrary, in the *Contributions* and elsewhere, Heidegger is pur-

suing and radicalizing the path of thinking which he had opened up for philosophy in 1927.

Certainly it was the metaphysics of Aristotle which dedicated philosophy to the question of being. All other sciences concern themselves with a particular object, a domain of entities, Heidegger would translate. What remains to philosophy is being, the universal (καθόλου), the *a priori*, or the πρότερον—in short, that which serves as a foundation or principle for all entities. At the conclusion of the long odyssey of metaphysics (during which this being never allowed itself to be seized), Heidegger comes to think being as *Kehre*, as the retreat or nonpresence of that which philosophy has sought or laid claim to from its first founding. If the object of philosophy is thought as a totalizing, universal, and absolute being, then it cannot but escape the grasp of a finite thinking, which is not able to build a bridge between its concepts or fictions and the being to which it aspires.[39] In fact, philosophy has never succeeded in capturing that which is called 'being', 'reason', '*a priori*', or 'truth', and which has fascinated it from the beginning. Is the thinking of the turn equivalent to a resignation of Philosophy? No, but perhaps to a resignation from this resignation, which means a resignation to the necessity of a constant self-criticism of the classic ambitions of philosophy, or of metaphysics. The discovery of the finitude of all philosophical thought is far from being antiphilosophical, for philosophy has always accompanied its most inaugural moments with self-critique, as demonstrated in the critique of metaphysics carried out by Aristotle (of or with Plato), Kant, and Wittgenstein. This discovery can encourage philosophy to return to the forgetfulness which constitutes it, i.e., that of the incommensurability of finitude and the *a priori* it continues to require. To put it otherwise, the universal, the *a priori*, the rational, being, and its inaccessibility, could be set under finitude itself, summoned to become the *a priori* the thinking of which would give sense to the philosophical enterprise. No one can predict the form that such a philosophy of finitude might take, but philosophical endeavor since Hegel has surreptitiously been carried out in its name. Of course, in a certain respect, this consciousness of finitude was never wholly absent in metaphysics. Plato was the first to say that no god philosophizes. But why has philosophy been unable to this day to establish itself except at metaphysics and except as beyond finitude? It is this retreat from metaphysics or the *a priori* that the philosophy of the turn offers to thinking.

Chapter 6

On the Sources of *Truth and Method*

Truth and Method (hereafter: TM) has been one of the very few classical works in the German philosophical tradition to emerge since Heidegger's *Being and Time*. In what follows, I will try to sketch out, in a rather "philological" fashion, the genesis of its composition and development. To this point in time, TM has hardly been discussed as a text which has a history. There are philologies for Plato, Kant, and even Wittgenstein and Heidegger, but not yet one for Gadamer. Is one needed? Philosophers have the habit of considering philology to be less important: they are concerned with the spirit, not with the letter. Given the pervasive disdain for philological work, an interest in Gadamer philology must therefore first be aroused. What is at stake? Can the philological viewpoint expose something which the philosophical reader would miss?

In spite of its prosaic character, TM is a very complicated work, especially in terms of its organization. Is there a stringent compositional development in the series of chapters and sections? Over time TM has earned the reputation of being a rather heterogeneous work. It is true that it offers many historical studies (e.g., concerning Greek tragedy, the "beautiful" in Plato, Augustine's doctrine of the *verbum*, Hegel's concept of "experience") about which one could often be of the opinion that they stand disconnected next to each other. Sometimes the suspicion even arises, and Gadamer has at times nourished it, that TM originated from *different* investigations—perhaps from works on art, history and language. In the beginning of his "self-critique" of 1985, Gadamer speaks of TM as "a theoretical project which united the initiated investigations from various sides into the unity of a philosophical whole."[1] Does TM then consist of three different analyses which came together, perhaps by chance, to form the unity of a philosophical opus? For each individual investigation the question also arises whether it was created as a whole; indeed, many chapters in TM do read like individual essays.

One recognizes what is at stake here: the question whether TM is a disparate whole. This suspicion, which will not be supported here, implies the further question of whether TM was conceived as a unified hermeneutic theory and, therefore, can be read as a coherent philosophy. If TM is to be understood as a unity, it remains to be demonstrated how the individual parts relate to the whole of the work. Simply put, what is the basic thesis of this work and in what manner is it argumentatively developed in the individual chapters?

What sources are available for such a philological examination of the text? There are different ones. First, a philology must pay attention to the specific conjunctions of the parts of the work. How is each transition from one part to the next or from one chapter to the next, accomplished? One must ask whether these transitions are arbitrary or consistent. Second, a philological analysis must pay special attention to the "preliminary stages" of the work. Before TM, Gadamer published several individual investigations which disclose his original intuitions at that time. Some of these essays are brought together under the title "Preliminary Stages" in the beginning of the second volume of his collected works. For example, one should be struck by the fact that Gadamer was then concerned with questions (i.e., such as the problem of truth in the humanities) which preoccupied him to a far lesser extent after the publication of TM when the debates with Betti, Habermas and Derrida presented his hermeneutics with completely new challenges. Third, Gadamer's autobiographical statements concerning the composition of his major work are to be consulted, including the verbal ones.[2] For TM itself says relatively little about the most important conjunctions of its parts. Our fourth and most informative source, however, is the longhand manuscript of TM. Gadamer presented this manuscript to the University of Heidelberg Library for an exhibit that marked the occasion of his eightieth birthday and that took place from February 11 to April 15, 1980.[3] It consists of approximately 80 closely written pages, 45 of which were numbered by Gadamer. This first draft of TM does not greatly depart from the published work of 1960 in either its development, its formulations and, to some extent, in its theoretical standpoint. But, most importantly, this manuscript may

illuminate the original theme of TM due to its short length. Therefore, on the basis of the four above-mentioned sources, this chapter
will present several theses concerning the composition of TM and
in particular its major conjunctions. For corroborative purposes, the
argument presented here will be based on the published texts of
Gadamer in so far as is possible.

To begin our philological examination of TM, a few points concerning the genesis of the work should be recalled. Gadamer presented his first major systematic work relatively late in life, when
he was 60. This is understandable due in part to the historical circumstances. Between 1933 and 1945, the period following the publication of his habilitation thesis in 1931, Gadamer could not consider
a larger publication. During this time he worked on a commentary
on Aristotle's *Physics* (parts of which may be published someday[4]).
Also a larger study of sophistic and platonic politics was at that time
"prudently" discontinued.[5] After the war he was appointed rector in
Leipzig, which must again have delayed any plans for a demanding
publication. After a two-year teaching appointment in Frankfurt, he
became the successor of Karl Jaspers in Heidelberg in 1949. Caring
for the intellectual rebirth of Germany, he then dedicated himself,
as a "passionate teacher,"[6] to his teaching and pedagogically oriented
publications (e.g., the translation of *Metaphysics* book Lamda, and
a new edition of Dilthey's *Outline of the History of Philosophy*). In
addition to these trying historical circumstances, it is also true that
Gadamer found writing difficult. In regard to this time, he writes
in his "self-presentation" of 1975 (the *Philosophical Apprenticeships*
of 1977 clearly discusses Gadamer's encounters with others more
than himself): "Otherwise writing remained a real torment for me
for a long time. I always had the damnable feeling that Heidegger
was looking over my shoulder."[7] In the semester vacations between
1950 and 1959, he wrote his "Hermeneutics" (this was clearly the
general working title).

The first draft of TM was presumably written in the year 1956,
before the Loewen lectures of 1957 that were published in French
under the title "Le Problème de la conscience historique" in 1963.
They were translated in English in the *Graduate Faculty Philosophy Journal*, but the German manuscript, which may be considered
a further draft of TM, has been lost. The original draft demonstrates
first that TM was written as a whole. It has neither a title nor titled
sections. Nevertheless, the main argument or the original argument
of TM, may be grasped in it. This argument, which will be summarized here, begins with the problem of the methodological self-
understanding of the humanities in Dilthey, Droysen and Helmholtz.
This is followed by a discussion of the humanistic guiding concepts

of education and taste. At the same time, it discusses the abstractions of both historical and aesthetic consciousness, before it deals separately with the aesthetic. The central point here concerns the isolation of the aesthetic image from the context of life out of which it sprang. This isolation of the work from its environment will be the cause of a certain disconfort which the romantic era will address and answer with a new appreciation of hermeneutics with Schleiermacher (whose task of reconstruction is criticized, although without the reference to Hegel's task of integration as occurs at the end of the first part of TM). From this point on, the original draft follows the development of the hermeneutic question in Schleiermacher and Dilthey up to the new formulation of the problem in Heidegger. Then, within one and the same paragraph the transition is made to the systematic and central part of TM, a transition made by means of the doctrine of the hermeneutic circle. In the original draft one finds next the idea of a mediation between history and the present, which the classical is called upon to illustrate. Here as well, the theory of the fusion of horizons builds the central aspect of the principle of effective history. On the basis of this principle, the critique of the philosophy of reflexivity is carried through. However, the 1960 sections concerning application, judicial herme-neutics and *phronesis*, which occur between the chapters on effective history and the philosophy of reflexivity, are absent in the original draft.[8] From this point in the argument, the universal aspect of language is developed. The important *Cratylus* und *Verbum* analyses follow, the latter, however, without reference to the Thomistic reception. The logic of question and answer is first discussed here (i.e., before the "third" part of TM). Furthermore, the reference to Humboldt is missing in what will be the third part of TM. Gadamer's discussion of the universal character of language in this section often addresses the problem of relativism and the hermeneutic character of philosophical statements, to which I will return. The proof of the metaphysical character of the beautiful in Plato, the actual conclusion of TM, also occurs near the end of the original draft. However, the manuscript, in its original form, returns finally to the problem of the humanities. Nonetheless, it soon becomes clear that one is concerned with a new editing of the first pages of the work. Sketched summaries follow, which are certainly indications of further working plans.

While the absence of subdivisions in the development of thought in the first draft often makes it difficult to follow, it does permit the unified character of the work and its original intention to be grasped in outline. Due to the later introduction of the tripartite division of the book, it is the ruling opinion that the first part concerns "art," the second "history" or the "humanities" (as if they were the same) and the third "language." However, by referring to the original draft, this generally held opinion can be put into question.

It is also true for the printed version that the first part does not only, and perhaps does not primarily, concern "art." The point of departure for the first part, and certainly for the whole work, is the problem of the methodological self-clarification in the humanities. In fact, the title of the first section of the first part serves as proof : "The Meaning of the Humanistic Tradition for the Humanities" (whose sub-sections are "(a) The Problem of Method; (b) Humanistic Guiding Concepts"). In the first 50 pages of TM, art is not even mentioned. Gadamer's problem is rather the correct self-understanding of the humanities in opposition to the natural sciences. In order to present this problem, Gadamer situates the discussion around Helmholtz's commemorative speech of 1862 on the relationship between the natural sciences and the humanities. Helmholtz's speech, by the way, is the one he delivered upon becoming pro-rector of the University of Heidelberg—which constitutes an auspicious relation to Gadamer's own place of work. In his presentation Helmholtz finds natural sciences to be characterized by the practice of logical induction which leads to universal rules and laws. The humanities, on the other hand, achieve their knowledge more by means of a psychological feeling of tact. Helmholtz speaks here of an artistic induction, of instinctive feeling and artistic tact, which proceed without clearly defined rules. With only a little exaggeration, one could claim that Gadamer's privileged conversation partner in the first part of TM is Helmholtz. At strategic points in the first part reference is made to Helmholtz.[9] Furthermore, should it be the case that one has understood a book when one has grasped the question to which it is the answer, then one could say that it was Helmholtz's question concerning the manner of cognition in the humanities which gave the impetus to TM.

It is especially evident that Gadamer is essentially in *solidarity* with Helmholtz. As is stated towards the end of the original draft:

At the end of all attempts to justify the unique method of the humanities, one finds oneself returning to the straightforward conclusions which Helmholtz made. What one terms method in modern science is exemplarily effective in the natural sciences. The method of the humanities has, fundamentally, actually nothing of its own. But the question arises as to how important method is here and whether there do not exist other conditions, which supervene here. Helmholtz correctly indicated exactly this point when he emphasized memory and authority and spoke of psychological tact, which here replaced conscious proving. What is the basis of such tact? How is it attained? Does not the scientific nature of the humanities lie finally more in this than in the use of "method"?[10]

Gadamer and Helmholtz agree that the humanities are fundamentally much more concerned with practicing a tact than with applying some sort of method. Although Helmholtz proceeded from the exemplary status of the natural scientific method—nothing else was possible in the second half of the ninteenth century—he still correctly grasped (according to Gadamer) the uniqueness of the humanities in 1862. One measures immediately the provocation of Gadamer's solidarity: by returning to 1862 and to an argument offered by the *natural scientist* Helmholtz, Gadamer skips over the epistemological discussions concerning the methodological uniqueness of the humanities, which were conducted toward the end of the nineteenth and in the beginning of the twentieth century by authors such as Dilthey, Misch, Rothacker and Weber and which were influenced by the ruling Neo-Kantianism. The point is surely that these protracted debates were possessed by the idea that the humanities must somehow also have their own method in order to elevate them to sciences. It appears to Gadamer, who follows Helmholtz here, much more appropriate to trace the uniqueness of the humanities back to something like tact, a "je ne sais quoi" which cannot be methodologized. Helmholtz, not Dilthey,[11] becomes thereby the silent representative of a hermeneutics which correctly exemplifies the specific mode of cognition in the humanities. In this spirit, TM conducts a fundamental critique of the methodological obsession apparent in the Neo-Kantian concern for the scientific nature of the humanities.

Accordingly, the initial thesis of TM is that the scientific character of the humanities may "be understood more easily from the tradition of the concept of education (*Bildung*) than from the modern idea of scientific method."[12] It is here that the meaning of the recourse to the humanistic tradition, which appears at the beginning of TM, is uncovered. In the heart of this tradition, the concepts which are able to correctly express the particular claim to knowledge of the humanities were developed. According to Gadamer, this tradition was very much alive before Kant and previous to its being supplanted by the foreign rule of the concept of method. So Gadamer must pursue the question: "how did this tradition became so impoverished and how did the human sciences' claim to know something true come to be measured by a standard foreign to it—namely the methodical thinking of modern science?"[13] How did this deteriorization of the humanistic tradition, which led to the sole rule of the idea of method dominated more and more by the natural sciences, take place? Gadamer answers that it occurred by means of the ominous aesthetization of the basic concepts of the humanistic tradition, especially judgment and taste, which previously were acknowledged to have a *cognitive* function. This was the act or effect (Gadamer varies somewhat in the characterization) of Kant's *Critique of Judgment*, which subjectivized and aestheticized taste and, what amounts to the same thing, denied it cognitive value. What could not satisfy the criteria of the objective and methodological natural sciences, was now seen as merely "subjective" or "aesthetic" (i.e., separated from the realm of knowledge). The Kantian subjectivization of the concept of taste, in "discrediting any kind of theoretical knowledge except that of natural science, compelled the human sciences to rely on the methodology of the natural sciences in conceptualizing themselves."[14] The humanistic tradition, in which the humanities could have recognized themselves, was thereby abandoned and the path of the aesthetization and subjectivization of judgment followed. One measures the loss for the humanities: "The importance of this cannot be easily overestimated, for what was here surrendered was the element in which philological and historical studies lived, and when they sought to ground themselves methodologically under the name of «human sciences» side by side with the natural sciences, it was the only possible source of their full self-understanding."[15]

This development also has important consequences for the textual structure of TM. For art or aesthetics is first introduced here, in the discussion of TM. Nevertheless, the exposure of the subjectivization and aesthetization of the fundamental supports of the humanistic tradition does not lose sight of the guiding question concerning the self-understanding of the humanities. Gadamer avidly pursues this guiding question when he decisively criticizes the development which led to the creation of a completely new and specific *aesthetic* consciousness. The middle of the first part of TM, therefore, consists in a "critique of the abstraction of aesthetic consciousness."[16] If the expression may be permitted, one might say that, in terms of the composition of TM, the path into the aesthetic represents a kind of "detour." In spite of all the positive insights into art, the initial confrontation of TM is rather an "anti-aesthetic" than an aesthetic. The creation of the aesthetic is nothing more than an abstraction, which needs—in the words of the early Heidegger—to be destroyed or relativized in order to (re-)gain an appropriate understanding of the mode of cognition in the humanities.

This regaining of the hermeneutic specificity of the humanities is accomplished in the following part of TM, especially in its systematic and major subdivision, which is preceded by a historical review. How stringent is the textual transition from the first part to the second part of TM? The opposition of Hegel and Schleiermacher constitutes the transitional point in the published version. While Schleiermacher understood the fundamental task of understanding to be a reconstruction and reproduction of a past act, Hegel saw it in the task of integrating history and the present. In this respect, Hegel more adequately presented the historical productivity of understanding than Schleiermacher. Gadamer wishes to follow "Hegel rather than Schleiermacher" and to urge the history of hermeneutics to "place its emphases quite differently."[17] For this reason the "dogmatic presuppositions" of the development of hermeneutics are to be exposed in the second part of TM. The transition is somewhat different in the original draft in which the reference to Hegel is completely missing. Schleiermacher's position is alone decisive. In this regard, Gadamer especially emphasizes the discomfort which follows the creation of the artistic consciousness and the associated isolation of the work of art from the horizon of its creation. Schleiermacher still had a keen sense about the "organic interdependence of the work of art and its situation of origination"[18] in his lectures on aesthetics. The task of historical understanding was therefore to reconquer this original world. Accordingly, he saw the historical understanding of the work of art "as a reconstitution of the uprooting which influenced the understanding of the work, therefore, history as a means to completely grasp the artistic meaning of the work—a restitution in and for the aesthetic consciousness."[19] The interest in the reconstitution of the original work was still a normative one; it concerned the rewinning of an exemplary stylistic ideal. Gadamer especially discusses the interest in the stylistic ideal of classical simplicity, which was persued by Winckelmann and Herder and which brought to life classical studies as well as the romantic interest in the Middle Ages. Exactly at this point the transition, which is still not yet one, occurs to the second part of TM:

> In this situation of a historical-normative interest in the romantic Middle Ages, an old discipline of Biblical theology and classical philology regains a new life. And the whole future of historical sciences will be influenced by it: hermeneutics. On

both paths, the theological and the philological, this art of understanding and interpretation developed from an analogous impulse: theological hermeneutics, as Dilthey has beautifully shown, as a self-defense of the reformation's understanding of the Bible against the attack of the Tridentian theologists and their appeal to the indispensability of tradition; the philological hermeneutics as an instrument for the humanistic claim to re-discover classical literature."[20]

The last lines are identical with the beginning of the second part in TM. Only the point of departure is somewhat different. For reasons of space, I must forgo a presentation of the very rich second part, as it appears in the original and published versions. Two remarks must suffice. First, the systematic second subdivision of the second part is to be viewed as a type of conclusion or response to the question of TM concerning the appropriate self-understanding of the humanities. This is not only due to the fact that in this subdivision the concepts are explicated which stand at the center of the discussion about philosophical hermeneutics (such as effective history, fusion of horizons, rehabilitation of prejudices, authority and tradition, application and the logic of question and answer). The fact that it is a response or a conclusion is already evident in the title of the systematic subdivision: "Fundamentals of a Theory of Hermeneutic Experience." For this title is almost identical with the original title of the book, which was relegated to being a subtitle during the printing: "Fundamentals of Philosophical Hermeneutics." There can be no doubt, therefore, that in this subdivision TM attains its goal as stated in the introduction, i.e., to situate the truth claims of the humanities.

Our second remark is precisely that this second part still concerns the problem of the humanities. In both the published as well as in the original version, Gadamer speaks in this section, continually and consequently, of his project as being one of a "hermeneutics of the humanities."[21] This must be emphasized because *after* the publication of TM, the problem of hermeneutics was considered to be one of a general theory of historicity, facticity, the life-world and dialogue. This development is quite correct, but the work of 1960 remains completely influenced and ruled by its initial problem, the humanities.[22]

Nevertheless, the development towards a *philosophical* hermeneutics, which leaves the "limited" problem of the humanities behind it, is already present in 1960. This is, however, to be accomplished in the third part of TM. There, the universal dimension of hermeneutics is to be brought to light. The basis of this universal aspect is, however, not immediately evident. The sure, but limited, means of philology alone certainly do not permit its discovery. Nonetheless there exists a certain consensus that this universality is to be accredited to "language," and so the third part of TM should be a discussion of "language."

To a certain extent, the means of philology do permit this consensus to be questioned. For some texts indicate that the actual discussion of the third part is to be about "philosophy." For example, on the first page (of the Introduction) of TM one reads about the goal of the investigation:

> Its purpose is to seek out those experiences of truth, wherever they may be encountered, which transcend the area of control of the scientific method and to question them concerning their own legitimacy. So the humanities are brought together with other ways of experiencing which lie outside science: with the experience of philosophy, with the experience of art and with the experience of history itself.[23]

Right at the beginning of TM this passage confronts us with the triad: philosophy, art and history. Is this perhaps a mistake by Gadamer, who forgot to emphasize language as the third and fundamental area of experience in his hermeneutics? Or does Gadamer thereby hit the nail on the head by identifying the subject matter which is to be considered within the context of the "ontological" turn of hermeneutics *following the guide* of language (the title of the third part)? However, what does "ontological" mean here? Primarily, it means that, following the lead of Heidegger, a turn of hermeneutics toward the philosophical is envisioned. The closing section of TM concerns hermeneutics' becoming universal, *that means* philosophical. It is precisely here that the transition is achieved from the "hermeneutics of the humanities" of the second part to an authentic "philosophical hermeneutics" in the third part, which is to be accomplished following the "guide" of language. From the text, it appears that a (hermeneutic) self-understanding is to be initiated here which draws on the consequences from the hermeneutics of the humanities in the second part.

This turn of hermeneutics towards the philosophical, I believe, is much clearer in the original draft than in the published work. On the first page of the original draft, the task of the investigation is already determined to be the exploration of a new basis for philosophy out of the self-understanding of the humanities. Since it has not yet been translated, it is of value to quote the first paragraph in its entirety:

> It is not only a need for logical clarity which connects the humanities with philosophy. To a greater extent the so-called humanities present philosophy itself with a problem. What one has stated and could say about their logical, epistemological foundation and about the justification of their scientific independence in opposition to the natural sciences, remains far behind what the humanities are and what they mean for philosophy. It could be nothing—or everything. Nothing, if they are considered as only an incomplete realization of the idea of science. For it follows from this that the idea of "scientific philosophy" will also be measured in terms of the complete determination of this idea of science as it is presented in the mathematical natural sciences, i.e., understood only, however, as a tool of these sciences. On the other hand, where the idea of the humanities is recognized as an independent type of science, whose reduction to the ideal of natural scientific knowledge is impossible, and where the idea of the greatest possible approximation to the methods and certainty of natural sciences is even recognized as absurd, there philosophy itself and all of its concerns are brought into play. It is doomed to fail, if the discussion of the methodological particularity of the humanities is limited to the methodological: it does not concern another, unique method, but rather a completely different idea of knowledge and truth. And philosophy, if it acknowledges this claim, will project for itself completely different goals than are demanded by the concept of truth in science. A true foundation for the humanities, as Dilthey sought to achieve, is, with inner necessity, a foundation for philosophy.

TM is opposed to the determination of the scientific character of philosophy which orients itself according to the methodological natural sciences. Philosophy can learn from the properly understood humanities that its knowledge is not based upon methodological distance, but rather upon the belongingness of the interpreter to its object and to its history. It is clear that a philosophy which accepts this "completely different idea of knowledge and truth" will also "project for itself completely different goals." Based upon the self-understanding of the humanities, which is presented in the first two parts of TM, a new, hermeneutical foundation for philosophy is to be made possible in the third part.

This transition becomes evident in the development of the original draft. As soon as the principle of effective history is established, Gadamer advances to the determination of the limits of the philosophy of reflexivity. In so doing, the third part of TM actually begins and the becoming philosophical of hermeneutical self-understanding which has been freed from methodological prejudices presents itself to the reader. The principle of effective history clearly implies becoming conscious of the continuing efficacy of tradition beyond our conscious awareness of these effects, and therefore, the impossibility of a complete self-awareness of consciousness about itself. Gadamer opposes such an understanding to the absolute claim of the philosophy of reflexivity. The power of history renders unattainable the speculative self-possession of consciousness, which the philosophy of reflexivity has envisioned up to the present. Gadamer states:

> But, properly considered, the power of history does not depend upon its being acknowledged. The power of history over finite human consciousness is exactly that it has its effect even when one, through the belief in method, denies one's own historicity. The demand to become conscious of this effective history is so urgent precisely because of this situation.[24]

The next task is to convince philosophy about this urgency. Philosophy, hermeneutically understood, is not exhausted by a system of true sentences. Its propositions may only be understood when one has referred them back to their motivational background. The content of philosophical propositions, as all propositions, cannot be read from their semantic-logical character.[25] To understand philosophically and hermeneutically one must proceed to the motivation of the spoken. In the classical terminology of Augustine, from whom alone the hermeneutic claim to universality in Gadamer's sense may be understood, one is concerned with the *actus exercitus*. This fundamental intuition, which is derived from Augustine, as seen through the early Heidegger,[26] is already found in the preliminary studies to TM. For example, in the important essay of 1957, "What is Truth?", Gadamer writes:

> I believe that one can principly state: there can exist no statement which is absolutely true (. . .). There exists no statement which one can grasp only from the context which it presents, if one wishes to grasp it in its truth. Every statement is motivated. Every statement has its presuppositions, which it does not express.[27]

This *universal hermeneutic* character of philosophical sentences
is the actual theme at the end of TM. Gadamer uses the adjective
"hermeneutic" here, as he later recognizes, "with reference to a manner of speech which Heidegger developed in his early period."[28] As
we can learn from the only recently available lectures of the young
Heidegger, the hermeneutical is to be understood as being distinct
from, but not unrelated to the "apophantical." While the apophantical retains only the level of sense which constitutes the form
of the logical proposition, the hermeneutical envisions the preceding, more original sphere of the unstated self-interpretation of *Dasein*
which motivates the apophantic. Through the universal hermeneutic
character of philosophical sentences, Gadamer supports the thesis
that philosophical sentences are not to be reduced to their logical
content, but are only to be comprehended in their total meaning from
their motivational background. I quote again from the original draft
and indeed from one of the last paragraphs, its *conclusio*, if one will:

It is necessary to also understand the propositions of philosophy in their propositional character, i.e., also they are not to
be organized as separated, absolute, and in a system of true
sentences, but are to be understood in their "meaning." This
meaning is in every proposition, as is to be remembered, a direction of meaning, results from its motivation. This reference
of all philosophical propositions to such a motivational background does not at all imply, therefore, that every proposition—
as always motivated—is correct. Rather, what is more
important is to establish the motivational level as such.[29]

The actual meaning of the claim for the universality of
hermeneutics lies in this motivational structure of language, in the
verbum interius, which is to be understood as the *actus exercitus* in its
complete meaning. The dialectic of question and answer is called upon
in order to clarify this motivational structure. It is no surprise that this
dialectic is contained in the original draft in the section on language
(the later third part). In the printed version it enables precisely the
transition from the hermeneutics of the humanities, contained in the
second part, to the philosophical or universal hermeneutics of the last
part. This dialogic, which replaces Hegel's dialectic aiming towards
completion, embodies "the hermeneutically primordial phenomenon,
that there exists no possible proposition which could be understood as
anything else but an answer to a question."[30]

This hermeneutically primordial phenomenon legitimizes the
universality of philosophical hermeneutics. It makes sense that this

"universal aspect," as TM almost paradoxically states, primarily concerns "language." For this reason language enjoys the guiding function in the last part of TM and so constitutes its central theme.
However, the discussion of a *philosophical* hermeneutics means
more: it is a new understanding of philosophy which results from
the hermeneutics of the humanities (in part II). The textual unity
of TM becomes evident here in that "the methodological self-
understanding of philology pushes towards a systematic questioning of philosophy."[31] One will understand and appreciate that this
hermeneutics, which has become universal, i.e., philosophical
hermeneutics, and which situates itself in the dialogical element of
language, will develop for itself completely different goals than those
which would be suggested by a methodical, self-certain and scientific philosophy of reflexivity. Its direction of attack will certainly in-
clude the need to "break the rigidity of the so-called chemically pure
concepts."[32]

The well-known, three-part division of TM ("art," "history," "language") therefore receives a new coherence. As it was noted above,
this division is also somewhat inexact. First of all, the opening section does not primarily concern art. Its point of departure is rather
the methodological problem in the humanities and the deterioration
of the humanistic tradition wherein the humanities could have been
able to recognize themselves, a deteriorioation which is due to the
ominous aesthetization of the concept of taste. The aesthetic, and
even autonomous art, which constitute abstractions, are criticized
in the first part for the purpose of a better hermeneutic evaluation
of the guiding concepts of humanism. After this "detour," the second part is dedicated to the problematic of a hermeneutics of the
humanities. Despite all the emphasis on historicity and effective history, it does not specifically concern "history" and avoids speculations
on the philosophy of history. Finally, while the third part certainly
deals with "language" and its universal hermeneutic dimension, it
implies the unspoken motivational structure of language, the dialogic of question and answer which conditions every proposition. In
short, it implies the *verbum interius*, a hermeneutical view which
finally aims at a new self-conception of philosophy.

Clearly, with these remarks the domain of pure philology has
been somewhat transgressed. In order not to break the boundaries
of our project, therefore, let's now return to the textual evidence of
TM and its third part. In relation to the corresponding discussions
of the original draft, the final part of TM might appear somewhat
unsatisfying. Even without reference to the original draft, this is
apparent in the vague use of language which other critics have al-

ready had reason to fault. In this regard, Gadamer employs extremely imprecise formulations in the third part and this stands in sharp contrast to the conceptual precision achieved in the second part. For example, the thesis that "Being which can be understood, is language," the idea of an "ontological turn" and a "universal aspect" of hermeneutics are formulations which are not very often understood. Furthermore, why were these theses also presented as historical interpretations of Augustine and Plato? What Gadamer wishes to say in the third part remains very difficult to pinpoint if one does not consider the motivational background of the original draft.

However, what accounts for this lack of precision in the published third part? Viewed in a purely philological manner, the comfortable expediency about an earlier or later edition of the third part could suggest itself. It is clearly customary in philology to explain away differing textual editions by means of periodizing. In order to discover whether my private feelings were perhaps misleading here, I finally asked Professor Gadamer himself about this vagueness in the third part. He answered in complete sincerity that indeed this third part even appears to himself to be linguistically very indistinct. Moreover, he explained that perhaps he had run out of breath at the end of his work on such a long text. The third part, therefore, was composed more hastily and the precision of the formulations was given less attention. While each is free to accept or reject this self-explanation, until a futher explanation is offered, it does have something to it.

Following this self-explanation, Gadamer has provided other small hints. Although the third part might appear to be inexact, he has made up for this in the years after TM through his work on the theme of language which was discussed in general in his 1960 publication. In fact, after 1960 Gadamer increasingly turned his attention to the theme of language, which previously was less the subject matter of detailed publications. Up to that point in time, his main theme was certainly the humanities, which still dominated in TM.[33]

If that is the case, one must recognize that the text of TM does not end in the year 1960, but continues beyond. This is supported by the interesting history of the title *Truth and Method*. As one can learn from his autobiography,[34] the book was originally to be called "Fundamentals of a Philosophical Hermeneutics." Gadamer's publisher found the title somewhat exotic. "Hermeneutics" was then clearly not a common term. So Gadamer decided to make the original title the subtitle. We should bear in mind however that the original title was "Fundamentals of a Philosophical Hermeneutics."

Gadamer announced his work to colleagues under this title, and TM was also sometimes reviewed under this old heading. In his debate with Gadamer, Emilio Betti continually quotes the book as "Fundamentals of a Philosophical Hermeneutics" as if the title "Truth and Method" did not exist.

At the time of the publication of TM, Gadamer also considered the title "Event and Understanding" which he perhaps rejected because of its similarity to a title of Bultmann's (*Faith and Understanding*). Only during the printing did the new, Goethesque title, "Truth and Method" occur to him. However, the matter does not end here. The book appeared between the years 1960 and 1975 in four editions. A fifth edition appeared in the year 1986 as volume I of the *Collected Works*. Until now it has been overlooked that the title was then silently somewhat modified. In fact, besides the first volume which presents the revised and corrected text of 1960, a second volume appeared with "supplementary material" that consists primarily of essays on philosophical hermeneutics which were published before and after TM. This second volume also bears the title *Truth and Method*. This title literally stands on the title-page of the two first volumes of the complete edition. The only thing which differentiates the first volume, with respect to the title, is the heading "Fundamentals of a Philosophical Hermeneutics." Consequently, the text of 1960 regains, de facto, its original title. The title "Fundamentals of a Philosophical Hermeneutics" applies only to the first volume (i.e., TM as it was published in 1960). Surreptitiously, "Truth and Method" became the title for the two volumes. In this manner, the prefaces and postscripts of the later editions could be accommodated in the second volume.

In this Gadamer gives an important hint for the understanding of his work: namely, that one should not limit TM to the work published in 1960. In fact, after 1960, Gadamer continued to work on TM, on his hermeneutics.[35] Only the "Fundamentals" of TM remained, necesarily, the same. Those who wish to understand to truly read TM, therefore, must also take into consideration both the works after and before TM. The composition of TM did not end in 1960 and, indeed, it still continues.

Chapter 7

Gadamer and Augustine:
On the Origins of the Hermeneutical
Claim to Universality[*]

The subtitle of this chapter alludes to hermeneutics' claim to universality. However, at first glance, it may be surprising that the title brings the name of Augustine into the context of this discussion. For Augustine is almost never referred to in the course of passionate debates raised by hermeneutics' claim to universality. In this regard, one is much more likely to be concerned with the limits of the hermeneutical "idealism of linguisticality" (Habermas), the scope of the psychoanalytical model and the legitimacy of a methodical, explanatory tendency in the social sciences. It is not very obvious how Augustine is relevant to these controversies.

   Nevertheless, the text which follows will attempt to expose why hermeneutics' claim to universality can only be adequately understood by referring to Augustine. However, before we turn our attention directly towards the details of Augustine's contribution, there are two pieces of textual evidence, which help to establish the Augustinian origins of Gadamer's notion of hermeneutical universality, that should be pointed out. First, we should note that the very

---

[*] This paper was given originally at a gathering of the Martin-Heidegger-Gesellschaft in 1990 at Heidelberg on the occasion of Hans-Georg Gadamer's 90th birthday. Translated by Brice Wachterhauser

last chapter of *Wahrheit und Methode*, which discusses "the universal aspect of hermeneutics" actually offers a discussion of Plato and Augustine in order to throw the "speculative" content of language into bold relief. This Platonic-Augustinian context was not really taken into consideration in the debate sparked by Habermas.

Secondly, in the third part of *Wahrheit und Methode* one finds a critique of the Western forgetfulness of language (*Sprachvergessenheit*), a forgetfulness that had already set in with Plato as language, understood instrumentally, fell into a completely secondary relationship to self-certifying thought. In terms of our discussion, it is important to note that Gadamer knows of just one exception to this forgetfulness of language: the Augustinian theory of the word (*Verbumslehre*). Only in the context of Christian thinking about the incarnation is Gadamer able to recognize that: "the forgetfulness of language in Western thought has not been complete."[1] In fact, Gadamer dedicates an important chapter in the last part of *Wahrheit und Methode* to this exception where he treats with compassion the early medieval speculations on the theory of the Trinity. However, given the singularity of this theological horizon, this section remained relatively unnoticed in the debates on the hermeneutic claim to universality. Still, it may be worthwhile to learn why it would occur that Augustine forms the single exception to the Western forgetfulness of language, especially since it is the task of the universal claim of hermeneutics to overcome this forgetfulness. In any case, it is enough for us to note the above two examples to hint at some closer than expected link between Augustine and hermeneutics.

In fact, Augustine has been an essential discussion partner for the hermeneutics of the 20th century[2]. The young Heidegger, who occupied himself with the phenomenology of religion, declared his interest in Augustine very early on. In the summer semester of 1921 he held an as yet unpublished lecture course on Augustine and Neo-Platonism and even in 1930, as his thinking was gripped by a "turn," he held a talk, likewise unpublished, that was entitled: "Augustinus: Quid est tempus? Confessiones lib. XI"; and again in 1960 he took as the basis of his seminar on "Image and Word" in Bremen, a citation from the 10th book of the *Confessions*.[3] Furthermore, the references to Augustine in *Sein und Zeit*, as well as those in the published lectures, come across as being generally positive, a fact worth emphasizing as Heidegger was already then committed to the program of a critical *Destruction* of the history of Western ontology. According to Gadamer's testimony, Heidegger welcomed Augustine as one, if not the most important, corroborator (*Eideshelfer*) in his conception of the complete meaning of the statement (*Vollzugssinn der Aussage*), a notion which he used against the metaphysical-idealistic tradition. It is with Augustine that we are lead back to the fundamental difference between the *actus signatus*, the predicative statement, and its completion (after the fact), in the *actus exercitus*. In this regard, according to Gadamer's account, Heidegger used Augustine's incantation very succesfully to charm his audience in Freiburg and Marburg, and indeed Gadamer himself[4].

As it comes out in the newly published lecture on the "*Hermeneutics of Facticity*" (1923), Heidegger highly valued Augustine's hermeneutical tract, *De doctrina christiana*, a text which Gerhard Ebeling has celebrated—not without justification—as the most historically influential work of hermeneutics.[5] At the beginning of this lecture, where Gadamer was in fact present, Heidegger distinguishes Augustine's work as "the first hermeneutics in the great style."[6] Heidegger contrasts this "hermeneutics in the great style" with the subsequent and, in his opinion, more formal hermeneutics of, for example, Schleiermacher, who "[reduced] the far-reaching, and living elements seen in the idea of hermeneutics (cf. Augustine) to an 'art of understanding' (*Kunstlehre*)."[7] In so far as it is fitting to catch sight of "the far-reaching and living elements seen in the idea of hermeneutics" in Augustine, it is not hard to detect them in the text of *De doctrina christiana*. Heidegger was surely impressed by the unmistakable connection that Augustine advances between simply understanding the text and the zealous stance of the person who not only seeks to understand, but whose singular concern is to seek the living truth. This connection lends his hermeneutics an unmistakable 'existential' tendency, which for a long time has earned Augustine the reputation for being a protoexistentialist. The desire to understand a written work is not an indifferent and purely epistemic process that occurs between a subject and an object. Rather, it is always a self-understanding that bears witness to the fundamental uneasiness and way of being of a *Dasein* who strives after meaning. The fact that understanding always simultaneously implies self-understanding is a notion which *Sein und Zeit* could use to expose the tacit epistemological boundaries of the hermeneutics of its time.

From this point of view we can understand Heidegger's (and Gadamer's) reliance on Augustine's distinction between an *actus signatus* and an *actus exercitus* (i.e., between what the statement simply says and the completion (*Vollzug*) that it encourages from the understanding person). Clearly, it is here that one finds the root of Heidegger's insight into the statement's fullness or "completion of meaning" (*Vollzugssinn*). The statement does not consist only and primarily in its propositional or semantic content, rather it consists in the achievement or completion (*Vollzug*) which it hopes to foster. Whoever wishes to truly understand linguistic utterances should not restrict her attention to the linguistic sign as such, but must rather be open to the offer of meaning (*Sinnangebot*) that each word contains. This Augustinian conviction was so essential to Heidegger that in *Sein und Zeit* he did not hesitate to speak boldly and provocatively of the "derivative character" of the proposition, which is to my mind one of the most fundamental and contemporary of Heidegger's ideas. The statement, as a secondary manifestation, is the propositional fallout (*Niederschlag*) of an existential (*daseinsmässigen*) relationship to the world whereby the proposition levels everything to the language of the given ("S is P"). Working behind the proposition, is that which Heidegger names the "hermeneutical." Before the apophantic (i.e., propositional) 'as' stands the more content-laden hermeneutical 'as.' This hermeneutical 'as' can only be acquired through a completion of meaning (i.e., by dealing with the motivation and context of interpretation). This is true Augustinianism.

Therefore, Heidegger also requires "hermeneutical concepts" or "formal indications" for his own philosophy. As Heidegger conceived things, the primary purpose of a "formal indication" is not to describe what is objectively given, but to enable *Dasein* to accomplish out of its very own situation a proper self-understanding which entails an always specific, or interpretive, "co-execution" (*Mitvollzug*)[8]. In the Jaspers Review, Heidegger characterizes "hermeneutical concepts" as expressions that do not simply intend to make a given, neutral fact present, but "are only accessible by always pursuing renewed interpretation."[9] Accordingly, for Heidegger, the 'hermeneutical' aims at that which stands behind every word and which alone makes its understanding possible. For his part, Gadamer agrees that he used the word 'hermeneutical' "in connection with a way of speaking developed by Heidegger in his early days,"[10] as he admitted in the important essay on "The Universality of the Hermeneutical Problem" (1966), which set in motion the debate with Habermas.

Gadamer, to whom we now turn, relies on the classical and certainly antiquated terminology of the Stoics and Augustine in order to express this state of affairs. Gadamer asserts that behind each word uttered, behind the λόγος προφορικός lies a λόγος ἐνδιάθετος, an inner word or a *verbum interius*. This essential insight was found by Heidegger and Gadamer in Augustine's *De trinitate*, a text highly valued by both, and which the chapter on the Christian theory of the word in *Wahrheit und Methode* brings into relief. Augustine turned to the Stoic distinction between the λόγος προφορικός and

ἐνδιάθετος in order to make the event of the incarnation more accessible to theological understanding. According to the fourth Gospel, God's son is viewed as the Wisdom or the λόγος of God who has
come into the world. For Augustine, as for every Christian theology,
the incarnation presents the most difficult of challenges for an understanding of the Christian gospel. What happened in this "becoming flesh" (*Fleischwerdung*)? If the word of Christ was the full
presence of God, then it must be explained how the eternal could
manifest itself within time. If Jesus had been originally only a human being, then he could not have been God in the full sense. Therefore, the theory of the Trinity must strike a path between the
Charybdis of a pure subordinationism (i.e., the notion that Christ
was a secondary manifestation of God) and the Scylla of Docetism
(i.e., the heresy that Christ's body was not human but one of celes-
tial substance).

With this objective in mind, Augustine calls upon the linguis-
tic-logical distinction between an outer and inner word or *verbum*.
Identifying that original speech or thought is an inner word or language of the heart, Augustine states: "*verbum est quod in corde
dicimus : quod nec graecum est, nec latinum, nec linguae alicujus
alterius.*"[11] This inner speech, which has no sensuous or material
form, is purely intellectual or universal. In other words, it has not
yet taken on the form of a *particular*, sensuous or historical language. When we hear a word in a particular language it is clear that
we do not attempt to understand it in its particular, accidental form.
Rather, we attempt to understand the *verbum* or the reason embodied in it (imperfectly, of course, as it is with every incarnation of the
intellectual among human beings). Therefore, it is necessary to transcend the sensuous, uttered language in order to reach the true, human *verbum* (*sed transeunda sunt haec, ut ad illud perveniatur
hominis verbum*)[12]. What one strives to reach is the *verbum*; and
while it does not offer itself in sound, it nevertheless dwells in all
speech and is presupposed in all signs into which it can be "translated." When this intimate word of the soul or the heart takes on the
sensuous form of a concrete language it will not be expressed as it is,
but as it can be seen from the standpoint of our physical being (*nam
quando per sonum dicitur, vel per aliquod corporale signum, non
dicitur sicut est, sed sicut potest videri audirive per corpus*)[13].

The theological gain that Augustine obtains from this theory
is considerable. This distinction between the inner and the outer
word also holds *per analogiam* for Christ, the Word of God. The
divine Word, which comes into the historical world at a particular
time, is not to be confused with the Word that is coeternal with God.

This difference allows Augustine to conceive of both the distinction between and the sameness of the historically revealed Word and the eternal Word of God. Just as a human utterance presupposes an inner word, a Word pre-exists with God before creation and the earthly appearance of Christ (a Word which the tradition understood as the *sapientia* or self-knowledge of God)[14]. It is also valid to say that this Word took on a sensuous form at a particular time in order that it might be communicated to human beings. Just as our language mediates no exact copy of our inner thoughts, it must be true for the Word of God that the outer, contingent and sensuous Word is separate from the inner, eternal and ideal Word of God as it is in itself. Nevertheless—and this we find only with God—the manifestation of the divine Word in the historical world was essentially the same as God's *sapientia* so that God could be thought to have been fully present in the utterance (*Veräusserung*) of his Word.

Augustine marks the limit of this analogy with the human word in that the essential sameness between thought and the concrete word almost never occurs for human beings. While the Word of God means the complete self-knowledge of God, the human word, on the other hand, does not have a comparable self-possession at its disposal. Only very seldom is our word a reflection of knowledge which is certain. In this regard, Augustine questions whether our word originates only from that which we know and from our science?[15] Indeed, is it not true that there is much we say without possessing final clarity about the knowledge we are using? In contrast to God's Word, our word is alloted no final self-evidence, and this comes from the fact that our being is not bound up with a pure and true self-knowledge (*quia non hoc est nobis esse, quod est nosse*). Our word is always created out of an implicit knowing, a "je ne sais quoi" (*quiddam mentis nostrae*)[16], which helps our thoughts to be expressed. However, this "je ne sais quoi," which Augustine invokes when he speaks about concrete languages is not something which is firmly formed, nor does it issue a clear vision. Rather, it is infinitely formable because it constantly assumes different forms (*hoc formabile nondumque formatum*). And it is in regard to this aspect in particular that Augustine highlights the contrast between the divine self-presence from which the Word of the Son is begotten and the implicit knowing from which the human word is derived.

However, for our purposes we may limit our interest to the hermeneutical consequences of this insight and how it has found partial entry in modern hermeneutics. In the first place, Gadamer views Augustine's distinction as a reminder that the word that one attempts to understand is not simply the one which we hear, but the one which is suggested by the utterance (i.e., the intended word, the thought, or ultimately, the word of reason itself in its universality)[17]. But what is the meaning of this inner word for contemporary philosophy? Does this imply a notion of "mental representation" with would threaten a relapse into mentalism and psychologism? Following Gadamer's lead, therefore, we must "inquire into the issue of what this inner word is."[18] We may proceed from Augustine's remark that that which is expressed in signs always has something contingent or material about it. It only makes an aspect of what is expressed appear and not the whole fact of the matter. The theory of the *verbum cordis* warns us against taking this linguistic sign as final. It always presents only an incomplete translation (*interpretatio*), whereby one is obliged to engage in further speech if one wants to try to get the whole subject matter in view. In this regard, Gadamer states: "The inner word certainly does not refer to a particular language and it does not at all have the character of words hovering before the mind, being called up out of the memory, rather it concerns a thinking through to the end of the subject matter (*forma excogitata*). In so far as it concerns a thinking through to the end, a moment of process should be recognized."[19]

This element of process concerns the word and its corresponding search for understanding. Every proposition offers only a piece of understanding cut off from the dialogue out of which language lives. The "subject matter thought through to the end," the *actus exercitus* of post hoc completion of speaking, lives only in this dialogue that demands understanding and cannot be limited to the palpable *actus signatus* or that which is literally expressed in speech. Gadamer learned from Augustine that the meaning language mediates does not imply "the abstractable logical meaning of the proposition but rather the interweaving (*Verflechtung*) that occurs in it."[20] The fixation of Western thinking on the proposition signifies a curtailment of language of its decisive dimension (i.e., the embeddedness of each and every discourse in a dialogue). The "logical" concentration on what is asserted abstracts explicitly from the irrevocable "answer-character" of the word[21] or from its reference to what is prior, namely, a question. The true universality of language lies in this dialectic of question and answer out of which a truly philosophical, that is universal, understanding can unfold. This fact was unmistakably understood by Gadamer in his essay entitled, "The Universality of the Hermeneutical Phenomenon" (1966), as the "hermeneutical ur-phenomenon," that is the most *original* insight of hermeneutics: "there is no possible assertation that cannot be understood as an answer to a question and indeed it can only be so understood."[22] This dialogical view echoes the Augustinian theory of the *verbum cordis* which Gadamer calls upon in order to help overcome the Western forgetfulness of language, namely the fixation on the proposition as final and along with it the abstraction from the event-character of meaning.

The truth of the proposition does not lie in itself or in the accidental signs of the given moment, but in the whole that it opens up. Gadamer states: "One may not take the word only for the particular meaning the sign intends but one must also simultaneously become aware of everything it carries with it."[23] Already in his pathbreaking essay from 1957, "What is Truth?," Gadamer wanted to free the truth claim of language from the limits of the propositional: "If one wants to grasp a proposition in its truth then there is no proposition that can be comprehended only in terms of the content that it presents. Every proposition is motivated. Every proposition has presuppositions that are not asserted."[24] From this it stands out clearly that the universality of language cannot be one of spoken language, but one of the "inner word" (as it may be expressed with Augustine, however awkward it might come across today). Furthermore, such an understanding does not imply a neglect of concrete language. Indeed, it serves to encompass language in its proper hermeneutical horizon.

According to Gadamer, the theory of the *verbum interius* leads to a "dialogical" conception of language, a conception which is, without doubt, directed against the hegemony of propositional logic. Indeed, its intent is to call into question the traditional fixation of philosophical thought on the theoretical λόγος ἀποφαντικὸς (i.e., on the referential propositional sentence which "is theoretical [in so far] as it abstracts from everything it does not expressly say"[25]). It would be a narrowing of language to want to nail it down to a theoretical statement. Following Heidegger, Gadamer believes that the "construction of the logic of the proposition" was "one of the most consequential decisions of Western culture."[26] And to work against it is the primary motive of his dialogical hermeneutics, whose main idea could be summarized as: "Language accomplishes itself not in propositions, but in dialogue."[27] Against propositional logic, for which the proposition offers a sufficient unit of meaning, hermeneutics reminds us that a proposition cannot free itself from the context of motivation (i.e., the dialogue in which it is embedded, and from which alone it gains meaning). The proposition is ultimately an abstraction that one never encounters in the life of a language. Thus Gadamer challenges: "When and where are there such pure propositional sentences?"[28]

This Augustinian-motivated critique gives the title of the work, *Wahrheit und Methode*, its full speculative significance. The distinction conferred on method by the modern consciousness is intimately bound up with the logical privilege of the proposition. The idea of method draws its strength from the fact that one can isolate certain fields or cases in an experiment in order to make them controllable.[29] The preferential position of the proposition is a consequence of the fact that one can free it from its dialogical context. However, such isolation does violence to language. Understanding a language is really not reducible to a subject's intellectual grasp of an objectifiable and isolated content. Gadamer's protest against the modern privilege of method, which he first carried through in the field of the human sciences, culminates in his analysis of language. This privilege is all too understandable, since it promised a control and with this a command of things which could be methodically isolated, repeated and re-used. However, it is questionable whether such isolation can really be successful in the case of language. Do we understand because and in so far as we control? Does not finitude succumb here to a self-delusion? Hermeneutics replies that when we understand, it is much more because of our capacity to be addressed by a tradition to which we belong, regardless of how loose that connection may seem to be.

Against the primacy of propositional logic, which conceives and mistakes understanding as some sort of control, Gadamer develops his hermeneutical logic of question and answer, which conceives of understanding as a participation in meaning, in tradition and, finally, in dialogue. In this dialogue there are "no" propositions, rather there are questions and answers that in their turn elicit new questions. According to Gadamer: "If one wishes to comprehend them in their truth then there are no propositions that can be comprehended solely on the basis of the content they present (. . .). Every proposition has presuppositions that it does not express. Only he who also grasps this presupposition can really measure the truth of a proposition. Now I maintain that the question is the ultimate logical form of such motivation for every proposition."[30] Here we touch at the heart of hermeneutical philosophy, that is, to quote Gadamer's penetrating formulation once again, at "the *hermeneutical ur-phenomenon*, that there is no possible proposition that cannot be understood as an answer to a question, and it can only be so understood."[31]

The ur-phenomenon of language (i.e, its universal dimension) is opened up by the dialectic of question and answer, which replaces the traditional logic oriented toward the given, abstract proposition.

This debt of linguistic expression to a preceding question reveals the horizon of inquiry and motivation of all propositions. It is no editorial accident therefore that the chapter on "The Logic of Question and Answer" makes up the last section of the second part of *Wahrheit und Methode*. Only from this perspective can one comprehend the transition to or the turning towards the universal hermeneutics of language in the closing part of the book. As is known, the second part deals predominantly with the project of a "hermeneutics of the human sciences" (as Gadamer often calls it). In this section, Gadamer's concern is the claim to truth made by knowledge in the human sciences, a knowledge which is to be kept from the seduction of method in the natural sciences. The pursuit of truth in the human sciences does not lie in the use of secured methods, but in the universality of the structure of question and application in the research situation. The scientific nature of the humanities does not manifest itself in some kind of methodology, but in the successful fulfillment of the dialectic of question and answer. This is *in nuce* the liberating result of the hermeneutics of the human sciences that Gadamer presents in the first two parts of his main work.

Furthermore, while the dialogical relationship between question and answer is exemplified by the human sciences in the first two sections, it is the third part that brings about a universalization of hermeneutics in so far as it proposes that the dialectic of question and answer is ultimately the essential achievement of language. This affirmation also results in the much-discussed "ontological" shift of hermeneutics, whereby "ontological" is consistently used as a synonym for "philosophical" and "universal." Making hermeneutics universal and philosophical in the last part of *Wahrheit und Methode* signifies that the scope of what up until now has been a strictly methodological hermeneutics has now been overcome in the direction of a hermeneutics that understands the dialectic of question and answer as the element of our thinking existence, a dialectic which Plato aptly described as the "dialogue of the soul with itself." Thus, the dialectic of question and answer, which is the conclusion of the hermeneutics of the human sciences (Part two of *Truth and Method*), also constitutes the beginning and even the capstone of the last part which turns to language. In this final section, Gadamer asserts that language can only be understood on the basis of dialogue and that to tie down language to the propositional implies an instrumental falsification of language.

We understand now why the third part of *Wahrheit und Methode* could find in Augustine's theory of the word the only evidence for the claim that "the forgetfulness of language in the West

had not been complete."[32] However, Gadamer's little noticed rehabilitation of this theory is not to be understood as a relapse into a
naive mentalism. Rather, it is a hermeneutical critique of the
method-oriented domination of the logic of the proposition. The Augustinian theory turns out, in fact, to be very graphic in that the
words we use cannot, just because they occur to us, exhaust what
we have "in mind" (i.e., the dialogue that we are). The inner word
"behind" the expressed word is nothing other than this dialogue or
this intimate connection of language with our inquiring and self-
inquiring existence. Furthermore, this inner word or dialogue—or
Da-sein in the terms of Heidegger—cannot be completely reproduced
by any proposition. In the words of Gadamer: "What is explicitly said
is not everything. What is unsaid first makes what is said into a
word that can reach us."[33] This unsaid is what one can name with
Augustine the *verbum cordis*. To what is this or that proposition an
answer? To whom is it directed? Why was it expressed at this particular time? Was it meant ironically? Etc. Obviously, no proposition
which is cut off from its context can answer for itself. As Plato asserted, the outer word runs the risk of going astray when it is set
loose form the *verbum interius* or from the soul of the word.

Finally, it should be emphasized, that this remains a hermeneutical theory of language and not some mysticism of the ineffable.
In order to discuss language correctly, not to circumvent or leap behind it, it is appropriate to invoke the non-propositional, inner dialogue. However, hermeneutics definitely takes the limits of language,
or better, of the proposition, as its point of departure. Gadamer
states: "Naturally, we cannot mean by the fundamental linguisticality of understanding that all experience of the world is carried
out as speaking and in speech."[34] This assertion refutes, once and
for all, the overly precipitated interpretation that ascribes to
Gadamer the linguistic-ontological thesis according to which everything that is must be expressible in propositional form.

Nevertheless, if a *fundamental linguisticality* of our experience
of language is maintained, it concerns only the claim that language
embodies the only medium for the (inner) dialogue that we are for
ourselves and for each other. Hermeneutics, therefore, sanctions a
sentence like "Being that can be understood is language." However,
the weight here should be placed on the "can."[35] For understanding,
which itself is always linguistically formed and issues from language,
must always attempt to invoke the whole content of language in
order to approach Being, which it helps bring to expression. The essential *linguisticality* of understanding manifests itself less in our
linguistic utterances than in our search for language, in our attempts

to express and even "press out" that which we struggle with in our souls. It is less important for the hermeneutical aspect of understanding that it results from language, which would be a banality, than that it lives from the never-ending process of the searching for words for what can never be entirely said or comprehended. For this process—and the corresponding invocation of the inner word—grounds the universality of hermeneutics.

Chapter 8

Gadamer on Humanism

In this section, I would like to try to understand Gadamer's step or leap beyond Heidegger by concentrating on a theme that might first appear somewhat remote from the major preoccupations of the two thinkers: the problem of humanism. While generalizations tend to be hazardous, one might claim that the issue of humanism was more closely attended to in Latin countries such as France and Italy, than in the German philosophical tradition. In this regard, the German tradition seems to be more concerned with history and the traditional tenets of Western metaphysics, according to which the "human" perspective takes a second seat to the divine or merely "logical" perspective and where man fits in through the use of reason. Nevertheless, the issue of humanism, far from being incidental, can enable us to understand what is profoundly at stake, and strikingly different, in the philosophies of Heidegger and Gadamer. For many, and it is true in many respects, Gadamer can be described as a Heideggerian. Indeed, in spite of his evident and often acknowledged debt to authors like Plato, Augustine and Hegel, the most dominant and persistent imprint on his philosophy and his intellectual development has come from Heidegger, his teacher and mentor. And while Gadamer has distanced himself from Heidegger on a wide variety of issues (such divergences have have been dealt with extensively in the literature) any work "on" Gadamer is still ultimately a study of his relation to Heidegger. Surely, Gadamer departs from Heidegger on many counts, but why he does so can, I submit, be grasped by focusing on the subterranean theme of humanism.

To put the thesis bluntly, Gadamer is a humanist and Heidegger is not. No moral judgment whatsoever is immediately implied by this (say, Gadamer is "humane," whereas Heidegger is not). Rather, I am proposing that a general philosophical orientation (i.e., humanism) can help us to understand why and at what point a Heideggerian such as Gadamer ceases to be Heideggerian. Such an approach should not be understood primarily in a biographical sense. It is certainly accurate to note that Heidegger was raised in a provincial form of Catholicism that was hostile to modernism and humanism in general, which was more often than not associated with atheism, and that Gadamer, a Protestant, profited from a rather open, classical and humanistic upbringing. My reference to humanism primarily concerns their philosophical outlook, that is, their appreciation of humanism as a leading force in Western culture.

The current literature on the theme of humanism usually singles out three major forms or "high points" of humanism.[1] The first to be identified is the "humanism" of the Renaissance. By resurrecting the accomplishments of human artistry and culture in the original works of the Greek and the Latin authors, the humanism of the Renaissance focused on "human" achievements, the *studia humanitatis*. This new focus was opposed, or added, to a God-centered perspective, the *studia divinitatis*,[2] that was said to be pervasive in the "Middle" Ages. Since the Renaissance was a "rebirth" of antiquity, one could trace back the seeds of humanism to Greek antiquity itself and, more specifically, to Socrates and his concentration on "merely" human affairs (exemplified, for instance, in the "know thyself" and in his turning away from the cosmological preoccupations of his predecessors). A second form of humanism, of which the Germans are well aware, was found in the Enlightenment and, more precisely, in the works of the German classics: Lessing, Schiller, Goethe and Winckelmann. All of these authors followed the Renaissance in viewing man as a being whose constant task consists in perfecting his own self, in fulfilling his latent possibilities, again against any heteronomous tutelage of reason. Finally, a "third" form of humanism emerged at the beginning of the twentieth century among classicists like Werner Jaeger who perceived in ancient culture the models of a truly humanistic education. Today, to enjoy a "humanistic" up-bringing, in Germany and elsewhere, means that one has studied the Greeks and the Latins.

However, in order to put the philosophical debate on humanism in its proper focus, one has to take into account the spiritual situation of Europe after the Second World War. It is safe to say that it was the sheer inhumanity of the Nazi regime and the World War that prompted a new discussion on the avenues of humanism. Had humanity exhausted all its possibilities after the death camps and the bloodiest of wars humanity had suffered? Was faith in humanity and its promises of self-formation still possible after Auschwitz? This feeling of disarray was echoed in Jean Beaufret's question to Heidegger in 1946: "How can we give a new meaning to the word 'humanism'?" This question was very typical of the general atmosphere of the times. The dominant philosophy was existential humanism (Sartre, Jaspers, Merleau-Ponty), a philosophy that concentrated exclusively on the human predicament. However, the issue, as much as existentialism itself, also went far beyond academia. The German constitution, drafted under the shock of the Nazi regime of terror, established as its first and guiding principle the "inviolable dignity of man" (*die Würde des Menschen ist unantastbar*).[3]

Nonetheless, what does it mean to adopt a "humanist" perspective after modernity led up to the barbarism symbolized by Auschwitz? Indeed, this is the question Jean Beaufret put to one of the leading, if isolated thinkers of the time, Martin Heidegger, whose philosophy of existence was also thought to be one of the roots of the new "humanism." Heidegger was himself so concerned by the problem that he immediately took up Beaufret's question (probably the first and only time he ever responded publicly to a query on his intellectual perspective) in an open letter that became one of the most outspoken testimonies of his philosophical "turn," the famous *Letter on Humanism*. Heidegger's reflections on humanism were not sparked by the events that led to the collapse of national-socialism. As if to document this, Heidegger published his *Letter* conjointly with his seemingly scholarly, yet momentous study of 1942 on *Plato's doctrine of truth*.[4] In this study, Heidegger argues that humanism is but the latest avatar of metaphysical thinking launched by Plato's subordination of everything there is to the instance of the *idea*, or the *eidos*. In this regard, *eidos* refers back to an "ideal" perspective, something that can be seen (*eidos* is etymologically linked to the verb *oida*, which means "to have seen," hence "to know") or grasped by a looking person and the human eye. For Plato, to understand reality as it is, is to comprehend it by way of its "idea" (i. e., through the general aspect it presents to the apprehending eye of the soul). Heidegger sees in Platonism the most decisive event in the adventure of human culture, which one could translate as a far-reaching "intellectualization" of all there is, or, as Heidegger puts it, as a "forgetfulness of Being." What is forgotten in this strictly human "idealization" of the world is the sheer gratuity of Being, that simply "is," and in which we are thrown into well before we even attempt to make sense out of it with our "ideas." Platonism erases, as it were, the naked evidence of Being and replaces it by the ontological precedence of the "idea," of the intellectual and, therefore, of the human outlook on what is. This surpassing of Being by reaching forth to the "idea" or "ground" behind it is what distinguishes metaphysics. Thus, metaphysics is characterized by the at first tacit rise to prominence of the human being who imposes himself as the source from which the whole of Being becomes accountable, an accountability that culminates in the essence of technology and technological manipulation (that was carried to its extreme by Facism). Metaphysics, humanism and the essence of technology form an intertwined whole for Heidegger. This is why Heidegger wants to take some distance regarding the blinding evidence of humanism. To Heidegger's mind, humanism is not what is going to save us from the impending catastrophe of humankind, rather it could very well be what got us into trouble in the first place. He thus rejects the implict premise of Beaufret's question, namely that humanism is a "good thing" and just needs to be redefined. Clearly swimming against the tide, his answer begins by stating: "Comment redonner un sens au mot 'humanisme'? [How does one give meaning to the word 'humanism' again?] The question proceeds from your intention to retain the word 'humanism.' I wonder whether that is necessary. Or is the damage caused by all such terms not already sufficiently obvious?"[5] Indeed, Heidegger will even recommend "an open resistance to 'humanism,' " that would help us to become dumbfounded by the traditional view of the "*humanitas* of the *homo humanus*" and its basis.[6] In this regard, we should keep in mind this idea of "resistance" since we will encounter a different version later on when we examine Gadamer's work.

Furthermore, the fact that Heidegger uses Latin titles when he describes humanism is by no means adventitious. According to Heidegger, humanism arose in the era of the Latins, that is, for him, at a time when philosophy had ceased to be a creative force and had degenerated into a hollow "technique" of "education." The notion of "*humanitas*" was first entertained, Heidegger claims, in the Roman Republic,[7] where the *homo humanus* was single-handedly opposed to the *homo barbarus*. The *homo humanus* proudly adopts the Greek ideal of education (*paideia*) by indulging in the *eruditio et institutio in bonas artes*. This understanding of education, which is embodied in the term *humanitas*, was renewed during the Renaissance of the 14th and 15th centuries as well as in the German Humanism of Goethe and Schiller. In this regard, humanism has generally been

understood as "the concern that man can become free for his own
humanity and in so doing find his dignity." Moreover, Heidegger asserts that humanism fosters a perspective that centers on humanity and can see nothing else besides it. Thus, he concludes that the
anthropocentrism of humanism prevents one from raising the question of Being or of its relation to humanity. Humanism presupposes
an unquestioned understanding of the human being as an *animal
rationale*, as a living being endowed with the power of reason that
assimilates it to divinity. It is this understanding, this self-distin-
guishing of humanity from the rest of Being—and its alleged supe-
riority—that Heidegger wishes to call into question. Indeed, what
is it that enables us to pose ourselves as something beyond animality,
as beings that must cultivate their reason and so forth? For
Heidegger, it is urgent to realize that man is not at the center of
the universe. He is perhaps a peripheral apparition in the whole of
Being, out of which he should gain a new understanding of itself
(e.g., as a pastoral "shepherd of Being") and its essential finitude,
or "thrownness" into Being and by Being. Heidegger thus urges us
to go beyond humanism, a transcendence suggested perhaps by the
"*über* " in the title "Letter on (*über*) Humanism," intended as a kind
of message thrown into a bottle at sea with the hope of paving the
way for what could come after the age of humanism or metaphysics
(in German, one might say: "*Brief über den Humanismus hinaus*").
   Heidegger's depiction of the Roman "*humanitas*" is markedly
sarcastic, both in tone and content. Underscoring time and again
that the rise of humanism is a typically Roman phenomena,[8] he appears to claim for himself a fresh path to the Greeks which is above
and beyond the "humanist" classicists of his time. He boasts that
the Greeks could still think without titles such as humanism and
did not even bother to label their thinking "philosophy."[9] Moreover,
Heidegger asserts that with both the later Greeks, who first invented
"schools of philosophy," and the Romans, "thinking came to its end."
Its disappearance therefore had to be compensated by the rise of
"philosophy," which was understood to be an "instrument of education that acquired value as a scholarly enterprise and as a cultural
institution." Philosophy was thus reduced to being a "technology destined to produce explanations out of the highest causes."[10]
   It is now time to confront Heidegger's massive critique of humanism with Gadamer's own philosophy. Even if Gadamer does not
deal directly with Heidegger's position on humanism (not even, if I
read correctly, in his collection of essays on *Heidegger's Ways* which
are devoted to the later Heidegger)[11] his philosophical perspective
can be understood to be a defense of humanism and, consequently,

as a response to Heidegger's repudiation of the humanistic tradition. This is obvious in at least two ways. First of all, Gadamer's
major work, *Truth and Method* (1960), is concerned with a legitimation of the "human" sciences and their importance for philosophy. While human or social sciences are called *Geisteswissenschaften*
in German, Gadamer is certainly dealing with the "humanities" or
humaniora that formed the cornerstone of the humanist conception
of education. Secondly, and perhaps more importantly, the book provokingly opens with a rehabilitation of the forgotten humanistic tradition. In the immediate context of the book, this rehabilitation is
directed against the Kantian outbidding of humanism which stripped
the humanities of the title of science. However, for a Heideggerian
such as Gadamer, it can and should also be read as an answer to
Heidegger's own overcoming of humanism.

In a way, Gadamer still follows the lead of Heidegger on this
issue. His critique of the overriding dominance of methodical science
in contemporary culture is Heideggerian in nature. Where Heidegger
denounces the pervasive essence of technology, Gadamer points to
the false claims of method. Yet the roots of their criticism are very
different and perhaps opposed to each other. Heidegger sees technology as the last flagpole of metaphysics or humanism that reduces
Being to its functionalism for human purposes. Unlike his mentor,
however, Gadamer interprets the dominance of method as the result
of the abandonment of the humanist tradition, which was motivated
by Kant. Gadamer's hermeneutics, therefore, will strive to build a
new bridge to this tradition.

Kant's importance in this debate cannot be underestimated.
Even if his inquiry into the possibility of metaphysics had a positive intent, its result and impact was to establish mathematics and
the natural sciences as the sole models of scientificity. Anything that
does not correspond to the methodological criteria of exact science
is deprived of any cognitive value. Common sense, judgment and
taste, which were cultivated by the humanistic tradition because of
their social, political, and indeed their cognitive importance, are thus
relegated to a merely subjective sphere that is devoid of scientific
import. Everything that is not "scientific" (i.e., verifiable by the
norms of methodical science) can only entertain a subjective or aesthetic validity. Gadamer's heroic effort in *Truth in Method* will start
off with a repudiation of this aesthetic trivialization of the human
sciences. He will call into question the Kantian methodological bias
that led thinkers of the 19th and 20th centuries to ground the
scientificity of the human sciences on rigorous "methods" that
are valid independently of the context and the observing subject

(i.e., similar to the way in which the natural sciences define their own "method").

Even if Gadamer does not wish to exclude method entirely from the realm of the humanities, it is his conviction that methods alone do not determine the scientificity and relevance of the human sciences. More importantly, he argues, the human sciences have to be understood as "the true advocates or emissaries of humanism," *als die wahren Sachwalter des Humanismus*.[12] This is the first occurrence of the term humanism in *Truth and Method*. It is introduced as a countermovement to the methodical (Heidegger would say: technical) model of knowledge represented by natural science. However, according to Gadamer, this tradition has been forsaken or forgotten as a result of the unquestioned domination, since Kant, of the model of exact science. Gadamer will thus have to reacquaint us with this tradition.

It is useful to follow Gadamer closely in his own depiction of the meaning of humanism. The first author Gadamer evokes in this context is Herder, who during his time was also an adversary of Kant. In 1941, Gadamer devoted a conference to Herder, that became one of the few articles he published during the Nazi era. Even though some parts of this conference contain elements which refer to the German idea of *Volk* (a notion that one could certainly find objectionable today)[13] the lecture courageously, in a time of inhumanity, portrayed Herder as a defender of humanism. Indeed, his philosophy of history is grounded on a "faith in the victory of reason,"[14] seeing in history "the spread and promotion of humanity, a humanity however which can only be found in the course of history."[15] It is important to note here that humanity has to *build* itself through history in order to reach its rational potential.

Humanism as a whole, and this idea is independent of Herder's specific views, is not so much defined by the notion that humanity distinguishes itself from animality through reason. Rather, it is the view that humanity constantly has to subdue the animality out of which it stems by education, which is actually nothing but the overcoming of animality and its barbaric forms in the history of mankind. Hence, the value of culture and tradition is crucial for humanism. Man never ceases to cultivate himself nor to learn because she or he is constantly threatened by the darker sides of animality that can break out anytime.[16] Humanism is thus an attitude of vigilance toward this animal side of human nature, that one can only contain through a process of education or formation, for which there are some models (the "classics" for example), but no scientific rules. Humanism, therefore, does not rest on a fixed notion of what it is to be human or to possess a reason. To be human is to have no such algorithmic notion of oneself. Humanism is rather an unending quest for civility in human affairs that can only be achieved or exercised in the process of culture and the cultivation of one's own talents.

Undoubtedly, there are theological roots to this conception of humanism that is characteristic of the Renaissance, if not of contemporary humanism. The "lower" side of our nature is to be found in the biblical notion that man was made out of ashes. What elevates humanity, on the other hand, is the belief that God created man according to his own image. Humanity, which carries the image of God within itself, thus lives up to its parentage by letting its talents flourish and by realizing what they are destined to accomplish, that is, by elevating mankind ever closer to the level of God.[17] The dignity of mankind resides for humanism in this idea that it is made in the image of God, a distinction it can only live up to by cultivating itself and domesticating its "animal" side.

It is therefore no surprise to see Gadamer's rehabilitation of humanism in *Truth and Method* start off precisely with this notion of culture, or *Bildung*, that takes on a historical dimension with Herder, but whose theological origins date back to the Renaissance and the Middle Ages. In the best humanistic tradition, Gadamer characterizes *Bildung* as the "properly human way of developing one's natural talents and capacities."[18] In short, humanity is not something one already has, or some skill one could learn once and for all. Rather, it is a sense or direction that one attempts to cultivate. Gadamer also evokes the theological context out of which this conception arose: "The rise of the word Bildung evokes the ancient mystical tradition according to which man carries in his soul the image of God, after whom he is fashioned, and which man must cultivate in himself."[19] What distinguishes man from the other animals is exactly this ability to develop himself, to surpass his provincial particularity and lift himself up to the universal. In this regard, Gadamer does not hesitate to follow Hegel's description of this human elevation above nature: "Man is characterized by the break with the immediate and the natural that the intellectual, rational side of his nature demands of him."[20]

Furthermore, one can hardly not notice the striking fact that Gadamer so candidly brings to life again the classical self-definitions of humanism that Heidegger rejected out of hand. In terms of substance, the depictions of humanism they use are the same. However, while Heidegger evokes them in a distanced and ironic way, Gadamer seems to have no qualms whatsoever with them. For

Heidegger, this idea that the *homo humanus*, as a "child of God," must devote himself to the *studium humanitatis* and cultivate the *eruditio et institutio in bonas artes* in order to master his *animalitas* serves as a caricature of humanism, as a view of man's "divine" and "cultivated" distinction that one cannot assume anymore. However, if one takes Gadamer at his word, and I believe one should, it is clear that he fully endorses the conception of humanism from which Heidegger distances himself. It is as if Gadamer is saying that while Heidegger is right in his understanding of humanism, one should nevertheless attempt to keep this tradition of humanism alive.

There is also another latent difference between Heidegger and Gadamer. In order to establish the solidarity of humanism with metaphysics, the "Letter on Humanism" repeatedly states that humanism undoubtedly rests on a "fixed" understanding of what man is.[21] One can surmise why Heidegger would want to claim this, but it is far from certain whether it is true or not. If man is a being that is constantly in the process of self-development, through learning, culture and civilization, then there is no such thing as a human "essence." There is no fixed idea of what man is, only an idea that man has to build himself, his world and his institutions in order to fight the evil, or "animality," that begets him. Considering what Heidegger himself writes on man in his *Letter on Humanism* (i.e., that he is a "shepherd of Being," that he has to understand himself out of his "essential (!) relation to Being," that he is "capable of a relation to the Gods and the sacred," that he "inhabits this world through language or poetry," and so on), then it is Heidegger, and not humanism, that has a clear and definite understanding of what man's essence really is all about. For humanism, it is precisely the "essence" of mankind not to have an essence since it is able to surpass any fixed essence one could assign to it.[22]

This is also the lesson that Gadamer draws from the humanistic tradition. If man never ceases to learn, then there is nothing fixed about his essence. Furthermore, if one has to "build" or "form" oneself through *Bildung*, one will naturally be open to other points of view, to different perspectives than one's own. The main characteristic of humanism is thus this thankful openness to the enlightening perspectives of others and of those who have preceded us and bequeathed to us the opportunity of their experience. Gadamer states: "That is what, following Hegel, we emphasized as the general characteristic of Bildung: keeping oneself open to what is other—to other, more universal points of view. It embraces a sense of proportion and distance in relation to itself, and hence consists in rising above itself to universality."[23] What distinguishes our humanity, is not a rational capacity that would catapult us into a divine world of pure ideas. Rather, it is the ability to go beyond our own particularity by taking into account the heritage that can help us grow above and beyond our limited selves.

When we take into account this heritage of tradition and the wisdom of others, that we always apply differently to ourselves and our situation, we acquire genuine truths, but such truths cannot be adequately described in the terms of methodical science. These are truths that simply help us become more "human," more open and also, negatively, more aware of the dangers that surround us. This truly human wisdom corresponds to the form of knowledge that is pursued in the humanities. Gadamer's rehabilitatation of the humanistic tradition thus enables him to account for the specific truth claim of the humanities. In this regard, Gadamer states: "What makes the human sciences into sciences can be understood more easily from the tradition of the concept of Bildung than from the modern idea of scientific method. It is to the *humanistic tradition* [the italics indicate Gadamer's emphasis] that we must turn. In its resistance to the claims of modern science it gains a new significance."[24] While Heidegger advocates a "resistance" *against* humanism, Gadamer unearths in the forgotten tradition of humanism an instance that can fuel a resistance against the illegitimate claims of modern science to encompass all there is to know.

As alluded to at the beginning of this chapter, the respective positions of Heidegger and Gadamer on humanism point to fundamental differences in their philosophical bearings. In his break with tradition, be it in his earlier or his later period, something in Heidegger always hoped for a new beginning, for a radical transformation of the relation between man and Being.[25] For Gadamer, on the contrary, there can be no such thing as an absolute beginning or a point-zero in human affairs where we could start everything anew. We can never leap over our shadows. This is why Gadamer puts so much emphasis on tradition and dialogue. They are the two instances that can help us (finite beings that we are, but who, fortunately enough, can learn from our mistakes) to make things better. Furthermore, Gadamer insists, in his important chapter on the hermeneutical experience, that most of our experiences are negative.[26] This aspect of Gadamer's humanism needs to be stressed against those who accuse Gadamer of nursing a continuous, harmonious and rosy understanding of tradition. Tradition is not the golden chain that bears witness to the rationality of history. Rather, as Hegel's *Phenomenology* taught, it is the memory of the deceptive experiences stored by our humanity. As a matter of fact, we do not learn anything through positive experiences because they only confirm what we already know. Hermeneutical insight only sinks in when we have been contradicted by events which force us to change or adjust our perspectives.

While it is true that Heidegger also spoke of tradition and dialogue, he did so in ways quite different from Gadamer. The bulk of tradition is neither less present nor heavy for Heidegger, than it is for Gadamer, but it is something that has to be destroyed if we wish to grasp the things themselves or to make way for a new dwelling on this earth. But how can we destroy that which supports us and allows us to critique the past, retorts Gadamer? With regard to dialogue, Heidegger was the first to call attention to Hölderlin's now famous passage on the "dialogue that we are." His seminal lecture of 1936, "Hölderlin and the Essence of Poetry," singled it out as one of the leading words of Hölderlin. In this context, Heidegger also wrote that "the being of man is grounded in language and that language only happens properly in dialogue."[27] However, Heidegger followed Hölderlin in understanding this "dialogue that we are" as a conversation going on between the mortals and the gods. Heidegger proclaims: "Since we are a dialogue—man has experienced plenty and has named many of the gods. Ever since language takes place properly as dialogue, the gods come to word and a world comes to the fore. But, again, one must see that the presence of the gods and the emergence of the world are not a consequence of the event of language. Rather, they happen at the same time as them. And this to such an extent that the true language that we are consists precisely in naming the gods and in the becoming-word of the world."[28] Yet, as R. Dostal has pointed out, in this alleged dialogue, where real conversation consists in the naming of the gods, "no consideration is given to the conversation among mortals about things mortal."[29]

Gadamer, however, is very attentive to this earthly dialogue between mortals. He takes Hölderlin at his word when we speaks of the "dialogue, that _we_ are." The dialogical essence of language[30] does not mean that we are primarily in constant exchange with the gods (who probably do not need conversation anyway), but that we have to rely on what others have to say and what lies there before us if we want to find some orientation in our earthly existence. What "we are" consists in the traditions that are alive within us. We are what has been bequeathed to us and, most importantly for a humanist, what we have made out of this tradition when we constructively applied it to our situation. We are also a dialogue in the sense that we live in a community in which we are exposed to a plurality of opinions. This plurality of views also lives within us, it constitutes

us and it accounts for our all too human stammering and hesitations. To be in a constant situation of learning means that we cannot entertain the hope of ultimate foundations in order to decide how
the world ought to be. All we have is the experience of those who
preceded us, the dialogue with others and our good judgment that
cannot but be chaneled by tradition and the ongoing conversation.

Hence, Gadamer's apology of humanism is not only a defense
of the human sciences, it is also a defense of the utter humanity of
our knowledge. The meaning of this is that we can never hope to
obtain any god-like wisdom, that is, a bird's-eye view that would enable us to transcend our finitude. To be human means to be deprived
of ultimate foundations and to have to educate and cultivate oneself to our possible humanity. In this regard, Gadamer takes on the
Socratic and, in his eyes, Platonic heritage of philosophy as an
exercice in not knowing. Gadamer writes: "So I was persuaded that
the Socratic legacy of a 'human wisdom' had to be taken up again
in my own hermeneutical theory-formation, a legacy which, when
measured against the god-like infallibility of science, is, in the sense
of *sophia*, a consciousness of not knowing."[31]

The focus on the issue of humanism also sheds a new light on
Gadamer's Socratic reading of Plato. As we saw earlier, Heidegger
linked the rise of humanism to Plato's metaphysics and to the subordination of all there is to the clarity of the intellectual idea. To
overcome humanism, for Heidegger, is tantamount to overcoming
metaphysics and Platonism. However, no such motive is to be found
in Gadamer. If he goes back to Plato, it is precisely to retrieve his
humanism, as a humanism of dialogue in the discipline of a merely
"human" wisdom. In this respect, Gadamer affirms: "From the
Greeks one could learn that thinking in philosophy does not, in order to be responsible, have to adopt as system-guiding the thought
that there must be a final grounding for philosophy in a highest principle; on the contrary, it stands always under the guiding thought
that it must be based on primordial world-experience, achieved
through the conceptual and intuitive power of the language in which
we live. The secret of the Platonic dialogues, it seems to me, is that
they teach us this."[32]

Gadamer thus heeded Plato's admonition in the *Symposium*
(204 a): "No god indulges in philosophy." Philosophy is a truly human and humanistic enterprise, conducted in the hope of gaining a
better understanding of ourselves and the world through dialogue
and by learning from tradition. In the eyes of Gadamer, Plato can
rightly stand as the father of humanism, as Heidegger also believed.
Yet, while Heidegger gave this humanism a negative metaphysical

interpretation, for Gadamer humanism is the only resource we have or attitude we can adopt in the absence of a cogent metaphysics.

From Gadamer, one can learn that humanism is not necessarily an anthropocentrism. It is not because the only perspective we can entertain is a human one that man is at the center of Being. As far as one can tell, the individual stands rather at the receiving end of Being, be it language, community or the cosmic order. An openness to tradition and dialogue in order to contain the animality that threatens us does not entail an anthropocentric view of things. In a way, it is very humiliating for mankind to constantly have to learn and to conquer its darker instincts. No triumph of reason or of man's centeredness is to be found here. In this regard, Gadamer truly follows the turn of the later Heidegger toward a more modest and peripheral understanding of our humanity. He fully assumes Heidegger's critique of metaphysical subjectivism, but he does not forfeit the focus on humanity involved in this process. It is perhaps Gadamer's achievement to have protested against the precipitated equation of subjectivism and humanism. He rejects, in the footsteps of Heidegger, the subject-centered philosophy of modernity without loosing sight of the pervading humanistic trend of Western civilization. Humanism is not an anthropocentrism. Rather, it is the acknowledgment that as finite beings we never cease to learn. And given that philosophical humanism is nothing but the modest openness to truths that can help us raise above our indigence, hermeneutics is a humanism.

Chapter 9

Humanism and the Hermeneutical Limits of Rationality

The problem of the limits of reason can be addressed in many different ways according to one's understanding of rationality and of what it is that it cannot comprehend. Perhaps the most common way of seeing these limits lies in the traditional opposition between reason and emotion. Conceived as a "cold" manner of arguing, reason would somehow be unable to grasp the true feelings that motivate the human heart. Let us call this problem that of the *emotive limits of rationality* (1). However, the limits of rationality may also be interpreted according to a "cosmological" perspective. In this regard, it is often believed that the project of rationality rests on the tacit expectation that reality is rational and thus open to scientific penetration. But what if the world is not rational? What if it resists all attempts to come to terms with it on a merely rational basis? The limits of rationality would thus lie in the profound chaotic or anarchic state of the universe. Let us call this understanding, which is characteristic of romanticism, that of the *anarchic limits* of rationality (2). There is a also more modest version of this anarchic sentiment which is to be found in the assumption that there are ultimately incomprehensible phenomena which reason cannot explain. These inexplicable happenings could surely be emotions (as in 1) or the chaotic substructure of the universe (2). However, what I am referring to here is simply the fact that rationality always leaves something unexplained and often inexplicable. A rational elucidation can never give a complete account of everything it is claiming. It must rely on hypotheses which go back themselves to other hypotheses and so on. Therefore, one cannot expect a thoroughly rational account of phenomena or one which could explain everything. This limit of rationality lies at the root of the unending process of explanation that is characteristic of modern science. Furthermore, even if the unexplained elements of a theory come to be elucidated by other theories, they will in turn have their own gray areas, and so forth *ad infinitum*. Let us call this understanding, which is characteristic of scientific explanation, the *explicative* limits of rationality (3). Beyond mere epistemological accounts, the limits of rationality can also be seen in a broader or sociological perspective. The rise of rationality goes hand in hand with a world that is more and more secularized. The questions of meaning that were long answered by religion, myth and metaphysics are now left to rationality alone. Yet, this modern and instrumental variant of rationality, more often than not appears unable to satisfy them. As Max Weber has shown, this rational, secularized and disenchanted universe induces social pathologies: lack of orientation, no real explanation of the purpose of human life or action, dissolution of the sense of community and authority, etc. A rationally dominated world is one in which the belief in a higher purpose would no longer be possible; while undesired, meaninglessness and nihilism would be the unavoidable consequences of a rationalized universe. Let us call this understanding, which is characteristic of the modern predicament, the *sociological limits* of rationality (4). Yet, another dramatic way of understanding the limits of rationality is to claim that the age of rationality is over and that rationality is no longer the compelling force it used to be (e.g., as it was for the Enlightenment or the whole of Western civilization). The "end" of reason would therefore usher us into something like postmodernism, and while there are various conceptions of this end of reason, according to what is understood as reason, one can speak here of the *historical* limits of rationality (5).

In this essay, I will discuss the limits of rationality from a somewhat different perspective: the perspective of humanism and the way it is represented by contemporary hermeneutic theory (following in great part the lead of Hans-Georg Gadamer). Where do the limits of rationality lie for a humanist? Mostly in the exclusive domination of the rational mode of knowledge that is exemplified by the exact sciences. According to humanism, and with it hermeneutics, the natural-scientific mode of knowledge has been wrongly heralded as the sole model of knowledge and science. Furthermore, as a result of its universal imposition, the truth claim of the humanities has often been measured in light of criteria that belong to the rational-scientific model of the exact sciences. Humanism, and hermeneutics, would argue that this does not do justice to the truth experience that is witnessed by the humanities. The humanities should not understand their scientific relevance according to this alienating model in which they end up loosing their vital specificity. Rather, they should understand their relevance according to the tradition of humanism, where truth is more a matter of education, culture or "formation" than a matter of certainty controlled by the means of methodical science. Finally, given that the humanistic foundation of the humanities has to a large extent been forgotten in the self-understanding of the humanities, it is the ambition of hermeneutics to retrieve it.

Before we discuss the hermeneutic approach to humanism, it might be useful to clarify first what is to be understood by the rational model of knowledge that one might call *scientistic* and, secondly, what is meant by humanism. It is only if we understand the limits of the rationality involved in this scientistic view that we can fully appreciate the contribution of humanism as it has been reactivated by hermeneutics.

Even if there is still quite a lot of debate in post-Kuhnian philosophy of science about the meaning of a rational or scientific explanation, one can characterize its undeniable success by highlighting some of its less controversial and still dominant features. Let us stress from the outset that it is not our purpose to call into question the legitimacy or success of the scientific outlook. While there is no denying that humanity owes much to what modern science has brought about, there are crucial limits to this model in that in cannot be applied without qualifications to the realm of the human sciences (or, for that matter, to the field of politics and the social sciences) in which a more humanistic approach has to be rediscovered or reintroduced.

The success of the scientistic approach resides primarily in its stress on method. Method is the objective instance which guarantees that the scientific results do not depend on the subjective prejudices of the observer. Method displays a step-by-step rigor which can be reproduced by any other observer, regardless of his or her standpoint. Therefore, it is by distancing the subject matter from the observer that method permits objectivity or a view of the object that does not depend on the subject. Through this distancing of the subject matter, in order to allow for objective verification, method aims at universality; and, unless there is an error in the methodology, its results are supposed to be valid for everyone. This is why most of the criticism that is practiced in the field of science is directed towards methodology. In this regard, one might refer to the trivial example of some opinion polls that are dismissed because of their flawed "methodology." What is important for method is that any independent observer can repeat the steps of scientific explanation in order to test the validity of the results. Mathematical formulas are a most convenient tool for such verification because they do not vary from one individual to the next. Beyond this appeal to mathematics, which often suffices to qualify truths as scientific, modern science also appeals to a critical and open discussion in which progress is achieved through falsification. A theory that excludes itself from such open criticism would cease to be scientific. As Karl Popper argued, a scientific theory has to put itself on the line by remaining open to outside refutation. There is much discussion on this controversial notion of refutation, which cannot occupy us here. If a theory itself is not susceptible of refutation, at least its empirical predictions must be. For instance, while the guiding hypotheses of the theory of relativity might never be confirmed, its predictions have to expose themselves to such testing.

A last feature of the scientistic picture, one which is linked to its hypothetical nature, is its commitment to general laws or regularities. A particular event is explained scientifically when it is shown to be the occurrence of a more universal law of events. In other words, something is demonstrated to be the result of an overall regularity which is in principle open to objective corroboration. Therefore, a simple description of events, which is devoid of explanation, is not thought to be scientific. A scientific explanation takes place when the particular event is traced back to a general constant which can itself be referred back to a still higher law, for the greatest coherence of the theory that is defended.

In short, method, independence from the observer and her individual prejudices, objective verification and testing, the search for universal laws are constitutive of the scientistic outlook which has imposed itself on our culture as the most reliable, if not the only model of knowledge. Now, what is humanism?

In a way, humanism and modern science have much in common. They were both developed in the Renaissance as means of emancipation from the tutelage of the Middle Ages and superstition. The search for objective, verifiable results based on observation is itself not foreign to the humanism that appeared in the Renaissance. In fact, the fathers of modern science, Copernicus, Galileo, Bacon, Descartes and even Gutenberg were great humanists. Yet, humanism espoused a view of knowledge that cannot be reduced to the scientistic outlook which has become so dominant in the last centuries that it threatens to exclude the humanistic perspective itself. In its inception, humanism rests on a theological understanding of man's position in the universe. There are two sides to human nature: a humiliating and a more elevating one. The humiliating aspect of our condition is found in the biblical notion that man has been made out of ashes. Our origins are very modest indeed. Nonetheless, it is also said in the *Genesis* (and this is unsettling as it is enhancing) that man was made in the image of God (*imago dei*). Mankind thus carries in itself an image which begets it upon a higher destiny. One might note here that the modern notion of human dignity, that is so often called upon today in ethical debates, rests entirely on what was originally a theological qualification. If something is to be respected in human nature, it is not its dusty, terrestrial or animal side, which it shares with all other creatures, but the challenging notion that man was created as an *imago dei*. Because of this and only this, man enjoys a dignity in the realm of creation that calls for some respect. The Renaissance seized upon this notion of man's dignity when it celebrated the human achievements in the arts, science and culture as so many attempts to live up to this higher calling. This brought about a liberation in the understanding of human knowledge and artistry. Science did not exhaust itself in the study of divine things or in the *studia divinitatis*. There was also a genuine science of human affairs, a *studia humanitatis* that reaped fruit from the human accomplishments of the classics in literature, culture and science. For the Middle Ages (at least, according to the way in which they were resented by the Renaissance) the pursuit of human knowledge was thought to stem from a mere curiosity (*curiositas*)[1] which was condemned as being a conceited and infatuated attempt by man to understand the world out of his own resources, that is, without relying on the traditional or biblical account which both revealed all that man needed to know and was accompanied by a severe repudiation of merely human wisdom. The entire effort and achievement of the Renaissance was to protest against this depreciating view of human wisdom by extolling the possibilities of the notion of *imago dei*, that assimilitated man's nature, and most prominently his "rational" nature, to divinity. There is thus a way in which mankind can develop its cognitive capacities without appearing to indulge in a presumptuous curiosity for its own sake. To let one's talents flourish is nothing other than the realization of man's higher calling as an image of God.

The early Renaissance was too dependent upon tradition to picture this self-elevation of man as something that could be achieved by the means of the autonomous human being (a possibility that, nevertheless, soon became a real temptation for Bacon and Descartes with their project of an entirely new beginning or *tabula rasa*). For humanism, which still heeded the admonition that man was made out of ashes and that his reason could be very presumptuous indeed, human culture needs models. These models were originally the classics, which were mostly found in antiquity and then the canon of works which modernity later developed on its own. Such classics are, so to speak, the privileged witnesses of man's experiences, and the ones that need to be studied if one wants to learn what it is to be truly human and to measure up to the ideal of man as an *imago dei*.

Furthermore, it is also important to note in this respect the concept of culture and education which the German classicists of the 18th century later called *Bildung* ("formation"). While *Bildung* means education, it also stresses the notion that education has to be achieved by a process of building, that is, by transforming what is originally an amorphous matter into an orderly structure. The word "culture" also retains this dimension if one recalls its agricultural origins. To cultivate the soil is to labor it or to prepare it for seeds that will let fruit blossom. For humanism, the true dignity of mankind does not reside in its actual state, but in the idea that it can be cultivated and elevated to its higher destiny by domesticating, as it were, its animal or earthly side. The very modern notion of an "unending process" and of the necessary development or unfolding of man's latent potential thus has theological origins. Gadamer will allude to these origins in his rediscovery of humanism at the beginning of *Truth and Method* (1960): "The rise of the word *Bildung* evokes the ancient mystical tradition according to which man carries in his soul the image of God, after whom he is fashioned, and which man must cultivate in himself."[2] What distinguishes mankind from the other creatures is precisely this capacity to develop itself and to surpass its provincial particularity by lifting itself up to the universal. Gadamer, relying on Hegel's later description of this human elevation above nature, also states: "Man is characterized by the break with the immediate and the natural that the intellectual, rational side of his nature demands of him."[3]

Universality, as an aim of knowledge, is something one achieves by broadening one's horizons, by going beyond the particularity of our given nature and by learning from others who have transmitted to us the wealth of their wisdom. This meaning of universality differs from the one we encountered in the scientific view. According to this conception, universality meant that a hypothesis is valid for all the occurrences of this or that general law. For humanism, universality resides rather in the unending task of overcoming one's particularity or situatedness; and it is important that it be understood as a task because it can never be achieved once and for all. Moreover, humanism asserts that one never ceases to learn and to rise above one's own indigence through learning. Evidently, this model of knowledge is very different from the scientistic outlook. Its purpose is to make us more human, not to yield mathematical laws. Yet, it is a genuine mode of knowledge and one which is attuned to our need for self-improvement or culture. However, what does one have to learn in order to become a better human being? There is no clear-cut answer to this question. If we had one, we would be situated outside the human condition and would therefore be able to fall back on the scientistic model of knowledge. So a humanistic formation has to constantly seek and rebuild its own culture by learning from tradition. For the early humanists, the only available models were those of the classics. Yet, while we have a great debt to them for rediscovering those forgotten models, it is unlikely that we can retain their normative notion of the ancients. But we can perhaps preserve something of their general notion of *formation* (i.e. the idea that education proceeds by learning first and foremost from the cultural achievements of humanity, the conquests of human reason that can be reaped from history, literature, art, philosophy, religion and all the human sciences). If one wishes to understand the "limits of rationality," it is important to note that through this humanistic "culture" (again in the agricultural sense of the word), we acquire a genuine *formation* and true knowledge. Yet, this is a truth that cannot be comprehended adequately under the scientistic model sketched above and which limits knowledge to the observation of objective and mathematical regularities, and where our situated selves have no bearing whatsoever on the scientific results.

The scientistic model aims at a detached notion of truth that does not relate to our human formation and concerns. What one makes out of a scientistic truth is irrelevant to its validity as long as it can be confirmed by methodical and mathematical means. However, truth means something different in the human sciences. One can speak here of a formative truth and of meaningful truths that can help us become more human by helping us rise above our particularity. Is methodical verification really that important here? Is mathematical certainty sought after? Are general laws the main concern of humanistic knowledge?

Clearly, these concerns are not central to the human sciences. Yet, it is by applying such criteria that one has judged the scientificity of the human sciences; and under such criteria, the human sciences have fared very poorly. Indeed, compared to the "hard" or exact sciences, they appear to be nothing other than "soft." Instead of producing mathematical and verifiable results, they seem content to ponder questions which will never be resolved. In all these judgments, which are wide-spread in the general population, but also among the human and social scientists themselves, the prevalence of the scientistic model remains unquestioned.

This is unfortunate since what is missed is the particular ideal of humanistic knowledge that has very little to do with the scientistic picture; and this is true despite the fact that the two were born out of the same motivation, that is, as means of emancipation. As we saw earlier, the founders of modern science came from the cradle of humanism. To ground knowledge on mathematical certainty and observation meant a deliverance from the yoke of superstition and clericalism. This liberation stood in the service of the emancipation of man. Nonetheless, it is worth asking whether this motive has remained central in our scientistic culture where the authority of exact science has staked an almost exclusive claim to the idea of knowledge and truth. It could very well be that this scientistic notion of truth, which rests on objective verification and mathematical method alone, has forced knowledge under yet another yoke which prevents other avenues of understanding from being explored.

In this context in which even the human sciences have tended to understand themselves in terms of the scientistic definition of knowledge, (and, indeed, in a rather deficient fashion), the philosophical hermeneutics of Hans-Georg Gadamer has tried to rediscover the humanistic dimension of the humanities. The human sciences, he contends, have to liberate themselves from the alienating methodology of the exact sciences and to understand themselves as "the true advocates or emissaries of humanism," *als die wahren Sachwalter des Humanismus.*[4]

It might seem rather tautological to claim that the humanities have to see themselves as the defenders of humanism. Yet, if this tautology needs to be repeated today, it is because the human sciences have increasingly fallen under an antihumanist spell. In fact, many scholars in the humanities actually pride themselves on being antihumanists. One must pose the question therefore: How did this anti-humanism creep into the humanities? It seems certain that is stems from a protest against the view that man is at the center of the universe. Modernity has indeed developed a notion of the human subject that seems to put it at the center of things. For Descartes, all certainty must derive from the authority of the *cogito,* the thinking subject. For Kant, to act morally is to follow a command that emanates from our autonomous reason. Clearly, the notion of the autonomous and independent subject has been a leading force in modern culture and humanism itself, which has generally been understood as a self-liberation of man.

However, many discoveries in both the natural sciences and in the humanities, have dethroned the human subject from the privileged position bestowed upon it by modernity. Geneticists have revealed to what extent human behavior depends on genetic codes, which one also finds in animals. Freudian theory has tried to establish that our conscious selves are creations of the libidinal realm of the unconscious to which psychoanalysis claims to have privileged access. In addition, Marxism has attempted to show that the consciousness of the individual was but a mere reflection of a class perspective. In other words, the real subject of history resides not in the individual but in class struggle. Similarily, structural linguistics has argued that language is not a creation or instrument of the human spirit. Rather, it is the other way around: What we are, or think we are, is a mere production of linguistic games that are alleged to be the truer, more fundamental "subjects." All these various "humiliations" of man's distinctiveness are well known and a host of others could be mentioned as well. If the human subject is more genetic code than autonomous subject, more unconsciousness than consciousness, more a member of a social class than an individual, more a function of language than its author, then it appears unwarranted to focus the humanities on the central position of mankind, which has been so undermined by recent insights of the hard and soft sciences.

This *Zeitgeist* or this spirit of the times accounts for the antihumanistic bent of today's humanities. Even if these specific insights are valid in themselves, I believe that the antihumanist perspective they seem to encourage is profoundly mistaken. For four main reasons: First of all, it rests on an ill-informed understanding of what humanism is all about. Secondly, it is itself, in a not so subtle way, a product of the scientistic picture of knowledge. Thirdly, it can be shown to be an overreaction to a form of existentialist humanism which was dominant in the first half of the century. Finally, it wrongly claims that the humanistic conception of knowledge is ideological or elitist. I will expand briefly on these points.

1) While it is often claimed that humanism rests on the reassuring view that man is at the center of the universe, humanism has never forgotten that man was made out of ashes.[5] If one can leave aside the theological context, one can claim for humanism the truism that man is but a grain of sand in the vast universe. This is

by no means comforting. Yet, man can build himself, make something out of his situation, transcend his provincial particularity and elevate himself to a more universal perspective. Of course, mankind can still do this even if it is not at the center of the universe anymore. Classical humanism attributed this elevation to the notion of *imago dei*. Even if mankind carries this image within itself, it is by no means certain that it will realize what it means and what it calls for. Indeed, for many centuries, the humanists believed, mankind neglected to develop its creative talents, preferring the, yes, comforting yoke of tradition (what Immanuel Kant called "man's self-imposed minority"). Formation or *Bildung* is there to help us conquer the darker sides of our nature which threaten us at every instant. It is not very reassuring to constantly have to domesticate and cultivate oneself in order to avoid barbarism. Yet, this is the human predicament. This remains true even if one relinquishes the theological concept of the image of God (a notion, in fact, which is far less encouraging than it is humiliating because of man's constant failing to measure up to this ideal). So, the antihumanism of today misunderstood humanism on a crucial point. Humanism never rested on the idea that man was at the center of things. Rather, as modern science has reminded us, the human subject stands at the receiving end of the cosmic order, of language and of its socio-historical community. A humanistic perspective is not therefore tied to an anthropocentric view of things. It is very demeaning for mankind to constantly have to be learning in order to conquer its darker instincts. Clearly, no idea of man's centeredness is to be found here. For humanism, the important point is the stock it places in the unending task of formation and education. In a way, it runs counter to the notion of man's central position in the universe. It is not therefore man's centeredness, but the promise of *Bildung* which is the key notion of humanism, a notion which is no less a requisite even in an antihumanist context.

　　2) By abandoning the tradition of humanism from which they could have gained a more appropriate understanding of their specific truth claim, the human sciences expose themselves to the alienating methodology of the exact sciences which is not at all attuned to the humanistic mode of knowledge. Willingly or not, antihumanism thus plays into the hands of the scienticist model; indeed, one might add that it is perhaps nothing other than its by-product. There is, in fact, a lot of reductive positivism in anti-humanism which is conspicuously reminiscent of scienticism. Surely, one cannot hide a certain uneasiness about the vagueness of the humanities which seem to confront us with unending discussion that hardly ever pro-

duces definitive or quantifiable results. Humanism deals with issues such as the best form of government, the meaning of human life and the lessons of history and human art, all of which are susceptible of infinite dialogue. Hence, there is the temptation to dismiss entirely this whole realm of knowledge as mere humanistic salivation and to adopt a reductive perspective that would explain the human achievements out of a single, all-encompassing and almost mathematical foundation, a foundation that would be beyond the scope of humanism, be it the unconsciousness, the class structure, the unending play of linguistic signs, and so on. This reduction of human concerns to an underlying structure could very well be a product of scienticism. It is perhaps less important for the humanities to adopt such a well-assured, objectified and antihumanistic stance than to continue discussing openly and to learn from each other and from tradition concerning the issues that matter most to our humanity; and while we may not come to any algorithmical results soon, we will arrive at some formative truths in the process.

    3) The context out of which antihumanism blossomed is often forgotten. Even if Marx, Darwin and Freud elaborated their theories some generations ago, antihumanism only emerged as an intellectual force in the sixties. It is in great part indebted to the literary and rhetorical success of the French structuralists or post-structuralists, whose most prominent intellectual figures are probably Michel Foucault and Jacques Derrida. Even if both authors are gifted philosophers, endowed with the best of humanistic educations (one which is often wanting in their disciples), they still delighted in proclaiming that man was nothing but a "recent invention" and one which would soon fade in light of the new positivism of linguistic structures. Undoubtedly, there is some humanistic truth to the idea that modernity's focus on man has been overblown and was nothing but a recent happening (dating back, for Foucault, to the postclassicist age which obviously started with Kant at the beginning of the 19th century). In the fiercely competitive context of French philosophy, this antihumanistic reading was leveled against the philosophy of existentialism which dominated the intellectual scene, at least in the *sixième arrondissement*, throughout the forties and the fifties. Sartre had proclaimed in his famous pamphlet, *Existentialism is a Humanism*, that every truth and every action imply a properly human context and subjectivity.[6] Again, this might appear tautological. Nonetheless, it was precisely the task of the antihumanists to show that the human perspective is inadequate if one wishes to understand how truth and knowledge are produced in our societies and how action and subjectivity are governed by

subterranean power structures. The demystifying authors referred to above (i.e., Marx, Freud, Darwin), whose findings were also confirmed by the intuitions of Nietzsche and the ethnological writings of Claude Lévy-Strauss, drove home the point that it was perhaps a limitation to concentrate on human subjectivity and its capacities of choice and decision heralded by the existentialists. While a humanist might agree to a large extent with this "eccentric" understanding of man, which one can oppose to an anthropocentric reading, one can still question whether it misses its target by attacking existentialism. As a matter of fact, it might even have concealed its own origins by distancing itself so massively from existentialism. As a matter of fact, even if existentialism devoted great attention to the human predicament, no idea is more essential to it than man's "throwness" into the universe. Heidegger spoke of man's *Geworfenheit* or his being thrown into a world in which he is left to himself, a situation French translators rendered by the dramatic notion of "déréliction." Therefore, man is not really at the center of his universe for the existentialists. He only has to gain a proper understanding of his limited and anguishing self out of this basic experience of being thrown into finite existence. The existentialists themselves were the first to investigate these broader structures into which mankind finds itself thrown. For example, Sartre explored the social webs of interaction in his *Critique of Dialectical Reason*, and the later Heidegger and Merleau-Ponty discovered to what extent language is a more primordial avenue for the understanding of man. In this way, the existentialists who developed the anti-Cartesian notion of "thrownness" were the first "post-existentialists." However, this fact was occulted by the devastating antihumanistic attack on existentialism that has remained a leading topos to this day (i.e, in the guise of deconstructivism and postmodernism). One might be tempted to ask if this antihumanism was nothing after all but an overreaction against humanistic existentialism and, moreover, one which ignored its genuine existentialist origins.

4) Finally, I would also like to address an objection to humanism that might seem extrinsic, but which nevertheless has a lot of appeal today: namely, the belief that humanism is vitiated by an elitist or ideological conception of knowledge. This criticism of humanism stems from a sociological critique which has been espoused in many different forms.

The interest in tradition is often viewed as ideological *per se*. Only an ignorance of humanism and its relationship to tradition could foster such a view. In fact, humanism started off precisely with a critique of tradition (in the classical sense of *critica*), which is dif-

ferent from the meaning understood today whereby critique is somehow identified with the capacity of each human being to express his
or her judgment on anything, even if he or she lacks the expertise
to do so. For the Renaissance, the *ars critica* was the discipline that
was concerned with the "critical" editing of ancient texts. If critical
judgment was called for in such an enterprise, it was because the
texts that were transmitted to us suffered alterations in the process
of transmission. In order to go back to the original texts and their
intended meaning, one had to critically identify and remove the misunderstandings that were imposed on the texts through their transmission. In our modern culture, to study tradition is *ipso facto* to be
critical of it; and while humanists study tradition because they hope
to learn from it, it is precisely this willingness that makes one suspicious of the ideology that has been sedimented throughout tradition. Furthermore, it is only if one has been trained to carefully treat
tradition and history that one can develop a sense for anything like
a "critique of ideology." Today, the critique of ideologies takes on a
very superficial level. It often simply consists in developing some
kind of conspiracy theory (hardly ever verifiable) which stems from
some feature of culture one happens to dislike. As is well known,
conspiracy theories are self-serving and self-immune, and are hence
unlikely to contribute to the development of a reflexive acumen.
What can contribute to that is, on the oppposite, direct and critical
commerce with the tradition.

    However, there is another point to the antihumanistic argu-
ment and its massive repudiation of the traditional bias, which is
made with some legitimacy. It alleges that the humanistic conception is one which fosters an elitist conception of knowledge, one
which is left to a small elite in society. Indeed, very few people know
Greek and Latin or have read Pico della Mirandola. The focus on
classical books or great names in history or the arts, which would
be constitutive of humanism, would therefore be ideological. For instance, it could ignore parts of the tradition which were characterized by bigotry against an oppressed majority, against women or
against minorities. In this regard, this general critique of tradition
is certainly a major part of the antihumanist atmosphere of today.

    However, this critique can be reconcilied with a humanistic out-
look on culture. Indeed, who ever claimed that a critique of bigotry
cannot be part of our humanistic relationship to history and tradition? On the contrary, there is nothing more characteristic of history than to point out the prejudices in the tradition which no longer
bind us; and there are certainly other ways to conceive of history
than to learn dates by heart and to study the feats of great men.

But, again, who ever said that our conception of history and our canon of great deeds had been fixed once and for all? In fact, critical acquaintance with tradition teaches that tradition itself is always studied and applied very differently from one generation to the next.

For humanism, it is not important that all human beings study a specific form of tradition, that they should read Plato, know some Latin or listen to classical music. That would be imposing a model of knowledge which one could label "elitist." The only insight that is essential to humanism—and if it is trivial, all the better—is that one never ceases to learn from one's encounter with tradition and that through the human sciences we can grasp truths we would never gain access to if scienticism were the sole mode of knowledge. This human wisdom is still part of our system of education, even if its realm appears to be shrinking in light of the advances made by the exact sciences. What is worth defending is not the specific content or canon of the human sciences, but the humanistic insight that the scientistic model of rationality has obvious limits.

The perspective that was defended in this chapter has been a hermeneutic one which follows the lead of Hans-Georg Gadamer in his defense of the human sciences. As is well known, the hermeneutic philosophy of Gadamer descends directly from Heidegger. However, as we have argued in the preceeding section, if Gadamer departs in any way from Heidegger, it is surely in his understanding of humanism as a living force in our civilization. The later Heidegger wrote an open *Letter on Humanism* in 1946 in which he responded to a query by a young intellectual, Jean Beaufret, who asked if it was possible after the Second World War and the death camps of the Nazis to give a new meaning to the word humanism. The underlying meaning of Beaufret's question was whether or not one could still have faith in human reason and its promise of emancipation after Auschwitz. If the question was addressed to Heidegger, it was because his philosophy of existence seemed to be one of the most outspoken representatives of humanistic philosophy. Heidegger perhaps surprised Beaufret and his readers, who were unaware of the shift that had already occurred in his philosophy, by asking in turn if it was indeed that necessary to retain the notion of humanism. In this letter, Heidegger espoused the view that humanism rests on some form of anthropocentricism in that it reduces every form of Being to the human perspective. In this respect, humanism would be following the metaphysics of Plato that reduced Being to the appearance (*eidos*) it had for the human eye or the eye of the apprehending soul. What Heidegger condemns in this form of metaphysics is its intellectualization and reduction of all there is to the idea that man can have of it. In this intellectual, metaphysical and humanist perspective, the sheer gratuity of Being which cannot be reduced to its functionality for human purposes is missed. Heidegger thus wishes to overcome both metaphysics and humanism, which concentrate on the human condition, in order to develop an outlook on Being which would not be subordinate to the requirements of human reason or functionality. Heidegger thus urges "an open resistance to 'humanism' "[7]; and it is precisely by such a resistance, or so Heidegger believes, that one will be able to transcend the age of technology and its anthropocentric understanding of Being.

It is exactly here that Gadamer's hermeneutics ceases to follow Heidegger. For if Heidegger abandons the tradition of humanism, on what ground can he still criticize the age of technology and the scientistic understanding of knowledge it sanctifies? In other words, Heidegger's "anti-humanism," of which the influence on French philosophy has been tremendous, would leave the entire field of knowledge to the empire of technology, and this perhaps despite Heidegger's basic instincts. What one can learn from Gadamer's defense of the human sciences and his apology of humanism is that the ground that enables Heidegger to dispute the advance of technology is to be found nowhere else than in the humanistic tradition itself. It is precisely in the context of humanism that Gadamer will indeed find an effective "resistance to the claims of modern science."[8] It is interesting to note that Gadamer uses the word "resistance" (*Widerstand*) when he alludes to the actual possibilities of the humanistic tradition. Whereas Heidegger advocated an open "resistance" *against* humanism, Gadamer unearths in the forgotten tradition of humanism an instance that can fuel a counterreaction against the hybrid claims of modern science to encompass all there is to know. Heidegger would in a way ignore the tacitly humanistic motive of his antihumanist attack on the sole empire of technology and its model of objectified science. Heidegger would thus be more of a humanist than he has led us to believe in his *Letter on Humanism*. In the view espoused by hermeneutics, the limits of the age of scientific rationality do not necessarily point to a new age that has yet to appear on the horizon of history. Such a utopian new beginning is not a real possibility for our humanity. Rather, the limits of rationality could reacquaint us with the tradition of humanism and the resistance it has always offered against the illegitimate claims of scienticism. We would do well therefore to rediscover its modest understanding of man as a being who is in constant need of learning from history. It is the recent notion of man as one who can destroy the tradition at ease which is shriekingly immodest.

Chapter 10

The Hermeneutical Intelligence of Language

One has spoken with a lot of irony, and not without justice, of an "inflation" of language in contemporary philosophy.[1] It is clear that this characterization is aimed in particular at classical analytical philosophy. Without necessarily subscribing to Wittgenstein's theory according to which all philosophical problems arise from abuses of language, which are all more on less correctible, analytical philosophers continue to view linguistic analysis as the privileged method by which one may orient oneself in the argumentative order of philosophical questions. However, language has also become an obsession for continental philosophy, of which the three most contemporary streams are probably: hermeneutical philosophy (Gadamer, Heidegger, to a certain extent Levinas) deconstruction (Derrida, but also Foucault) and transcendental pragmatics (Habermas, Apel), the heir of the critical theory of the Frankfurt School. It is also true for these continental philosophies that everything which can be thought must also be of linguistic nature. Indeed, Habermas' *Theory of communicational activity* bases its conception of rationality and its critical theory of society on universal or *a priori* presuppositions which would be invested in the use of every discourse (to engage oneself in an act of discourse would be to recognize the universal requisites, whether they be effectively respected or not, of the communicative order and of its implicit rationality). Thus is heralded a major revo-

141

lution of which future generations will have to measure the real scope: henceforth, "reason" no longer finds itself in the world order, nor in the head of thinking subjects, but in language which imposes its positivity on contemporary philosophy. For its part, Derrida's deconstruction, while it starts with the same phenomenon (i.e., the dominion of language), arrives at diametrically opposed conclusions. What deconstruction finds fascinating in the vertiginous universe of language is the fact that meaning (the "real presence" of the thing) is continually deferred. It is this very "deferring," *différance*, which governs the infinite, but arbitrary order of signs and which would exclude any type of extra-textual reference. Such a reference is only itself an "indicated" real presence, or only "promised" by the signs. Yet, these signs never return to an observable objective world. Rather, they refer back to other signs, to other oppositions of which the dominion would define what we are rightly able to hold for real (a dominion which corresponds a little to what Foucault understands as *epistèmè*, or to what Derrida alludes to when he speaks of the language of metaphysics). The world, Being, reference, truth, in short, all the notions which would claim to offer us access to something beyond language would themselves be nothing other than "effects of discourse."

One would easily find confirmations of this inflation of language in the hermeneutical phenomenology of Heidegger and Gadamer. In Heidegger's later writings, all access to the world appears to have become the affair of language, which to a certain degree inherits *Dasein's* function as the "there of Being," which remained man's prerogative in *Being and Time*. Gadamer appears to follow the later Heidegger when he professes at the end of *Truth and Method* (1960) that "Being which can be understood is language." The universal ontology of hermeneutics would thus also appear to reconduct everything which is and which can be thought to the imperial order of language.

What the critical idea of an inflation of language suggests is that the attention devoted to language has gone a little far in its referential or ontological blindness and that the real does not perhaps limit itself to what discourse is able to say about it. Furthermore, if one is still permitted to speak of error and lies, it is because everything does not reduce itself to a linguistic universe closed on itself. In this regard, the critique of "linguistic inflation" is a very healthy undertaking indeed.

What I would like to show in this chapter is that the hermeneutical conception of language that one finds with the "first" Heidegger and Gadamer is diametrically opposed to the inflationist celebration of language which prevails in philosophy. In fact, what distinguishes the hermeneutical intelligence of language could very well be its thesis on the "secondarity" of propositional language. For hermeneutics, the discourse of statements appears derivative in regard to the hermeneutical experience of understanding (which is always more a striving for understanding than a definitive comprehension). To hermeneutically understand language is precisely to pierce through the facade of uttered language in order to bring attention to the things which our words attempt to share, but without fully succeeding, hence their indigence or "secondarity."

The thesis on the secondary nature of language finds its clearest expression in the title of § 33 of *Sein und Zeit*, "The proposition as a derived mode of interpretation." At first sight, this notion appears rather naïve, *a fortiori* if one compares it to what seems to correspond to an "inflation" of language in the later writings of Heidegger. Paul Ricœur has faulted Heidegger for bestowing such a secondary status on language is his master work.[2] It is necessary, however, to note that § 33 only speaks of the derived status of the statement (*Aussage*), but not of "language" itself (*Sprache*). If Heidegger wants to distance himself from the statement, the *Aussage*, it is only in the hope of rekindling a more hermeneutical intelligence of language which does not let itself be confined to the order of statements. However, is there therefore a sphere of discourse which no longer pertains to statements? Is not language the entirety of that which allows itself to be stated? It is this evidence, on which classical logic reposes, that the earlier Heidegger wishes to challenge. What Heidegger wants us to see, is that the human statement proceeds from an experience of meaning which is never entirely stated in the attributive proposition studied by logic. Heidegger's classic example is well-known: "The hammer is heavy." Such an exclamation can come to the lips of an exhausted worker in his workshop. However, what the statement states is only that the predicate "heaviness" finds itself applied to the subject "hammer," as if the statement were only a theoretical deposition concerning a subsisting object at hand which would have nothing to do with our *Dasein*. If Heidegger evokes the derived status of the statement, it is because the predicative act is entirely secondary with respect to the original hermeneutic experience and which even risks being lost in the enunciation. What the statement means, is not that the "hammer" possesses the physical quality of heaviness, but that *Dasein* suffers in its commerce with the tool. This context alone permits an understanding of the tenor or the content of the statement, which may want to say several things; for example, it could translate an immediate expression of suffering, signify a request for assistance, etc.

In this regard, the statement is clearly secondary or "derived." It stems from the suffering worker's self-interpretation which precedes the statement and which perhaps does not even need to express itself in words. For example, sighs or expletives could be just as expressive, as would simply putting the hammer aside. "Out of the absence of words, one should not necessarily conclude the absence of interpretation."[3] The "pre-enunciative" interpretation is what Heidegger qualifies as properly "hermeneutical."[4] For the "hermeneutical" alludes to the self-understanding of *Dasein* which is at play within every encounter with Being and indeed with language itself. When this self-understanding comes to be expressed in words, one passes from the realm of the hermeneutical to the apophantic, predicative, or enunciative exposition.

The motivational or hermeneutical background can effectively be lost or poorly conveyed in the bulkiness of objective statements. This is why it is legitimate, according to Heidegger's perspective, to speak of its "secondarity." This does not mean however that Heidegger entirely ignores the importance of language for understanding. There is a mode of language which is not secondary in *Sein und Zeit*: *Rede*, the speech or discourse which the *Dasein* uses daily. This speech affirms itself as "co-original" with comprehension (*Verstehen*).[5] This speech embraces all the "primitive" forms of discourse in which our practical Being-in-the-world states itself out: linguistic tics, mannerisms, small-talk, innuendos, sighs, laughs, etc. While all these forms of speech appear to be primitive, it is for the young Heidegger precisely according to this mode that language is first and indeed most often present. Confronted with these most elementary "language games" (to take up the expression of the later Wittgenstein), the proposition appears as an "abstraction" which only characterizes the "theoretical" discourse in the strict sense. Heidegger's polemical intention is to relativize the privilege enjoyed by the statement or the proposition in traditional logic. In Heidegger's view, traditional logic impedes an adequate comprehension of how language functions, as the practical mode of the Being-in-the-world, which manifests itself less in the predicative statement than in the speech which bursts forth in the sphere of one's daily preoccupations and whose "logic" would in some way be "pre-predicative."[6]

There is thus something like a "contempt" for the realm of mere statements in the earlier Heidegger. One also encounters here one of the first motivations of what he understands phenomenology to be. For him, the phenomenological approach stands and falls with the simplicity of a "return to the things themselves." Without exag-

gerating, on could say that it is the only injunction which truly interested him in phenomenology. To engage in phenomenology or to
hold oneself to the things themselves, as volume XIX of the
Gesamtausgabe has recently confirmed, is to fight against the seduction and the ease of commonly received "discourses" which re-
lieve us from the necessity of a direct recourse to the things
themselves. The double task of philosophy, Heidegger insists, is precisely to find a renewed access to the things themselves, but at the
same time to destroy the discourses which cover up the elementary[7]
(a double task, positive and negative, which will continue to support the architecture of the two parts of *Sein und Zeit*, the Analytic
and Destruction).

It is not incidental that Heidegger expresses his radical dis-
may with regard to prevailing "discourses" in a course on the *Sophist*. The sophist was already for Plato the one who attempts to teach
how to be competent in the art of the *logoi*, but under complete abstraction from the discourse's claim to truth. Given the indigence of
the *logoi* for the knowledge of truth, the *Seventh Letter* and the
Phedrus go as far as condemning the usefulness of writing, even of
language, in philosophy. Heidegger's solidarity with Platon on this
point is total.[8] Written discourse, or even public discourse, risks being distorted from its original meaning if the author is not there to
defend its intentions. The essential is not to believe that one has
attained philosophical truth in some proposition, but to "see" the
things, and to only use discourse in order to arrive at an immediate
meaning of the things themselves. At the limit, as a manuscript
note of Heidegger reveals, philosophy, to the extent that it seeks after a "seeing," is "in a certain sense liberated from the *logos*"
(*Philosophie . . . in gewissem Sinne logos-Frei*).[9]

For Heidegger, the tendency to remain at the surface of the
logos corresponds to a certain inauthenticity of *Dasein*. Our being,
inasmuch as it is a virtual *Dasein*, or a being "there," is called upon
to be "there" where the things discover themselves, and even to secure this very discovering. Blindly following the *logoi* which circulate around us without taking upon oneself the effort of a direct
vision of the things themselves is to cease to be "there," to cease to
be *Da-sein*. In his 1929/30 course, and then again in the *Beiträge*,
Heidegger spoke here of a *Wegsein*[10]—of a *Dasein* which is not there,
but "away," elsewhere, that is, in the *logoi*. The surrounding *logoi*
obstruct the access of *Dasein* to itself. A discourse devoid of a corresponding or sought-after vision amounts only to chatter: "It is evident that the *logos* is dependent on a *horan*, a seeing, and that it
therefore enjoys a derived status; it is also evident, on the other

hand, that the *logos*, to the extent to which it accomplishes itself in an isolated manner, that it is the way according to which one is only able to speak, that is to chatter about things, is precisely what, in the being of man, obstructs the possibility of seeing the things themselves; the *logos* has precisely this tendency, to the extent that it simply floats in the air, to spread a presumed knowledge favoring a simple repetition of what is said and which itself no longer has anything to do with the things."[11] Heidegger clearly speaks here of the *logos* to the extent that it proceeds "in an isolated manner," that is, to the extent that it takes the place of an access to the things. It is precisely this autonomy that Heidegger wishes to debunk with the unique lever of phenomenology, i.e., the return to the things themselves.

If it is difficult to conceive of a discourse that would legitimately be able to speak authoritatively of the "things themselves," the polemical scope of Heidegger's position is clear. Its aim is to attack the widespread tendency which consists, in philosophy as in other modes of discourse, in holding idly to a jargon, to "what people say" (*das Man*), to the gossip which is present in our surroundings and in function of which we orient ourselves to varying degrees. It is this "deficient" mode of comprehension that the course on the *Sophist* labels the "*Verfallen*" upon the *logoi*," the falling to the level of discourses alone.[12] This excellent formula, the falling prey to the *logos*, translates one of Heidegger's most fundamental insights. One "falls," one descends into received discourses, as one falls into a snare. One cedes to the easiness of jargon which procures a vague and general orientation, evidently convenient, but which does not result from a direct encounter. In order to combat this drift towards the *logoi*, this thirst for gossip, phenomenology calls for an access to the things which are to be the object of an autonomous conquest, and thereby of a concrete legitimization. This evidence, phenomenology will always be able to call upon it and, in the best of cases, to produce it itself. It is far less crucial, if one wishes to do phenomenology to subscribe to its particular theses on the hierarchy of reductions or the constitution of transcendantal noesis. It is also useful to remind one of this to counteract the tendency in contemporary phenomenology which strives to reconstruct with much care and meticulousness the relationship between Husserl's and Heidegger's endeavors. To insist excessively upon the theoretical subtilties of this relation, is perhaps to miss what is essential, or to engage in phenomenology without hermeneutics. It is not the phenomenological doctrines which count, but the necessity to see the things themselves. This is how Heidegger understood phenomenology. It is moreover on behalf of such a primitive conception of phenomenology that he could accuse some aspects of Husserl's philosophy of being "non-phenomenological."[13] One's introduction to phenomenology, Heidegger wrote in 1924, is not accomplished by reading phenomenology's literature, but by the concrete work directly relating to the things themselves.[14] One sees that Heidegger subscribes here, *nolens volens*, to a conception of truth as *adaequatio*: true discourse is that which corresponds to the things themselves. Despite Heidegger's insistence upon the act of discovery which is incumbant upon *Dasein*, whose essence—as the being capable of being "there"—is to discover the things in their truth, this truth only allows itself to be thought as an adequation, if it wishes to "conform" to the "things themselves." The destruction of tradition sets itself the task of identifying the *logoi* which take possession of our vision. Yet, how does one destroy the aberrations of tradition without understanding truth as correspondence?

This polemical import of Heidegger's phenomenology is precious. It efficaciously denounces the jargon of received evidences which are not based upon any real experience, or on any "vision," and of which, of course, phenomenology itself is not exempt. However, the positive side of Heidegger's thesis presents some difficulties. One can indicate three: 1) What exactly is the direct vision of things which phenomenology attempts to advance? Does not the catch-word of a "return to the things themselves" itself remain purely declamatory? Heidegger's does not ignore it. It is precisely why he took so much care to demonstrate that the most essential phenomenon is that of being,[15] devoting all his phenomenological energies to the destruction of the successive overlappings of the question of being which metaphysics practiced. But how does one assure oneself of the authenticity of a return to the things themselves if it must be achieved through the intermediary of a question which itself remains "traditional," i.e., that of being? 2) One can also question whether Heidegger's critique of the "statement" does not somewhat neglect effective discourse and its positive potentialities in discovering the things themselves. If there is a lot of jargon or ideology in the discourses that we recite, it still remains that discourse does serve to discover Being and to present to us the things such as they are experienced. Without claiming along with a certain current of contemporary philosophy that language represents our only access to reality, if not a prison, language certainly remains the privileged mode of our comprehensive opening to the world. And does not discourse always deploy itself in an enunciative mode? 3) The third difficulty relates to what one can call the existential devalorization of the order of statements. As we have already seen, and this is even more manifest in the 1924–25 course than in *Being and Time*,

Heidegger appears to assimilate the predominance of the *logos* to a certain decline or fall of *Dasein*. In this regard, Paul Ricœur spoke of an "ontological degradation" in the "objectivization" of the statement. In abandoning oneself to jargon which is in current use, *Dasein* closes itself off to a certain extent to itself. It no longer assumes the responsibility of revealing its being to itself, rather it prefers to let it be dictated by commonly accepted discourses (those of the "everyone," Heidegger said in 1927). Often, writes Heidegger, propositions come thus to replace the truth.[16] A true discovering of the phenomena themselves would enable *Dasein* to fight against the *Verfallen* or the decline on the level of *logoi* alone.[17] Everything happens a little as if the realm of statements was one that one would absolutely have to fight against. For Heidegger, *Dasein* is from the start and indeed most often closed to itself, to the extent that it orients itself exclusively according to common discourses. *Dasein's* self-transparence appears to be conquered only at the price of a permanent battle against the *logos*. In this regard, one might have the feeling here that Heidegger grafts the opposition of the statement and the truth onto his dichotomy of the inauthentic and the authentic. However, is it legitimate to support a conception that one might call, at our risk and peril, a "moralizing" of discourse? Is the statement really in itself more of a covering-up than a discovering?[18]

Gadamer has often written about the fascination exerted upon him by the courses of the young Heidegger in the twenties. As we have seen, he recognizes having been particularly taken over by the use that Heidegger made of the Augustinian distinction between the *actus signatus* and the *actus exercitus*, that is to say between the significative act of discourse, that which is expressed by the signs which comprise a statement, and its effective exercise, or its comprehensive "accomplishment." The term "accomplishment," however, only conveys inadequately the German notion of *Vollzug* (literally: to pull to its fullness). "To accomplish" the discourse, the *actus exercitus*, means two things: to go to the end of pronounced discourse, in sounding out its secret motivation and background, but also to know how to apply that which has been uttered to one's own situation, to translate it into our concrete situation. It is in this spirit that the young Heidegger introduced his own concepts as simple "formal indications" which are not linked to any precise terminology, but which call for an expressed appropriation in order to be understood. Philosophical concepts are only adequately understood if one succeeds in applying them to one's existence, in piercing again the semiotic surface of the discourse with a view to its interior motivation. Indeed, in philosophy it does not suffice to know how to repeat formulas or theorems, this would simply be staying on the level of the *actus signatus*, it is necessary to make a specific effort of comprehension which aims as much at the motivation underlying the statement as its application to existence. Thus it concerns as much what follows as that which precedes the discourse. Only the effort of the *actus exercitus* permits one to arrive at the fuller meaning of propositions. When Gadamer employs the term hermeneutics, it is precisely to echo this hermeneutical conception of language extolled by the young Heidegger.[19]

In this perspective, "hermeneutics" characterizes perhaps less a specific philosophical doctrine than a way of understanding discourse. However, one can already note a slight difference between Heidegger and Gadamer on this hermeneutical intelligence of language. While, for Heidegger, the hermeneutical order sometimes appears to refer to something "beyond discourse," to the suffering of the worker when she sighs that "the hammer is heavy," Gadamer alludes rather to the interiority of language itself, to the will of meaning and to the motivation of effective discourse. What is common to the two authors is the idea that the statement cannot be considered as a self-sufficient semantic entity. Assuredly, Gadamer follows Heidegger in his opposition to the empire of the statement: "the concept of statement (. . .) stands in the most extreme opposition to the essence of the hermeneutical experience and the linguisticality of the human experience of the world."[20] The privilege of the statement is not however opposed to a "beyond language," but to the *Sprachlichkeit*, to the original "linguisticity" of our hermeneutical experience of the world. What is, however, the nature of this hermeneutical experience? It finds its clearest illustration in what Gadamer calls the logic of question and answer. It expresses what Gadamer holds as "the most original hermeneutical phenomenon" (*das hermeneutische Urphänomen*), the most universal feature of language, namely "that no statement is possible which could not be understood as an answer to a question—and that the statement can always be understood *only in this way*."[21] Whoever wishes to understand a proposition must first of all strive to understand the question which it is attempting to answer, or the horizon of questions that bring the proposition about. Gadamer speaks of a "logic" of question and answer, and this logic, as a discipline of truth in discourse, aims at superseding the predicative logic which confines itself to the positivity of statements. The dialogic of the question and answer invites one to look at the truth of the discourse which is at work in advance of our utterances, at the dialogue out of which such statements "emerge."

Nonetheless, it is important to see that, for Gadamer, this "in advance" or "upstream" from the statement, still pertains to language or more exactly, to *Sprachlichkeit* as such. The Gadamerian notion of *Sprachlichkeit* has not always been well understood. It does not uniquely designate the "linguistic character" of our experience of the world, since this general characteristic would also hold for the logic of the statement. Indeed, if such were the case, Gadamer would definitely appear as one of the culprits for the inflation of language in contemporary philosophy. The notion of *Sprachlich*keit designates rather the linguistic virtuality, the search for meaning, and the need of that which seeks to be understood to become language. What is universal in hermeneutics is not merely the linguistic character of our comprehension, because very often we are not fully able to say what we believe we understand. It is rather the search for language which is universal and this search is a never-ending one. It would only cease when we would stop to be a dialogue with and for ourselves; that is, when we would no longer be there.

The original hermeneutical experience is therefore less that of language than that of the *limits* of language.[22] It is because language never succeeds in exhausting everything that wants to be said and understood that our understanding always remains in a permanent quest of language. The constitutive insatisfaction of *Sprachlichkeit* corresponds to what Gadamer names the "speculative" structure of language, which is studied in the second to the last chapter of *Truth and Method*, the chapter which prepares for the universalization of the hermeneutical experience at the end of the book. The "speculative" dimension refers to everything which is not said in that which is effectively said or to the entire sphere of the unsaid which is only mirrored (the term *speculative* comes from *speculum*, mirror) or reflected in effective discourse. As we have argued throughout this book, there is a willed meaning which never achieves its full crystallization in the proposition. The speculative understanding encourages a comprehensive accomplishment of meaning which takes into account this "unsaid," the motivational background, the context, in short, the dialogue which precedes the given discourse. The speculative dimension is at work as much at the level of the speaker as of the listener. The speaker "risks" statements, he "commits" himself (in this regard one might say that stammering is language's most honest form of statement) while knowing perfectly well that his words do not exhaust his willed meaning. The speaker whose propositions are taken literally knows herself to be poorly understood. She can take a certain distance with regard to her own propositions while looking for others so that she can express what she really wants to

say, or all that which it would be necessary to state in order to be
adequately understood. It is precisely with regard to this excess of
meaning that one can continue to speak of a secondarity of the effective statement. What is required of the listener who attempts to
understand, is to retrace the path of the enunciation, of the
hermeneia that the Ancients already held for an act of *"interpretatio"*:
returning from what is said to what remains unsaid. To start from
what is said in order to understand that which wishes to be said, is
by its nature to speculate, to seek understanding. The speculative
dimension of *Sprachlichkeit* thus presupposes a labor with language
which does not remain at the "positivity" of discourse, but knows
that propositional language can only be understood by way of a
Vollzug von Sinn, a pursuing to an end of meaning, which is not itself stated in the proposition.

Gadamer's account of this speculative element of language merits being quoted in full length: "Language itself has something speculative—not only in the sense Hegel intends, as an instinctive
pre-figuring of logical reflection—but, rather, as the realization of
meaning, as the event of speech, of mediation, of coming to an understanding. Such a realization is speculative in that the finite possibilities of the word are oriented toward the sense intended as
toward the infinite. A person who has something to say seeks and
finds the words to make himself intelligible to the other person. This
does not mean that he makes "statements." Anyone who has experienced an interrogation—even if only as a witness—knows what it
is to make a statement and how little it is a statement of what one
means. In a statement the horizon of meaning of what is to be said
is concealed by methodical exactness; what remains is the "pure"
sense of the statements. That is what goes on record. But meaning
thus reduced to what is stated is always distorted meaning." The
task of a hermeneutical penetration of language is to reconquer the
speculative density of discourse by putting in the balance the unsaid which reflects itself in what had been uttered. One sees that
the hermeneutical intelligence of language, understood in the subjective sense of the genitive, is more an intelligence which distinguishes language itself than it is our own. What this intelligence
requires of us is an understanding, even a compassion, in the hope
of awakening the speculative truth which attempted to express itself in the limited (although intelligent) terms of discourse. Gadamer
continues: "To say what one means (. . .) to make oneself understood—means to hold what is said together with an infinity of what
is not said in one unified meaning and to ensure that it is understood in this way. Someone who speaks in this way may well use

only the most ordinary and common words, but he is just the same able to bring to language what is not said and must be said."[23] To know how to convey in what is said all that which cannot be said, this is truly the perilous task of discourse, but also that of comprehension which attempts to take the proper measure of that which gets said. To understand is therefore to enter into dialogue with what has been uttered, of course also with what an author wanted so say, but also with everything she was not able to say. Speech and understanding thus emerge as "speculative" processes whose success is nothing less than fragile. To understand is to bring out the unsaid which is necessary in order to accomplish that which was said. Hermeneutics must therefore, in a certain sense, leave the realm of statements, which are so secondary that they are always in need of supplementary explanations in order to be adequately seized. Its element is thus less that of language, which remains occupied by or even obstructed by statements, than that of *Sprachlichkeit*, that is, the virtuality of meaning which dwells within language. Human comprehension operates in this universal element of dialogue, of the search for language which precedes the objective world of statements.

However, does Gadamer's hermeneutics expose itself then to the criticism which Heidegger's theses on the derived character of the proposition seem to invite? As we have seen above, Heidegger's conception appears to presuppose a direct vision, *"logos-frei,"* of the things, but whose possibility or nature has perhaps not been positively provided. We have also argued that the secondarity of the statement could have the effect of screening out the real discourses of *Dasein*, which appear condemned to take the form of statements, as imperfect as they are. Finally, Heidegger's thesis seems to subordinate the tension between the truth and the discourse to a dichotomy between the authentic and the inauthentic.

In a somewhat older article, but one which is nonetheless very penetrating, as it has been one of the few to perceive the ultimate orientation of Gadamer's notion of *Sprachlichkeit*, the theologian Wolfhart Pannenberg accused Gadamer of too severely condemning the enunciative character of our linguistic experience.[24] Pannenberg is in agreement with Gadamer in recognizing that the horizon of the unsaid is essential to an appreciation of any discourse. However, Gadamer would have neglected two things. 1) The just understanding of the horizon of the unsaid must necessarily start from what was said, thus from the statement. There would therefore be no reason for putting the primacy of the statement into question for hermeneutics. 2) The elucidation of the realm of the unsaid could in turn only be accomplished through the intermediary of statements. Thus, hermeneutical understanding, the accomplishment of the meaning which works in advance of the proposition, would still pertain to the order of the enunciation.

While such criticisms are indeed just, I believe that they may still be reconciled with what Gadamer is saying. It is clear that it is necessary, in most cases, to start from the statement when one attempts to understand or to interpret. Hermeneutics does not contest this. Its thesis on the secondarity of the statement only wants to point out the indigence of the statement with regard to the infinity which attempts to express itself and of which real language is only the *speculum*. What it condemns, is not the fact of the statement, which would constrain it to an absolute silence (a "sigetics" which appealed to the later Heidegger), but the fixation on the statement as an autonomous entity of meaning. If the statement can be called an "abstraction" for Gadamer, it is because the exclusive concentration on the logic of the statements risks abstracting them from their dialogical horizon (contextual, motivational, etc.).[25] The statement is "secondary" only in relation to this essential dialogical horizon. "Real" language, as Pannenberg reminds us, takes on the form of statements, which are more or less articulate—and the more the discourse stammers, the more it is human, linguistic *aisance* serving in a certain way to mask the essential distress of human discourse. The only question is if these statements can be understood if one ignores this distress and the questions which underly it.

Pannenberg also had reason to say that the comprehensive elucidation of propositions can only be made through other enunciations. One cannot escape them. However, the hermeneutical explanation of the motivation of the statement is never exhausted by the explanations which are offered up and which only emphasize some of its aspects. Furthermore, the statements which one can venture about other statements participate themselves in the speculative structure of language. No explanation ever says everything. And what it affirms is in its turn susceptible to multiple readings. In the finite terms which the explanatory statements mobilize, an infinity of meanings are still hiding, as well as possible misunderstandings. Is it really everything that the proposition wanted to say? Does the context, for example, explain everything the original statement wished to convey? Such are the issues which preoccupy the hermeneutical attending to language.

It is possible that Pannenberg's criticisms reach Heidegger more than Gadamer. Indeed, Gadamer does not envisage a "beyond language" when he conceives of a hermeneutical intelligence. The hermeneutical is not opposed directly to the apophantic, it simply carries it. Gadamer does not therefore neglect the effective discourse, as Heidegger perhaps did in some of his formulas where he evoked an understanding which would be *"logos-frei,"* freed of *logos*. If Heidegger could underline that *Rede* was co-original to understanding, it was because life's everyday speech makes it easier to discern the practical embededness of *Dasein*'s understanding than the theoretical discourse of propositional enunciation. However, what one must understand remains beyond the statement, a practical suffering that the effective language of statements almost fatally lacks, because of the domination of the ontology of subsisting being (*Vorhandenheit*) and the propositional logic which commands it.

It is for another reason that Gadamer relies himself on the elementary experience of language which characterizes what he calls our hermeneutical experience of the world. It is not first of all because the practical concerns of our *Dasein* would be more visible here than in the realm of theoretical propositions, but because the necessity to go back up from the statements to their motivational background is already the way in which the understanding of language is lived and practiced in everyday life. The hermeneutical intelligence does not allude therefore to a sophisticated procedure or "method" that would be unique to philosophical hermeneutics: "The first step of the hermeneutical endeavor, namely the requirement that understanding must return from the statements to the underlying questions which motivate them does not demand a particular artifice, it describes, on the contrary, our most common practice (. . .). What would be artificial, would be not to reflect on these presuppositions. It is, on the contrary, very artificial to imagine that statements would fall from the sky and could be submitted to analytical analysis without even taking into account why they have been said and in what manner they are responses to something."[26] The speculation on language already inhabits our "linguisticity," our hermeneutical relation to language. The element of *Sprachlichkeit* is not therefore an invitation to leave the circle of statements, but to enter into them in an appropriate manner.

By linking the hermeneutical comprehension of language to the daily practice of understanding, to the intelligence of language, Gadamer also avoids the dichotomy of the authentical and the inauthentical which appeared to lend a rather elitist orientation to the phenomenological radicalism of Heidegger: the *logoi* in current use are from the start suspected of being inauthentic, pertaining to a *Dasein* which falls upon the banks of chattering, while truth pertains to phenomenology or its *Destruction*, that is, to a legitimation by the things themselves which is assured by a philosophy which knows how to destroy tradition.

Gadamer's hermeneutics succeeds in preserving the critical scope of Heidegger's thesis on the secondarity of the statement while avoiding its hazards. It does not oppose the order of language to a direct vision of things. The element of understanding is not that of immediate vision, but that of "linguisticity" where language is somehow able to surpass itself and the limits of any given statements, but while remaining entirely within the horizon of intelligibility which can be nothing other than pivoted upon a possible language. Hermeneutics thus reminds phenomenology that one cannot eliminate the sphere of possible statements and that the confirmation by the things themselves must itself be the object of an enunciative and dialogical effort. Riveted to the real practice of comprehension, it can also contend with effective discourse without the intervention of any notion of authenticity or decline (*Verfallen*). Thus, Gadamer's philosophical hermeneutics admits again the multiplicity of human *logoi* whose stammerings stem less from an existential forfeiture than from the finitude of our dialogical reason.

NOTES

Note to Introduction

1. Cf. Theodore Kisiel, *The Genesis of Heidegger's Being and Time*, Berkeley: University of California Press, 1993, 498.

Notes to Chapter 1

1. On this new foundation, see my earlier studies on Kant: *Kant et le problème de la philosophie: l'a priori*, Paris: Vrin, 1989; "The Conclusion of the *Critique of Pure Reason*," in *Graduate Faculty Philosophy Journal*, 16, 1993, 165–78. For the transition from Kant to the idealists, which cannot interest us directly here, compare "The A Priori from Kant to Schelling," in *Idealistic Studies*, 19, 1989, 202–221.

2. See the reconstruction of this perplexity in my "De Kant à Fichte," in *Proceedings: Sixth International Kant-Congress* (Penn State 1985), ed. by G. Funke and T. M. Seebohm, Washington: The University Press of America 1989,vol. II/2, 471–492.

3. See F. Schleiermacher, *Hermeneutik und Kritik*, hrsg. von M. Frank, Frankfurt: Suhrkamp, 1977, 92: "Die laxere Praxis in der Kunst geht davon aus, daß sich das Verstehen von selbst ergibt und drückt das Ziel negativ aus: Mißverstand soll vermieden werden. (. . .) Die strengere Praxis geht davon aus, daß sich das Mißverstehen von selbst ergibt und das Verstehen auf jedem Punkt muß gewollt und gesucht werden." On the religious background of Schleiermacher's hermeneutics, compare the excellent study of Ben Vedder, "Schleiermacher's Idea of Hermeneutics and the Feeling of Absolute Dependence," in *Epochè. A Journal for the History of Philosophy*, 2, 1994, 81–103.

4. On Schlegel's metaphysics and its impact on the development of hermeneutics, compare J. Zovko, *Verstehen und Nichtverstehen bei Friedrich Schlegel. Zur Entstehung und Bedeutung seiner hermeneutischen Kritik*, Stuttgart: Fromann-Holzboog, 1990.

5. On this universality of misunderstanding, see the Schleiermacher chapter of our *Introduction to Philosophical Hermeneutics*, New Haven: Yale University Press, 1994.

6. Hans-Georg Gadamer, *Wahrheit und Methode* [WM], in *Gesammelte Werke* [GW], I, Tübingen: J. C. B. Mohr (Paul Siebeck), 1986, 472 (Der Begriff der Aussage (. . .) steht nun in einem äußersten Gegensatz zu dem Wesen der hermeneutischen Erfahrung und der Sprachlichkeit der menschlichen Welterfahrung überhaupt); *Truth and Method* [TM], Second Revised Edition, New York: Crossroad Publishing, 1989, 468 (our emphasis).

7. WM in GW, I, 472–73; TM, 469.

8. GW, II, 226; "The Universality of the Hermeneutical Problem," in H.-G. Gadamer, *Philosophical Hermeneutics*, transl. by D. E. Linge, Berkeley/Los Angeles: University of California Press, 1976, 11.

9. WM, in GW, I, 464; TM, 460.

10. A more detailed historical account will be provided in the following essays on "The Task of Hermeneutics in Ancient Philosophy" and "Gadamer and Augustin."

11. See H.-G. Gadamer, "Heidegger und die Sprache der Metaphysik," in GW, III, 229–37. The subsequent debate between the two thinkers on this has been documented in the correspondence between them published in the *Nachwort* to J. Habermas/H.-G. Gadamer, *Das Erbe Hegels*, Frankfurt: Suhrkamp, 1979, also published in H.-G. Gadamer, GW, IV, 474–483.

12. Compare A.D. Schrift, *Nietzsche and the Question of Interpretation. Between Hermeneutics and Deconstruction*, New York/London: Routledge, 1990, 63: "One could argue that it is Heidegger who, in proclaiming the unity of the metaphysical tradition and dogmatically reducing all thinking to thinking of Being, is the consummate metaphysician."

13. H.-G. Gadamer, GW, III, 236: "Ist nicht Sprache immer Sprache der Heimat und der Vollzug des Heimisch-Werdens in der Welt?"

14. J. Habermas, *Nachmetaphysisches Denken*, Frankfurt: Suhrkamp, 1988.

Notes to Chapter 2

1. On this relation between the Renaissance and the hermeneutic imperative, see C. von Bormann, article Hermeneutik, in *Theologische-Realencyclopädie*, vol. XV, New York/Berlin: de Gruyter, 1986, 131–37.

2. On J. C. Dannhauer see H.-E. Hasso Jaeger, "Studien zur Frühgeschichte der Hermeneutik," in *Archiv für Begriffsgeschichte*, 18, 1974, 35–84.

3. W. Dilthey, *Das hermeneutische System Schleiermachers in der Auseinandersetzung mit der älteren Hermeneutik*, in W. Dilthey, *Gesammelte Schriften*, XIV/1, 597.

4. See G. Ebeling, "Die Anfänge von Luthers Hermeneutik," in *Zeitschrift für Theologie und Kirche*, 48, 1951, 174.

5. A fresh edition of the last version of Melanchton's hermeneutically oriented rhetoric was provided by J. Knape, *Philipp Melanchtons "Rhetorik,"* Tübingen: Niemeyer, 1993. For a recent, thorough account of Melanchton's importance in this regard, compare J. R. Schneider, *Philip Melanchton's Rhetorical Construal of Biblical Authority. Oratio Sacra*, Lewiston: The Edwin Mellen Press, 1990. For an appraisal of the significance of the rhetoric tradition for the history of hermeneutics, see our article "Hermeneutik" in the *Historisches Wörterbuch der Rhetorik*, Tübingen: Niemeyer, 1996.

6. Nevertheless, in German translations and commentaries, the *Peri hermeneias* has often been referred to as Aristotle's *Hermeneutik*. See for instance, in a recent as well as important occurrence: H. Flashar, Aristoteles, in Ueberweg-Praechter, *Grundriss der Geschichte der Philosophie: Die Philosophie der Antike*, 3, Basel/Stuttgart: Schwabe, 1983, 203, 237.

7. "Hermeneia und Hermeneutike. Ursprung und Sinn der Hermeneutik," in K. Kerényi, *Griechische Grundbegriffe*, Zürich: Rhein-Verlag, 1964, 42–52. While it is instructive and philosophically suggestive, it gives very few verifiable indications on Greek ἑρμηνευτική itself, concentrating instead on the art of interpretation in the Jewish tradition, the importance of tradition (παράδοσις), the art of divination in Greek religion and ending with reflections on Pindar's poetry.

8. See P. Chantraine, *Dictionnaire étymologique de la langue grecque*, Paris: Klincksieck, 1983, vol. I, 373. Despite popular tradition, there seems to be no etymological link whatsoever between the Greek god Hermes and the art of ἑρμηνευτική.

9. Platon, *Oeuvres complètes*, Paris: Bibliothèque de la Pléiade, Gallimard, II, 1950, 1137.

10. Plato, with an English translation by W. R. M. Lamb, vol. VIII, London/New York: Loeb, 1927, 433.

11. Bouché-Leclerq, A., *Histoire de la divination dans l'antiquité*, 4 volumes, Paris, 1879–82; Halliday, W. R., *Greek Divination. A study of its methods and principles*, 1913 (repr.: Chicago, 1967); Persson, A. W., "Die Exegeten und Delphi," in *Lunds Universitets Årsskrift*, 14, 1918; Oliver, J. H., *The Athenian Expounders of the Sacred and Ancestral Law*, Baltimore: John Hopkins University Press, 1950; for more recent literature see

W. Burkert, *Greek Religion*, Oxford: Blackwell, 1985, 391 and the extensive bibliography in Irad Malkin, *Religion and Colonization in Ancient Greece*, Leiden: Brill, 1987.

12. Compare F. Pfeffer, *Studien zur Mantik in der Philosophie der Antike*, Meisenheim am Glan: Verlag Anton Hain, 1976, 6–42; L. Brisson, "Du bon usage du dérèglement," in *Divination et rationalité*, Paris: Seuil, 1974, 220–48

13. See. W. Burkert, *op. cit.*, 116.

14. L. Taran, *Academica: Plato, Philip of Opus, and the Pseudo-Platonic Epinomis*, American Philosophical Society, Philadelphia, 1975, 224.

15. On Dannhauer, see our *Introduction to Philosophical Hermeneutics*, New Haven: Yale University Press, 1994.

16. In a famous passage of the *Symposium* (202 e), Eros is also praised as a ἑρμηνεῦον, an "hermeneut" or a go-between, that mediates between the gods and the mortals. As if to confirm the immediate association of "hermeneutics" with μαντική, Plato, or rather, the priestess of Mantinea (in itself an allusion to *mantikè*), goes on to say that it is through this mediation that the art of divination was instituted (203 a).

17 See J. Pépin, article Hermeneutik, in *Reallexicon für Antike und Christentum*, vol. 14, Stuttgart, 1988, 726 (with numerous references)

18. See the common edition Aristotle, *The Poetics*; Longinus, *On the Sublime*; Demetrius, *On Style*, Cambridge/ London: Loeb, 1927, 4th ed. 1946).

19. Accordingly there are almost no studies on the problem of translation for the Greeks. The only one I am aware of was written by J. Kakridis, "The Ancient Greeks and Foreign Languages," in *Hellenica*, 1966, 22–34. It confirms that the Greeks had no passion for translation. See esp. 24: "The ancient Greeks were entirely indifferent to foreign languages. No foreign language was ever taught in their schools; throughout the history of Greek literature we find only one book translated into Greek from a foreign language." The only translation that has come down to us was done in the 4th century B.C. It is a translation of an amazing story of an expedition by the Carthaginians on the west coast of Africa. The translator is not known (J. Kakridis, *op. cit.*, 29). I gratefully acknowledge the help provided on this subject by my colleague Luc Brisson (CNRS, Paris).

20. J. Kakridis, *op. cit.*, 30.

21 On the posterity of this notion of the *translatio studiorum* in the Middle Ages, when science was passed over to the Byzantine, the Arab and "back again" to the Latin world, see A. De Libera, *La philosophie médiévale*, Paris: P.U.F., 1993.

22. J. Kakridis, *op. cit.*, 34.

23. Eric A. Havelock, *The Literate Revolution in Greece and Its Cultural Consequences*, Princeton University Press, 1982; *Preface to Plato*, Cambridge: Harvard University Press, 1963, 2nd printing, 1982; *The Literate Revolution in Greece and Its Cultural Consequences*, Princeton University Press, 1982; *The Muse Learns to Write. Reflections on Orality and Literacy from Antiquity to the Present*, New Haven: Yale University Press, 1986.

24. See E. Havelock, *The Muse Learns to Write. Reflections on Orality and Literacy from Antiquity to the Present*, 112–13: "It is only as language is written down that it becomes possible to think about it. The acoustic medium, being incapable of visualization, did not achieve recognition as a phenomenon wholly separable from the person who used it. But in the alphabetized document the medium became objectified. There it was, reproduced perfectly in the alphabet, not a partial image, but the whole of it, no longer just a function of "me" the speaker but a document with an independent existence. This existence, as it began to attract attention, invited examination of itself. So emerged, in the speculations of the sophists and Plato, as they wrote about what they were writing, conceptions of how this written thing behaved, of its "parts of speech," its "grammar" (itself a word which defines language as it is written)."

25. *Theaitetus* 184 e; *Sophistes* 263 e, 264 a.

26. *De interpretatione*, 16 a 4, on this see the instructive new article of H.-G. Schmitz, "Die Eröffnung des sprachphilosophischen Feldes. Überlegungen zu Platons Kratylos," in *Hermes. Zeitschrift für klassische Philologie*, 119, 1991, 43–60, spec. 46 f.

27. *Stoicorum vetorum fragmenta*, ed. Armin, Leipzig, 1903, II, 135; Karlheinz Hülser, *Die Fragmente zur Dialektik der Stoiker*, Stuttgart: Frommann-Holzboog, 1987, vol. II, fr. 528–35. See M. Pohlenz, "Die Begründung der abendländischen Sprachlehre durch die Stoa," in *Nachrichten von der Gesellschaft der Wissenschaften zu Göttingen*, Philologisch-Historische Klasse, Neue Folge, 3. Band, 1938–39, 151–98 (spec. 191 f.). Augustine, *De trinitate*, XV.

28. 16 a 4–6 (translation used: Aristotle, *Categories and De Interpretatione*, translated with notes by J. L. Ackrill, Oxford: Clarendon Aristotle Series, 1963, 43).

29. On this inner truth of the word and its hermeneutical actuality, see H.-G. Gadamer, "Von der Wahrheit des Wortes," in *Jahresgabe der Martin-Heidegger-Gesellschaft*, 1988, 7–22.

30. H.-G. Gadamer, GW, II, 193: "Wir reden von Aussage in der Verbindung, Aussagelogik, Aussagekalkül, in der modernen mathematischen Formalisierung der Logik. Diese uns selbstverständliche Ausdrucksweise geht letzten Endes auf eine der folgenschwersten Entscheidungen unserer abendländischen Kultur zurück, und das ist der Aufbau der Logik auf der Aussage."

31. To the "spirit" again, and not to the letter, of Platonism, because, as *Truth and Method* will establish, Plato retained an instrumental conception of language, that Gadamer seeked to overcome by relying on the help of Augustine's doctrine of the verbum as the exteriorisation of the inner word. For a fuller account, see our study on Gadamer and Augustine.

32. See J. Tate, "Plato and Allegorical Interpretation," in *Classical Quarterly*, 23, 1929, 142–154.

33. Compare J. Pépin, *Mythe et allégorie. Les origines grecques et les contestations judéo-chrétiennes*, Paris, 1976, 159–167; H.-J. Klauck, *Allegorie und Allegorese in synoptischen Gleichnistexten*, Münster, 1978, 45–53.

34. J. Tate, "On the History of Allegorism," in *Classical Quarterly*, 28, 1934, 105–114.

35. The invention of writing can also be held responsible for the rise of allegorical interpretation. In an oral culture, there was no discrepancy between the myth and its present meaning: the story told was only present as it was recited and tacitly adapted to its audience. There was no way to control the "accuracy" of the present-day story-tellers, since the only available version of the myth was its latest oral presentation. See on this L. Brisson, "Mythes, écriture et philosophie," in *La naissance de la raison en Grèce*, éd. par J.-F. Mattéi, Paris: P.U.F., 1990, p. 51: "Car si on la compare à l'écriture, où il est interdit d'utiliser d'autres mots que ceux qui ont été retenus et même de modifier l'ordre de ces mots, la parole présente, comme moyen de communication, une grande souplesse qui permet une modification lente, mais constante, du message transmis dans son fond comme dans sa forme, la dernière version d'un mythe étant la seule disponible." But as the myth was fixed in writing, one became aware of a distance between these stories and the (scientific) requirements of the later times. A bridge, or a hermeneutical mediation, became necessary between the letter and its intended, presupposed meaning, its ὑπόνοια. Again, as J. Tate has stressed, the original purpose of these allegorical interpretations of Homer was not to inject different or more pious, "hidden," meanings into his texts, but to expound what he really wanted to say.

36. *Stoicorum veterum fragmenta*, ed. Armin, Leipzig, 1903, II, 135; Karlheinz Hülser, *Die Fragmente zur Dialektik der Stoiker*, Stuttgart: Frommann-Holzboog, 1987, vol. II, 582 (fr. 528–29).

37. I owe this necessary specification to the excellent commentary on an earlier draft of this study provided by Professor Christopher Smith. I am in full agreement with him when he states that the speaker stands more or less in the dative case when she comes to speak. This accounts for the lack of satisfaction we can feel towards our own words: they hint at part of what strives to be said, without fully exhausting it. This struggle with language is thus a battle with ourselves, with our own self-understanding. This struggle forms the core of the inner word.

38. A. N. Whitehead, *Process and Reality*, New York, 1929, 63.

Notes to Chapter 3

1. P. Ricoeur, "Phénoménologie et herméneutique," in his collection *Du texte à l'action, Essais d'herméneutique II*, Paris: Seuil, 1986, 39–73.

2. "The Phenomenological Movement," in H.-G. Gadamer, *Philosophical Hermeneutics*, University of California Press: Berkeley 1976, 143 (GW, III, 116). Cf. already M. Heidegger in 1924, *Platon : Sophistes*, Gesamtausgabe vol. 19, Frankfurt: V. Klostermann, 1992, 9 : "One's introduction to phenomenology is not done by reading phenomenological literature."

3. Cf. O. Pöggeler, "Die Krise des phänomenologischen Philosophiebegriffs (1929)," in *Phänomenologie im Widerstreit*, edited by C. Jamme and O. Pöggeler, Frankfurt: Suhrkamp, 1989, 225–76. In reciprocative fashion, Heidegger demonstrated the same indifference with regard to the publications of his "master": when he acknowledged his debt to Husserl at the end of the Introduction to *Being and Time*, Heidegger was content to allude to "Husserl's demanding personal direction" and to the "generosity with which he offered us access to his unedited research"(§ 7).

4. H.-G. Gadamer, "The Phenomenological Movement," 142 (GW III, 116).

5. *Formale und transzendentale Logik*, in *Husserliana* XVII, p. XXII, 21. As the recent edition of Husserl's correspondence reveals (*Briefwechsel*, Dordrecht: Kluwer, 1993, vol. 5, p. 186), Husserl found his own reflections on time consciousness which Heidegger edited quite "unreadable" (*literarisch fast unmöglich*).

6. L. Landgrebe, *Vorwort des Herausgebers* to E. Husserl, *Erfahrung und Urteil*, Prague: Academia, 1939, V–XI.

7. E. Fink, *VI. Cartesianische Meditation*, ed. by H. Ebeling, J. Holl and G. van Kerckhoven (2 volumes), Dordrecht: Kluwer Academic Publishers, 1988 (Husserliana-Dokumente Band II/I et II/2). The German text of Husserl's five conferences appeared only in 1950 in the *Husserliana* edition.

8. This is the very likely hypothesis proposed by K. Schuhmann, "Zu Heideggers Spiegel-Gespräch über Husserl," in *Zeitschrift für philosophische Forschung*, 32, 1978, 603. In this regard, Schuhmann cites a letter from Husserl to Ingarden (dated the 2nd of December 1929). After the latter had evoked the results of his study of Heidegger, Husserl responded laconically: "I accord therefore so much more weight to the deployment of the integral German edition of the *Cartesian Meditations*." Cf. also H.-G. Gadamer, "Europa und die Oikumenè," in *Europa und die Philosophie*. hrsg. von. H.-H. Gander, Frankfurt: V. Klostermann, 1993, 68: "Nicht zufällig hat Husserl später in der Abgrenzung gegen Heidegger und andere seine "Cartesianischen Meditationen" verfaßt" ("it is not by chance if the later Husserl published "Cartesian Meditations" in order to distinguish himself from Heidegger").

9. *Logische Untersuchungen, Husserliana* XIX / I, § 2, 10. For the right meaning of this watch-word, that one can compare to the "*ad fontes*" of the

humanists and the "return to Kant" of the Neo-Kantians, cf. H. Spiegelberg, *The Phenomenological Movement. A Historical Introduction*, 3rd Edition reviewed and augmented, The Hague / Boston / London: Martinus Nijhoff, 1982, 109. Cf. also G. Heffernan, *Am Anang war die Logik. Hermeneutische Abhandlungen zum Ansatz der Formalen und tranzendentalen Logik von Edmund Husserl*, Amsterdam: Verlag B.R. Grüner, 1988, 13, who underlines the hermeneutic implication of the Husserlian ascent "from the words to the things themselves." As Heffernan observes, it was Heidegger who imposed on phenomenology the more lapidary formula "to the things themselves."

10. On Heidegger's fight against the propositional regime, see the last study of this volume on "The Hermeneutical Intelligence of Language."

11. *Op.cit.*, 60.

12. M. Heidegger, *Platon: Sophistes, Gesamtausgabe* 19, Frankfurt: V. Klostermann, 1992, 19, 27, 47 et *passim*.

13. M. Heidegger, *Sein und Zeit*, § 32, 153. One will note in this regard that the hermeneutic problematic of understanding and of interpretation in SZ (§ 28 to 34) finds itself framed within the analysis of the "one" (§ 27) and that of chattering (§ 35). In this respect, the necessity of an explicitating interpretation starting from the things themselves aims at combatting that which Heidegger calls the "dictature of the one" (SZ, 126) and of which the chattering constitutes the most deafening articulation.

14. On the recurrent motif of inauthenticity and its corollary, decline, in Husserl, cf. exemplarily: *Formale und transzendentale Logik, Husserliana* XVII, 32 : "*We speak of an* authentique *consciousness, of an* authentique *science, of an* authentique *method. The logical ideas are from the start ideas of authenticity* (Echtheit). *The authentic is that towards which in the last instance reason aims at, even in the declining mode* (Verfallsmodus) *of unreason*" (all the underlines are Husserl's).

15. Compare his "fundamental phenomenological maxims" in the 1919 course, *Grundprobleme der Phänomenologie, Gesamtausgabe*, Bd. 58, Frankfurt: V. Klostermann, 1993, 219.

16. *Husserliana* III, 51.

17. One understands therefore that phenomenology is, from a methodological point of view, hostile to theology (at least, the theology which stems from metaphysics). Cf. in this regard, the polemic essay of D. Janicaud on *Le tournant théologique de la phénoménologie française*, Paris: L'éclat, 1991 which has the double merit of finding a common denominator to the most recent developments in French phenomenology and of confirming the critical actuality of phenomenology.

18. In the *Ideen*, the important Chapter IV devoted to this thematic already spoke of *phänomenologische Reduktionen* in plural from. Cf. *Ideen*, § 56 to 62.

NOTES 165

19. Cf.the useful analysis by F. Dastur in her presentation of Husserl in *La philosophie allemande de Kant à Heidegger*, under the direction of D. Folscheid, Paris: P.U.F., coll Premier Cycle, 1993, 273: *"In the phenomenlogical attitude, consciousness experiences its constitutive power, which does not however say that it is supplied with a creative power which would equate it with divine thought. Husserl always clearly underlined that constitution does not mean for him a creation ex nihilo, but a giving of meaning."*

20. Cf. H.-G. Gadamer, "The Phenomenological Movement," 165 (GW III, 135).

21. This is, of course, the thrust of Heidegger's critique of Husserl's phenomenology in his Marburg lectures, which has been the subject of ample literature since Giorgio Corà's study, "Ripetizione e superamento della fenomenologia in Martin Heidegger," in *Verifiche* 12, 1983, 371–409; 13, 1984, 19–53, 281–316. In France, one might think especially of the work of J.-L. Marion, *Réduction et donation. Recherches sur Husserl, Heidegger et la phénoménologie*, Paris: P.U.F., 1989 and of J.-F. Courtine, *Heidegger et la phénoménologie*, Paris: Vrin, 1990. In Germany, cf. the collection already cited *Phänomenologie im Widerstreit*. Everything occurs a little as if the publication of the young Heidegger's courses rendered possible for the first time the debate that the later Husserl wished to conduct with or against Heidegger concerning the ultimate orientation of phenomenology.

22. GA 24, 229–246: *"The more radical interpretation of intentionality with a view to explain the daily comprehension of being: the Being-in-the-world as the foundation of intentionality."*

23. GA 58: *Grundprobleme der Phänomenologie*, (1919/1920), Frankfurt: V. Klostermann, 1993. 54, 59 sq., 69, 76, 250, 261 and *passim*. The term often appears in the courses which followed.

24. *Husserliana* VI, Beilage XXVIII to §. 73.

25. With regard to this radical temporality which represents the point of departure (*"Being and Time"*) of Heideggerian phenomenology and its veritable breakthrough with regard to Husserl, see the first essays of our *L'horizon herméneutique de la pensée contemporaine*, Paris: Vrin, 1993.

26. Cf. H.-G. Gadamer, TM, 256 (WM in the GW I, 261): "Thus it was clear that Heidegger's project of a fundamental ontology had to place the problem of history in the foreground. But it soon emerged that what constituted the significance of Heidegger's *fundamental ontology* was not that it was the solution to the problem of historicism, and certainly not a more original grounding of science, nor even, as with Husserl, philosophy's ultimate radical grounding of itself; rather, *the whole idea of grounding itself underwent a total reversal.*"

Notes to Chapter 4

1. Compare the observations, influenced by Levinas, of R. Bernasconi, "Habermas and Arendt on the Philosopher's 'Error': Tracking the Diabolical in Heidegger," in *Graduate Faculty Philosophy Journal*, 14/15, 1991, 3–24, especially p. 3: "The scandal arising from Heidegger's political involvement with Nazism and from his postwar silence on the holocaust refuses to go away, but the evident glee of Heidegger's philosophical opponents in the consequent damage to his reputation is misjudged. It is not only Heidegger, both the man and his thought, who is diminished by the whole affair, but also, and perhaps primarily, philosophy itself."

2. *De l'esprit* (Paris: Galilée, 1987).

3. M. Heidegger, *Wegmarken* (Frankfurt: V. Klostermann, 2nd ed. 1978), 353. On the equation of the ontology of *Dasein* with ethics, cf. GA 22: *Die Grundbegriffe der antiken Philosophie* (Frankfurt: V. Klostermann, 1993), 148.

4. Both references from a letter of August 19, 1921 to Karl Löwith, published in *Zur philosophischen Aktualität Heideggers*, ed. by D. Pappenfuss and O. Pöggeler, vol. 2 (Frankfurt: V. Klostermann, 1990), 29.

5. M. Heidegger, *GA: 63* (1988). On the anything but accidental acquaintance of ontology and hermeneutics in this programme title, see my "Die Hermeneutik der Faktizität als ontologische Destruktion und Ideologiekritik," in *Zur philosophischen Aktualität Heideggers*, vol. 2, 163–78.

6. M. Heidegger, *Vom Wesen der menschlichen Freiheit. Einleitung in die Philosophie*, GA 31 (1982).

7. See the contributions of C. F. Gethmann and G. Prauss in the volume *Heidegger und die praktische Philosophie* (ed. by A. Gethmann-Siefert and O. Pöggeler, Frankfurt: Suhrkamp, 1988).

8. M. Heidegger, "Phänomenologische Interpretationen zu Aristoteles. Anzeige der hermeneutischen Situation," ed. by H.-U. Lessing, in *Dilthey-Jahrbuch*, 6, 1989, 241.

9. *Sein und Zeit*, § 32, 148

10. *Ibid.*

11. For this reading of hermeneutics as a self-interpretation of interpretation, compare C. F. Gethmann, *Verstehen und Auslegung. Das Methodenproblem in der Philosophie Martin Heideggers* (Bonn: Bouvier, 1974), 117, and R. Thurnher, "Hermeneutik und Verstehen in Heideggers *Sein und Zeit*," in *Salzburger Jahrbuch für Philosophie*, 28/29 (1984), 107.

12. Even though it was more preponderant in the early lectures, the expression *Selbstdurchsichtigkeit* also appears here and there in *Sein und Zeit* (144, 146). On the importance of this notion of self-transparency in

Heidegger's earliest period, see H.-G. Gadamer, "Heideggers 'theologische' Jugenschrift," in *Dilthey-Jahrbuch*, 6, 1989, 232. See also from H.-G. Gadamer, "Heidegger und die Griechen," in *Zur philosophischen Aktualität Heideggers*, ed. by D. Pappenfuss and O. Pöggeler, vol. 1 (Frankfurt: V. Klostermann, 1991), 62: "Heidegger meinte mit *Hermeneutik der Faktizität*, wie er sich damals ausdrückte, Erhellung. Er meint, daß das Dasein sich erhellt, sich hell wird."

13. GA 29, 94 ff.; *Beiträge*, GA 65, 301, 323 ff.

14. *Ontologie (Hermeneutik der Faktizität)*, GA 63, 15: "Die Hermeneutik hat die Aufgabe, das je eigene Dasein in seinem Seinscharakter diesem Dasein selbst zugänglich zu machen, mitzuteilen, der Selbstentfremdung, mit der das Dasein geschlagen ist, nachzugehen."

15. *Ibid.*, 16: "Thema der hermeneutischen Untersuchung ist je eigenes Dasein, und zwar als hermeneutisch befragt auf seinen Seinscharakter im Absehen darauf, eine wurzelhafte Wachheit seiner selbst auszubilden."

16. *Wegmarken*, 336.

17. Compare J. Derrida's sly deconstruction of this situation and its ideological implications in his *Spectres de Marx*, Paris: Galilée 1993.

18. GA 21, 410: "Sie indizieren nur Dasein, während sie als ausgesprochene Sätze doch zunächst Vorhandenes meinen (. . .). Sie indizieren das *mögliche* Verstehen und die in solchem Verstehen zugängliche mögliche Begreifbarkeit der Daseinsstrukturen.(Als diese ein ἑρμηνεύειν indizierende Sätze haben sie den Charakter der *hermeneutischen* Indikation)." Compare GA 63, 80: "Die *formale Anzeige* ist immer mißverstanden, wenn sie als fester, allgemeiner Satz genommen (. . .) wird." That Heidegger retained this notion of formal indication after *Being and Time* is confirmed by the lecture course of 1929/30, GA 29, 421–35.

19. "Anmerkungen zu Karl Jaspers' *Psychologie der Weltanschauungen*" (1919/21), in *Wegmarken*, 10–11.

20. See on this O. Pöggeler, "Heideggers Begegnung mit Dilthey," in *Dilthey-Jahrbuch*, 4, 1986–87, 134. Compare also H.-G. Gadamer, "Heidegger und die Griechen," in *Zur philosophischen Aktualität Heideggers*, vol. 1 (Frankfurt: V. Klostermann, 1991), 70: "Es geht wahrlich nicht darum, Heideggers Sprache zu wiederholen. Dagegen hat sich Heidegger immer mit Entschiedenheit gewehrt. Anfangs war er sich der Gefahren solcher Wiederholung so sehr bewußt, daß er das Wesen philosophischer Aussagen geradezu 'formale Anzeige' nannte. Damit wollte er sagen, man könne im Denken höchstens die Richtung zeigen. Aber man müsse selber die Augen aufmachen. Dann erst werde man die Sprache finden, die das sagt, was man sieht."

21. On this, we are following a suggestion of Manfred Riedel, "Seinsverständnis und Sinn für das Tunliche. Der hermeneutische Weg zur

'Rehabilierung der praktischen Philosophie,' " in *Hören auf die Sprache. Die akroamatische Dimension der Hermeneutik* (Frankfurt: Suhrkamp, 1990), 131–62.

22. Compare GA 29, 52 ff, § 10: "Die Bildung der Schuldisziplinen Logik, Physik, Ethik als Verfall des eigentlichen Philosophierens."

23. Grußwort an die Teilnehmer des zehnten Colloquiums vom 14.–16. Mai 1976 in Chicago, in *Jahresgabe der Martin-Heidegger-Gesellschaft*, 1989, 13: "...die Möglichkeit eines gewandelten Weltaufenthaltes des Menschen vorzubereiten."

24. See the opening sentence of M. Heidegger, "Anruf an die Deutschen Studenten (3. Nov. 1933)," in *Martin Heidegger und das 'Dritte Reich,'* edited by B. Martin (Darmstadt: Wissenschaftliche Buchgesellschaft, 1989), 177: "Die nationalsozialistische Revolution bringt die völlige Umwälzung unseres deutschen Daseins."

25. See on this connection I. M. Fehér, "Fundamental Ontology and Political Interlude: Heidegger as Rector of the University of Freiburg," in *Knowledge and Politics. Case Studies in the Relationship Between Epistemology and Political Philosophy*, ed. by M. Dascal and O. Gruengard (Boulder/San Francisco/London: Westview Press, 1989), 316–51.

Notes to Chapter 5

1. "Die Leute warten immer auf den zweiten Teil von *Sein und Zeit,* sie kennen eben das Kantbuch nicht." Quoted by Walter Schultz, "Die Aufhebung der Metaphysik in Heideggers Denken," *Heideggers These vom Ende der Philosophie* (Bonn: Bouvier, 1989), 37.

2. Jürgen Habermas, *Der philosophische Diskurs der Moderne* (Frankfurt: Suhrkamp, 1985), 185; *The Philosophical Discourse of Modernity*, trans. F. G. Lawrence (Cambridge: MIT Press, 1990), 156.

3. Jean Grondin, *Le tournant dans la pensée de Martin Heidegger* (Paris: Presses universitaires de France, 1987).

4. Martin Heidegger, *Zur Sache des Denkens* (Tübingen: Niemeyer, 1969), 24.

5. See J.-F. Mattéi, "Les deux versants de la pensée," *Dialogue* 27 (1988), 676.

6. Martin Heidegger, *Beiträge zur Philosophie (Vom Ereignis) [Contributions to Philosophy (Of Propriation)]*, Gesamtausgabe 65 (Frankfurt: Klostermann, 1989), 64. Henceforth, cited as *GA 65* with page reference and referred to as the *Contributions*.

7. Martin Heidegger, "Brier über den Humanismus," *Wegmarken* (Frankfurt: Klostermann, 1978), 159; "Letter on Humanism," trans. F. A.

Capuzzi and J. G. Gray in M. Heidegger, *Basic Writings*, D. Krell, ed. (New York: Harper & Row, 1977), 207 (translations will be modified without further notice). Henceforth, cited as *LH* with page reference.

8. William J. Richardson, *Heidegger: Through Phenomenology to Thought* (The Hague: Nijhoff, 1963), xix.

9. See the Afterword to Martin Heidegger, *Sein und Zeit, Gesamtausgabe* 2 (Frankfurt: Klostermann, 1977), 582.

10. Martin Heidegger, *Die Grundprobleme der Phänomenologie, Gesamtausgabe* 24 (Frankfurt: Klostermann, 1975), 1 (emphasis added); *The Basic Problems of Phenomenology*, trans. A. Hofstadter (Bloomington: Indiana University Press, 1982), 1. Henceforth, cited as *GA 24* with German and English page references, respectively.

11. See Friedrich-Wilhelm von Herrmann, *Hermeneutische Phänomenologie des Daseins. Eine Erläuterung von 'Sein und Zeit'*, volume I (Frankfurt: Klostermann, 1987), 404.

12. On this subject, see my essay, "Le sens du titre *Etre et temps*," Dialogue 25 (1986), 709–25.

13. Martin Heidegger, *Sein und Zeit* (Tübingen: Niemeyer, 1977), 19; *Being and Time*, trans. J. Macquarrie and E. Robinson (New York: Harper & Row, 1962), 40. Henceforth, cited as *SZ* with german and English page references, respectively.

14. I refer the reader to my book, *Le tournant dans la pensée de Martin Heidegger*: chapter 3, "De la temporalité du *Dasein* à celle de l'être"; chapter 4, "L'intention de 'Temps et être' à l'époque de *Sein und Zeit*"; and chapter 5, "L'échec de 'Temps et être' et la radicalisation de la finitude."

15. Here, we follow Hans-Georg Gadamer, *Heideggers Wege. Studien zum Spätwerk* (Tübingen: J. C. B. Mohr [Paul Siebeck], 1983), 109 (*GW 4*, 277). Gadamer writes in relation to *Die Grundprobleme der Phänomenologie*, 459, now in *Heidegger's Ways*, trans. J. W. Stanley (Albany: SUNY, 1994, 128): "Here the entire problematic of the reification of being is evoked, the problematic which led Heidegger to the 'turn'." ("Hier klingt die ganze Problematik der Vergegenständlichung des Seins an, die Heidegger zur 'Kehre' geführt hat.")

16. See F.-W. von Herrmann, *Hermeneutische Phänomenologie des Daseins*, 401, who offers an illuminating interpretation and also locates the turn that is announced around 1930.

17. On the subject of the turn, see my *Le tournant dans la pensée de Martin Heidegger*, chapter 7, "Le tournant dans l'être."

18. Martin Heidegger, "Die Kehre," *Die Technik und die Kehre* (Pfullingen: Neske, 1962), 40; "The Turning," trans. W. Lovitt, *The Question Concerning Technology and Other Essays* (New York: Harper & Row, 1977), 43.

19. "Die Kehre," 37; "The Turning," 37.

20. See *Being and Time*: "In such being-towards-its-end, *Dasein* exists in a way which is authentically whole as that entity which it can be when 'thrown into death.' This entity does not have an end at which it just stops, but it *exists finitely*. The authentic future is temporalized primarily by that temporality which makes up the meaning of anticipatory resoluteness; it thus reveals itself as *finite*" (*SZ*, 329–330/378). Also, from *Being and Time*: "Free for its ownmost possibilities, which are determined by the *end* and so are understood as *finite*, *Dasein* dispels the danger that it may, by its own finite understanding of existence, fail to recognize that it is getting outstripped by the existence-possibilities of Others, or rather that it may explain these possibilities wrongly . . . " (*SZ*, 264/308; the emphasis is Heidegger's own).

21. Martin Heidegger, *Kant und das Problem der Metaphysik* (Frankfurt: Klostermann, 1973), pp. 222–23; *Kant and the Problem of Metaphysics*, trans. J. S. Churchill (Bloomington: Indiana University Press, 1962), 237.

22. Martin Heidegger, *Die Grundbegriffe der Metaphysik. Welt— Endlichkeit—Einsamkeit, Gesamtausgabe* 29/30 (Frankfurt: Klostermann, 1983). This privileged positioning of finitude is surely unique in the history of metaphysics. It could be said that it is on the basis of its radicalization that Heidegger first broaches his overcoming of metaphysics.

23. To limit ourselves only to works which have recently appeared, we note that 'finitude' appears neither in Martin Heidegger's 1924 lecture, *Der Begriff der Zeit* (Tübingen: Niemeyer, 1989), nor in his *Phänomenologische Interpretationen zu Aristoteles. Anzeige der hermeneutischen Situation*, H.-U. Lessing, ed., *Dilthey-Jahrbuch* 6 (1989), 237–69, two major texts which may be considered first drafts of *Being and Time*.

24. See Hans-Georg Gadamer, "Der eine Weg Martin Heideggers," in *Gesammelte Werk* 3 (Tübingen: J. C. B. Mohr [Paul Siebeck], 1987), 423; and "Anfang und Ende der Philosophie," *Heidegger's These vom Ende der Philosophie*, M. F. Fresco, ed. (Bonn: Bouvier, 1989), 18.

25. Martin Heidegger, *Metaphysische Anfangsgründe der Logik im Ausgang von Leibniz, Gesamtausgabe* 26 (Frankfurt: Klostermann, 1978), 199ff. The notion of "metontology" had also appeared in a course of 1926 (*GA 22*, 106), but remained absent from Heidegger's *publications*.

26. See Robert Bernasconi, " 'The Double Concept of Philosophy' and the Place of Ethics in *Being and Time*," *Research in Phenomenology* 18 (1988), 44, where he writes, "Heidegger's characterization is so swift, the moves he makes so abrupt, that one can only assume that he is drawing on an earlier discussion."

27. On the changes in the existential analytic of *Dasein* that take place in this lecture, see Jean-Luc Marion, "L'angoisse et l'ennui. Pour interpréter *Was ist Metaphysik?'* *Archives de philosophie* 43 (1980), pp. 121–46.

28. The thinking of the turn in this writing has been well analyzed by Alberto Rosales, "Zum Problem der Kehre im Denken Heideggers," *Zeitschrift für philosophische Forschung* 38 (1984), pp. 241–62; and by R. Hosokawa, "Heidegger und das Problem der Kehre," *Studies in Philosophy* 4 (Fukuora, Japan) (1989), 1–23.

29. See Martin Heidegger, *Vom Wesen der Wahrheit. Zu Platons Höhlengleichnis und Theätet, Gesamtausgabe* 34 (Frankfurt: Klostermann, 1988).

30. We are adopting the expression of I. M. Fehér, "Heidegger's politisches Intermezzo: Rektor der Universität Freiburg," *Annales Universitatis Budapestinensis de Rolando Eötvös Nominate* 19 (1985), pp. 123–48.

31. See Carl F. Gethmann, "Heidegger's Konzeption des Handelns in *Sein und Zeit*," A. Gethmann-Siefert and O. Pöggeler, eds., *Heidegger und die praktische Philosophie* (Frankfurt: Suhrkamp, 1988), 174: "So far as is known today, there are no philosophical (but only 'political') writings by Heidegger from the time between these essays [from 1929–1930] and the essay on the work of art (1935)." In agreement with Pierre Aubenque ("Encore Heidegger et le nazisme," *Le Débat*, No 48 (1988), 120), we do not find the Rectoral Address to be an extraordinarily *philosophical* text.

32. Martin Heidegger, *Das Rektorat 1933/34. Tatsachen und Gedanken*, which appeared at the same time as the new edition of the Rectorial Address: *Die Selbstbehauptung der deutschen Universität* (Frankfurt: Klostermann, 1983), 39; "The Rectorate 1933/34: Facts and Thoughts," trans. K. Harries, *Review of Metaphysics* 38 (March 1985), 498: "In no way shall it be denied that at the time I believed in such possibilities and for this reason renounced the thinker's most proper vocation in order to help realize them in an official capacity."

33. See Hans-Georg Gadamer, *Heideggers Wege*, 15 (*GW 4*, 183; *Heidegger's Ways*, 11): "His later works did in fact always present new ways and new thought experiments. He began working on these ways years before his political involvement, and after the short episode of his political blunder, he continued without a visible break in the direction he had already begun." ("Tatsächlich sind es immer neue Wege und immer neue Denkversuche, die sein späteres Werk darstellt. Er begann diese Wege Jahre vor seinem politischen Engagement, und setzte sie nach der kurzen Episode seines politischen Irrtums ohne sichtbaren Bruch in der Richtung fort, die er vorher schon eingeschlagen hatte.")

34. Alexander Schwan, "Verliebt in Untergang und Abgrund," *Rheinischer Merkur* 17, April 28, 1989, 15. See also Friedrich-Wilhelm von Herrmann, "Technik, Politik und Kunst in den 'Beiträgen zur Philosophie'," in *Wege und Irrwege des neueren Umgang mit Heideggers Werk* (Berlin: Duncker & Humblot, 1991), 29–41.

35. *GA 65*, p. 102: "... aus der wesenhaften Nichtigkeit des Seins (Kehre) ... " ("... out of the essential nothingness of being (turn) ... ").

36. We have borrowed this term from Gilbert Hottois, *Le signe et la technique. La philosophie à l'épreuve de la technique* (Paris: Aubier, 1984).

37. *GA 65*, 407: "What is this originary turn in appropriation (*Ereignis*)? Only the attack of being as appropriation of the there brings the there-*being* to itself and thus to the consummation (sheltering) of the standing-internally grounded truth in the being which, in the lighted concealing of the there, finds its place." ("Was ist diese ursprüngliche Kehre im Ereignis? Nur der Anfall des Seyns als Ereignung des Da bringt das Da-*sein* zu ihm selbst und so zum Vollzug (Bergung) der inständlich gegründeten Wahrheit in das Seiende, das in der gelichteten Verbergung des Da seine Stätte findet.")

38. The same thesis is to be found in F.-W. von Herrmann, "Technik, Politik und Kunst in den 'Beiträgen zur Philosophie'": "The phenomenological glimpse of the turn into the event, the turn relation in the holding sway of the truth of being, led to the turn, to the transformation of the transcendental-horizonal formulation of the question of being into one based on the history of being." See also, by the same author, "Das Ende der Metaphysik und der andere Anfang des Denkens. Zu Heideggers 'Kehre'," a lecture held in Messkirch in September 1988: "The turn from the thinking of fundamental ontology to that of the history of being is grounded for its part on the turn which itself belongs to the holding sway of being, to the event. Thus, Heidegger speaks of the 'turn into the event' [*GA 65*, 255]. The glimpsing of the holding sway (i.e., the historicity of being) in the event and thus of the turn which belongs to the event, makes the turn from the thinking of fundamental ontology to the thinking of the history of being necessary."

39. On this subject, see my essay, "The A Priori from Kant to Schelling," *Idealistic Studies* 19 (1989), 202–221.

Notes to Chapter 6

1. GW II, 3.

2. At this point I would like to thank Professor Gadamer for his willingness to discuss our questions concerning the sources of TM.

3. The first sections of this original draft were published under the title "Wahrheit und Methode. Der Anfang der Urfassung (ca. 1956)," in the *Dilthey-Jahrbuch*, 8, 1992–1993, 131–42.

4. GW II, 487.

5. GW II, 489.

6. GW II, 492.

7. GW II, 491.

8. A trace of this insertion of the three named sections is preserved in the published work of 1960. If one moves from the end of the chapter

entitled "The Principle of Effective History" (WM, in GW I, 316; TM, 307) to the beginning of the chapter entitled "On the Limitations of the Philosophy of Reflexivity" (GW I, 346; TM, 341), the continuity of the flow of thought and questioning is evident. The incompletability of effective historical reflection, which Gadamer advocates, constitutes the main thread. From this idea the classical (and modern) philosophy of reflexivity may be overturned.

9. See GW I, 11–14 (TM, 5–9, the beginning of the work), 47 (TM, 41, end and summary of the first section), 90 (TM, 84, transition to the critique of aesthetics). In addition, Helmholtz is present in the published preliminary studies for TM. See the essay of 1953 "Truth in the Humanities," in GW II, 39.

10. Original draft, p. 44 (the end of the quotation is identical to GW I, 13; TM, 8).

11. See GW I, 170 (TM, 165: "Today's task could be to free ourselves from the dominant influence of Dilthey's approach to the question and from the prejudices of the discipline that he founded: namely "*Geistesgeschichte*" (intellectual history)." Oublier Dilthey?

12. GW I, 23; TM, 18.

13. GW I, 29; TM, 24.

14. GW I, 46; TM, 41.

15. GW I, 46; TM, 41.

16. This is the title of a section, GW I, 94; TM, 81. A preliminary study for TM was the Venice-lecture of 1958, "The questionability of aesthetic consciousness" (in D. Hendrich/W. Iser (eds.), *Theorien der Kunst*, Frankfurt: Suhrkamp, 1982, 59–69; translated in H.-G. Gadamer, *The Relevance of the Beautiful*, edited by R. Bernasconi, New Haven: Yale University Press, 1987), to which TM (GW I, 100; TM, 94) refers.

17. GW I, 177 (TM, 173, first line of the second part). Oublier Schleiermacher?

18. Original draft, 13. See also GW I, 171; TM, 166.

19. Ibid.

20. Original draft, after 13.

21. See GW I, 264, 286, 314, 316, 319, 330, 464 (respectively: TM, 259, 282, 309, 311, 314, 324, 460). GW I, 286; TM, 282 can be quoted as exemplary: "These thoughts raise the question of whether in the hermeneutics of the human sciences the element of tradition should not be given its full value" (Where Gadamer is referring to his own philosophical project in the second part).

22. This was in part correctly grasped by Leo Strauss (see his correspondence with Gadamer in *Unabhängige Zeitschrift für Philosophie* 2, 1978,

174   Notes

5–12) as the source of the hermeneutic problematic for Gadamer, in opposition to Heidegger, although Strauss over-emphasized the fixation on Dilthey (see GW I, 170; TM, 165, and above the footnote 10). Gadamer later recognized in this a shortcoming of his original intuitions for which he was responsible. For this see the self-critique at the beginning of the second volume of GW.

23. GW I, 1–2; TM, xxii.

24. GW I, 306; TM, 301 (= Original draft, 37 a).

25. Recently, Manfred Riedel has explored this "acroamatic" character of hermeneutic experience which depends upon the understanding reception. See his study, "Zwischen Platon und Aristoteles. Heideggers doppelte Exposition der Seinsfrage und der Ansatz von Gadamers hermeneutischer Gesprächsdialektik" in *Allgemeine Zeitschrift für Philosophie*, 11, 1986, 1–28; "Die akroamatische Dimension der Hermeneutik" in *Philosophie und Poesie. Otto Poeggeler zum 60. Geburtstag*, ed. A. Gethmann-Siefert, Stuttgart: Fromann-Holzboog, 1988, 107–119, reprinted in M. Riedel, *Hören auf die Sprache. Die akroamatische Dimension der Hermeneutik*, Frankfurt: Suhrkamp, 1990. See also the essays in the collection of the same author, *Für eine zweite Philosophie*, Frankfurt: Suhrkamp, 1988.

26. See Gadamer's reference to Heidegger's use of "actus exercitus" in his lectures, in H.-G. Gadamer, "Erinnerungen an Heideggers Anfänge," in *Dilthey-Jahrbuch*, 4, 1986/87, 21.

27. GW II, 52.

28. "Die Universalität des hermeneutischen Problems" (1960), in GW II, 219; The Universality of the Hermeneutical Problem," in H.-G. Gadamer, *Philosophical Hermeneutics*, transl. by D. E. Linge, University of California Press, Berkeley/Los Angeles, 1976, 4.

29. Original draft, after 13.

30. Die Universalität des hermeneutischen Problems, in GW II, 226; H.-G. Gadamer, *Philosophical Hermeneutics*, 11.

31. GW I, 478 (TM, 474, which is the last line before the concluding chapter). See also GW I, 479; TM, 476: "Hermeneutics is, as we have seen, to that extent *a universal aspect of philosophy* and not merely the methodological basis of the so-called humanities." (Gadamer's emphasis).

32. GW II, 90.

33. Between 1936 and 1959, Gadamer often held lectures under the title or subtitle "Introduction to the Humanities" (SS 1936, SS 1939, WS 1941/42, WS 1944/45, WS 1948/49, SS 1951, SS 1955). Clearly the first sketches for TM refer back to these lectures.

34. H.-G. Gadamer, *Philosophische Lehrjahre*, Frankfurt: V. Klostermann, 1977, 182.

35. One should also consider the additional references in the third part to the supplementary material in volume II, introduced in the fifth edition of 1986. See especially the addition (of 1986) to footnote 102, in GW I, 465; TM, 461: "Concerning the priority of the conversation before all propositions see the requisite supplementary material in vol. 2 of the Collected Works, 121–217" (similarily, the addition to GW I, 447; TM, 443). Also the propositions of TM are not to be reduced to their predicative character. Who thinks along hermeneutically, must also consider what lies behind them and what has happened to them in the further development of hermeneutics.—Asked about the philosophy of dialogue he developped in the last part of TM and in the words thereafter, Gadamer remarked in a recent interview (*Hans-Georg Gadamer im Gespräch*, herausgegeben von C. Dutt, Heidelberg: Universitätsverlag C. Winter, 1993, 36): "Indeed, this was the true work of the last thirty years" (*Ja, das ist die eigentliche Weiterarbeit der letzten dreißig Jahre*).

Notes to Chapter 7

1. Hans-Georg Gadamer, WM, 395 (GW I, 422).

2. In addition to Heidegger and Gadamer, we should also remind ourselves of Karl Jaspers, *Augustine*, München, 1983 (Selection from *The Great Philosophers*, München, 1975), Hannah Arendt who wrote a dissertation with Jaspers, co-inspired by Heidegger, on the concept of love in Augustine (Berlin, 1929), Edmund Husserl, whose lecture on inner time-consciousness begins with Augustine, Paul Ricœur, whose main work, *Temps et récit*, (3 vols., Paris, 1983–1985), begins with a reflection on Augustine and, lastly, on the periphery of phenomenology, the beginning of Wittgenstein's *Philosophical Investigations*.

3. Cf. O. Pöggeler, "Kunst und Politik im Zeitalter der Technik" in *Heideggers These vom Ende der Philosophie*. Verhandlungen des Leidener Heidegger Symposiums, April 1984, edited by M. F. Fresco, R. J. A. van Dijk, and H. W. P. Vijgeboom, Bonn: Bouvier, 1989, 111.

4. Hans-Georg Gadamer, "Erinnerungen an Heideggers Anfänge," in *Dilthey-Jahrbuch*, 4, 1986–1987, 21.

5. Gerhard Ebeling, "Hermeneutik" in *Religion in Geschichte und Gegenwart*, 1959, Band III, 249.

6. Martin Heidegger, GA 63: *Ontologie (Hermeneutik der Faktizität)*, 12.

7. *Ibid*, 13.

8. Martin Heidegger, GA 21: *Logik. Die Frage nach der Wahrheit*, 410.

9. Martin Heidegger, "Anmerkungen zu Karl Jaspers' 'Psychologie der Weltanschaungen'" in *Wegmarken*, 2. Auflage, Frankfurt: V. Klostermann, 1978, 10–11.

10. GW II, 219. I describe in my *Introduction to Philosophical Hermeneutics*, New Haven: Yale University Press, 1994, just how far Gadamer himself relies more on the early, and even "oral" Heidegger, that we today are getting to know from the published lectures, from the twenties, than on Sein und Zeit.

11. *De trinitate*, XV, chap. X, 19.

12. *Op. cit.*, XV, chap. XI, 20.

13. *Ibid.*

14. The tradition was following here 1 Corinthians 1:24. Cf. *De trinitate*, IV, chap. XX, 27; VI, chap. I, 1; VII, chap. III, 4–6; XV, chap. XII, 22, and others.

15. *De trinitate*, XV, chap. XV, 24: "numquid verbum nostrum de sola scientia nostra nascitur?"

16. *De trinitate*, XV, chap. XV, 25. In the absence of anything better, we are following the French translation here : *La Trinité, Œuvres de Saint Augustin*, vol. 16, Paris, 1955, 497.

17. Cf. WM, 398 (GW I, 425).

18. WM, 398 (GW I, 425).

19. WM, 399 (GW I, 426).

20. WM, 404 (GW I, 431)

21. Cf. WM, 404 (GW I , 431).

22. GW, II, 226.

23. Hans-Georg Gadamer, "Von der Wahrheit des Wortes," *Jahresgabe der Martin-Heidegger-Gesellschaft*, 1988, 17.

24. GW II, 52. Compare further on the same page: "It's not the judgement but the question that has primacy in logic, as the platonic dialogue and dialectical origin of greek logic also attest. But the primacy of the question over against the proposition signifies that the proposition is essentially an answer. There is no proposition that does not present some form of answer."

25. GW II, 195.

26. *Ibid.*

27. H.-G. Gadamer, "Grenzen der Sprache" in *Evolution und Sprache. Über Entstehung und Wesen der Sprache*, Herrenalber Texte, 66, 1985, 98 (GW VIII, 359).

28. GW II, 193.

29. Cf. GW II, 49, 186–7.

30. GW II, 52.

31. GW II, 226 (our emphasis).

32. WM, 395 (GW I, 422).

33. GW II, 504.

34. GW II, 496.

35. Which is already implied in the subtile notion of linguisticality when Gadamers alludes to the universality of *Sprachlichkeit*. The universal dimension of hermeneutics is not so much one of language itself (which would amount, say, to a linguisticism of sorts), but of an openness or quest for understanding in a mode which is less actual language itself than a striving for words for what urges to be said and heard.

Notes to Chapter 8

1. For a general survey of the problem, see the collective volume *Humanismus*, ed. by H. Oppermann, Darmstadt: Wissenschaftliche Buchgesellschaft, 1970, 2nd enlarged edition 1977. Most important in this respect is the work of W. Jaeger, *Paideia. Die Formung des griechischen Menschen*, Berlin: de Gruyter, vol. I, 1933, vol. II, 1944, vol. III, 1947. Cf. also his earlier essay *Antike und Humanismus* (Leipzig, 1925), reprinted in the Oppermann volume. It is to be noted that Werner Jaeger was also a mentor of Gadamer. One of his first publications happened to be a critique of Jaeger's genetic interpretation of Aristotle ("Der aristotelische 'Protreptikos' und die entwicklungsgeschichtliche Betrachtung der aristotelischen Ethik," in *Hermes*, 63, 1927, 138–64, reprint in H.-G. Gadamer, GW 5, 164–86). This essay enjoyed extensive notoriety since it was one of the first to criticize Jaeger's interpretation, whose importance is second to none in the Aristotelian studies of the last century. Gadamer also wrote a separate review of Jaeger's *Aristoteles* in 1928 (see GW 5, 286–94). Even if he maintained the trust of his truly ground-breaking criticism of Jaeger, the later Gadamer could not hide a certain uneasiness about the candour of his early essay in which an immature student attempted to criticize the major work of a renowned scholar. In this regard, all evidence indicates this is how Jaeger took Gadamer's criticism (compare H.-G. Gadamer, *Philosophische Lehrjahre*, 48). The two scholars remained close in the thirties and forties. Gadamer visited Jaeger often when he travelled through Berlin. Compare also Gadamer's tribute to Jaeger's teacher, Ulrich von Wilamowitz-Moellendorff, in GW 6, 271–77.

178 NOTES

2. On this distinction see the article *Humaniora*, in the *Historisches Wörterbuch der Philosophie*, vol. III, Basel/Stuttgart: Schwabe, 1974, 1215. Unfortunately, the following article in the HWdP on "humanism" is far too one-sided, centering almost exclusively on the marxist interpretations of humanism.

3. The text of the first article reads: "The dignity of man is inviolable. To respect and protect it shall be the duty of all state authority."

4. M. Heidegger, *Platons Lehre von der Wahrheit. Mit einem Brief über den Humanismus*, Bern: Francke, 1947.

5. See M. Heidegger, *Brief über den Humanismus*, in *Wegmarken*, 2nd edition, Frankfurt: V. Klostermann, 1978, 313; English translation: M. Heidegger, *Basic Writings*, Harper & Row, New York, 1977, 195.

6. *Basic Writings*, 225; *Wegmarken*, 342: "Oder soll das Denken versuchen, durch einen offenen Widerstand gegen den 'Humanismus' einen Anstoß zu wagen, der veranlassen könnte, erst einmal über die Humanitas des homo humanus und ihre Begründung stutzig zu werden?"

7. We are now following *Wegmarken*, 317–8; *Basic Writings*, 200–201.

8. *Wegmarken*, 318; *Basic Writings*, 201: "We encounter the first humanism in Rome: it therefore remains in essence a specifically Roman phenomenon which emerges from the encounter of Roman civilization with the culture of late Greek civilization." On Heidegger's interpretation of "romanity," compare GA 54: *Parmenides*, 1984, 57 ff. (course of the Winter semester of 1942/43, thus contemporary of the lecture on Plato's doctrine of truth and the context out of which the *Letter on humanism* was written). For a critique of Heidegger's letter on humanism, see the incisive and vehemently anti-modern article of G. Krüger, "Martin Heidegger und der Humanismus," in *Studia philosophica*, 9, 1949, 93–129, reprinted in *Theologische Rundschau*, 1950, 148–78. In some regards, specially in its critique of Heidegger's reading of Plato, Krüger's analysis anticipates, or echoes, the position of Gadamer. But Krüger goes beyond Gadamer when he faults Heidegger for failing to acknowledge a theological grounding of Being and accuses him of "humanizing" Being, an excess against which the Ancients and Plato could immunize us.

9. *Wegmarken*, 313; *Basic Writings*, 195–96.

10. *Wegmarken*, 315; *Basic Writings*, 197.

11. H.-G. Gadamer, *Heidegger's Wege*, J. C. B. Mohr (Paul Siebeck), Tübingen, 1983, repr. in GW 3, 1987 (English translation: *Heidegger's Ways*, SUNY Press, Albany, 1994). However, in 1965 and 1968/69, Gadamer devoted his proseminar at the University of Heidelberg to Heidegger's "Letter on Humanism." Gadamer's last and insisting pronouncement on the question of humanism can be found in his "Humanismus heute?", *in Humanistische Bildung*, 15, 1992, 57–70.

12. H.-G. Gadamer, WM, GW I, 1986, 14; TM, 9.

13. See the original version of *Volk und Geschichte im Denken Herders*, Frankfurt: V. Klostermann, 1942. The questionable passages were left aside in the new editions of the conference, retitled "Herder and the Historical World," in the *Kleine Schriften* III (Tübingen, 1971, 101–17) and the GW 4 (318–35). G. Warnke, *Gadamer. Hermeneutics, Tradition and Reason*, Stanford University Press, 1987, 71, has usefully discussed these critical passages.

14. *Volk und Geschichte im Denken Herders*, 20 (slightly changed in GW, 4, 332). This passage merits being quoted in its original version since one can glimpse through it a political indication as to what was needed in 1941: "In der Tat mag der Glaube an den Sieg der Vernunft und der Billigkeit nicht nur dem leidenden Teil der Menschheit wie ein Trost beiwohnen, sondern auch den Helden der Geschichte in ihren Plänen und harten Entschlüssen voranleuchten." In this respect, it is worth remembering that Gadamer was a close friend of the former mayor of Leipzig, Gördeler, who was convicted and executed because of his involvement in the assassination attempt against Hitler. We will not credit Gadamer with any heroic implication in this failed assassination attempt, that obviously remained a closely guarded secret amongst the plotters, but can only recall that Gördeler was regularly present in Gadamer's *Gesprächskreis* in Leipzig.

15. *Volk und Geschichte im Denken Herders*, 17 (GW 4, 330): "Er sieht in der Geschichte Ausbreitung und Beförderung der Humanität. Humanität aber eben in der Geschichte."

16. Compare the insightful development of this intuition and its application to the whole of the Western and Roman tradition in the recent essay of R. Brague, *Europe, la voie romaine*, Paris, Criterion, 1992. This book can serve as a useful antidote against the negative view of Romanity espoused by Heidegger and others.

17. On these theological and forgotten roots of humanism, see H. de Lubac, *Le drame de l'humanisme athée*, Paris, 1944; 7th. ed, Paris: Cerf, 1983, 15ff.

18. "Bildung gehört jetzt aufs engste mit dem Begriff der Kultur zusammen und bezeichnet zunächst die eigentümlich menschliche Weise, seine natürlichen Anlagen und Vermögen auszubilden" (WM, 16; TM, 10).

19. WM, 16 ("Der Aufstieg des Wortes Bildung erweckt vielmehr die alte mystische Tradition, wonach der Mensch das Bild Gottes, nach dem er geschaffen ist, in seiner Seele trägt und in sich aufzubauen hat."); TM, 11.

20. WM, 17 ("Der Mensch ist durch den Bruch mit dem Unmittelbaren und Natürlichen gekennzeichnet, der durch die geistige, vernünftige Seite seines Weses ihm zugemutet ist."); TM, 12.

21. *Wegmarken*, 319; *Basic Writings*, 202: "The first humanism, Roman humanism, and every kind that has emerged from that time to the present, has presupposed the most universal 'essence' of man to be obvi-

ous" ("Der erste Humanismus, nämlich der römische, und alle Arten des Humanismus, die seitdem bis in die Gegenwart aufgekommen sind, setzen das allgemeinste "Wesen" des Menschen als selbstverständlich voraus"), *et passim*.

22. On this idea that for humanism, contrary to what Heidegger and Derrida contend, there is no human essence, see L. Ferry and A. Renaut, *Heidegger et les Modernes*, Paris: Grasset, 1988. In this, they are following Jean-Paul Sartre. Compare also H. Arendt, *The Human Condition*, The University of Chicago Press, 1958, 10: "It is highly unlikely that we, who can know, determine, and define the natural essences of all things surrounding us, which we are not, should ever be able to do the same for ourselves— this would be like jumping over our own shadows. Moreover, nothing entitles us to assume that man has a nature or essence in the same sense as other things. In other words, if we have a nature or essence, then surely only a god could know and define it."

23. WM, 22 ("Eben das hatten wir, Hegel folgend, als das allgemeine Kennzeichen der Bildung hervorgehoben, sich derart für Anderes, für andere, allgemeinere Gesichtspunkte offenzuhalten. In ihr liegt ein allgemeiner Sinn für Maß in bezug auf sich selbst, und insofern eine Erhebung über sich selbst zur Allgemeinheit."); TM, 17.

24. WM, 23 ("Was die Geisteswissenschaften zu Wissenschaften macht, läßt sich eher aus der Tradition des Bildungsbegriffs verstehen als aus der Idee der modernen Wissenschaft. Es ist die *humanistische Tradition*, auf die wir zurückverwiesen werden. Sie gewinnt im Widerstand gegen die Ansprüche der modernen Wissenschaft eine neue Bedeutung."); TM, 18.

25. It was this utopianism, out of which one can also understand some aspects of Heidegger's entanglement with National Socialism, that we had in mind in the section on "The Ethical and Young Hegelian Sources in Heidegger's Hermeneutics of Facticity."

26. WM, 359; TM, 353. The hermeneutical primacy of negativity in ethics has recently been stressed by H. Krämer, *Integrative Ethik*, Frankfurt: Suhrkamp, 1992, 234.

27. M. Heidegger, *Erläuterungen zu Hölderlin's Dichtung*, GA 4, 1981, 38 ("Das Sein des Menschen gründet in der Sprache; aber diese geschieht erst eigentlich im Gespräch").

28. *Ibid.*, 40 ("Seit ein Gespräch wir sind—hat der Mensch viel erfahren und der Götter viele genannt. Seitdem die Sprache eigentlich als Gespräch geschieht, kommen die Götter zu Wort und erscheint eine Welt. Aber wiederum gilt es zu sehen: die Gegenwart der Götter und das Erscheinen der Welt sind nicht erst eine Folge des Geschehnisses der Sprache, sondern sie sind damit gleichzeitig. Und das so sehr, daß im Nennen der Götter und im Wort-Werden der Welt gerade das eigentliche Gespräch besteht, das wir selbst sind.").

29. R. Dostal, "Friendship and Politics: Heidegger's Failing," in *Political Theory*, 20, 1992.

30. In this, Gadamer also stands in the footsteps of humanism. On the humanistic conception of language, compare K.-O. Apel, *Die Idee der Sprache in der Tradition des Humanismus von Dante bis Vico*, Bonn: Bouvier, 1963, and E. Grassi, *Einführung in philosophische Probleme des Humanismus*, Darmstadt: Wissenschaftliche Buchgesellschaft, 1986.

31. H.-G. Gadamer, "Reflections on my Philosophical Journey," in *H.-G. Gadamer*, ed. by L. E. Hahn, The Library of Living Philosophers, forthcoming.

32. *Ibid.* Gadamer's dialogical interpretation of Plato is now extensively documented in volumes 5, 6 and specially in the more recent volume 7 (under the title *Plato im Dialog*, 1991) of his GW.

Notes to Chapter 9

1. Compare the classical study of Hans Blumenberg, *The Legitimacy of the Modern Age* (1966), Cambridge/London: M.I.T. Press, 1983.

2. Hans-Georg Gadamer, WM, in GW I, 16; TM, 11.

3. WM, 17; TM, 12.

4. H.-G. Gadamer,WM, 14; TM, 9.

5. For an incisive critique of the notion that the earth's position at the center of the universe had any dignifying aspect for the Middle Ages and the Renaissance, compare R. Brague, "Le géocentrisme comme humiliation de l'homme," in *Herméneutique et ontologie*, Hommage à P. Aubenque, Paris: P.U.F., 1990, 203–23. By relying on an impressive and wide variety of texts, Brague comes to the convincing conclusion that man was more often than not viewed as a humble piece of "dirt" (we are prudishly avoiding another four-letter word which frequently appears in the medieval texts quoted by Brague) at the very bottom of universe. For the Middle Ages, the sheer quest for autonomous knowledge was a very presumptuous undertaking for such an undeserving being as man, that could only be saved through grace. The Renaissance introduced a new perspective by valorizing knowledge, but it was still grounded on the notion that man was at its base nothing but a piece of mud. It is only by building itself, in the humanist understanding of the word, that it could hope to achieve any kind of grandeur, yet one which is primarily reminiscent of its divine creator.

6. J.-P. Sartre, *L'existentialisme est un humanisme* (1947), Paris: Nagel, 1968, 12: "Nous entendons par existentialisme une doctrine qui rend la vie humaine possible et qui, par ailleurs, déclare que toute vérité et toute action impliquent un milieu et une subjectivité humaine."

7. M. Heidegger, *Basic Writings*, New York: Harper & Row, 1977, 225.

8. WM, 23; TM, 18.

Notes to Chapter 10

1. Cf. G. Hottois, *L'inflation du langage dans la philosophie contemporaine. Causes, formes et limites*, Éditions de l'Université de Bruxelles: 1979; see also *Le signe et la technique*, Paris: Aubier, 1984.

2. Cf. P. Ricœur, *Du texte à l'action. Essais d'herméneutique II*, 93; "Heidegger's philosophy—at least that of *Sein und Zeit*—is so little a philosophy of language that the question of language is only introduced after those of situation, comprehension, and interpretation. Language, during the time of *Sein und Zeit*, remains a secondary articulation, the articulation of explicitation in the form of statements." See also the manuscript (available at the Library of the University of Louvain) of the "Course on hermeneutics" given by P. Ricœur in 1971–1972, 115, in which Ricœur underlines the "degradation" which is accomplished by the statement: "It is undoubtable that, for Heidegger, it is by degradation that one passes from that which is still immanent to the interpretation to the determination of abstract properties. Logical clarification is thus payed by an ontological obscuring. The statement is one of those places where one can identify the advance of the forgetting and hiding. It is not therefore, to say it again, the promoting of logic which matters, but its derivation by ontological impoverishment."

3. SZ 157; also GA 20, 414–15; GA 21, 187–88.

4. For this important distinction between the apophantic order of statements and the hermeneutical order, touched upon in SZ (158), but which one finds everywhere in the courses of this period, of GA 21, 143–61.

5. SZ 161.

6. A student of Husserl and Heidegger, Hans Lipps (1889–1941), attempted to develop on this basis a "hermeneutical logic" that would take into account the situatedness of every discourse and bring about a relativization of classical logic. See his *Untersuchungen zu einer hermeneutischen Logik*, Frankfurt: V. Klostermann, 1938. For an appraisal of Lipps contribution to hermeneutics, cf. the volume of the *Dilthey-Jahrbuch* (Bd. 6/1988) devoted to his work.

7. Cf. M. Heidegger, GA 19: *Platon : Sophistes*, 1992, 16.

8. *Ibid.*, 340–48.

9. *Ibid.*, 628.

10. GA 20/30, 95; GA 65, 301.

11. GA 19, 339–40 ("Es ist deutlich geworden, daß *der logos auf das horan angewiesen ist*, daß er also einen *abgeleiteten Charakter* hat, daß er andererseits, sofern er *isoliert* vollzogen wird, sofern er die Weise ist, in der man einzig über die Dinge spricht, d.h. schwätzt, gerade dasjenige im Sein des Menschen ist, was ihm die Möglichkeit, die Sachen zu sehen, *verstellt*,

daß er in sich, sofern er *freischwebend* ist, gerade die Eignung hat, vermeintliches Wissen zu verbreiten im Nachreden, das selbst kein Verhältnis zu den Sachen hat"). This potent statement already made a strong and lasting impression on the young Hannah Arendt, who quoted it in *The Life of the Mind* (San Diego/New York/London: Harcourt Brace Jovanovich Publ., 1978), vol. I, 118 (the wording differs slightly from the text recently published in the *GA*).

12. GA 19, 27, 47 and *passim*.

13. GA 20, 147 and *passim*.

14. GA 19, 9.

15. This phenomenological primacy of the question of being is more and more contested today. We are referring here to the recent works of J.-L. Marion, *Réduction et donation*, Paris: P.U.F., 1989; K. Held, "Heidegger und das Prinzip der Phänomenologie," in A. Gethmann-Siefert and O. Pöggeler, *Heidegger und die praktische Philosophie*, Frankfurt: Suhrkamp, 1988, 111–39; E. Tugendhat, *Philosophische Aufsätze*, Frankfurt: Suhrkamp, 1992. The first to put it into question from a phenomenological point of view was E. Levinas, "L'ontologie est-elle fondamentale?," *Revue de Métaphysique et de Morale*, 56, 1951, 88–98. The critique of Heidegger's question of being has, of course, been a common place of analytical philosophy. Its most recent instance has been provided by H. Philipse, "Heidegger's Question of Being and the 'Augustinian Picture' of Language," in *Philosophy and Phenomenological Research*, 52, 1992, 251–87, which attempts to show that Heidegger's interrogation remains emprisoned by a referential concept of being (the verb being would correspond to a real object), following the Augustinian and Husserlian conception of language. We hope to have shown here that there is a better picture to be grasped from Augustine.

16. GA 19, 25, 197.

17. Cf. GA, 19, 47.

18. Heidegger's thesis on the secondarity of the statement also governs his confrontation with the great authors of the metaphysical tradition, all of whom are interpreted in function of a singular question, that of Being, which often they have not themselves posed. One might think here of the beginning of the essay on *Plato's Doctrine of Truth* where Heidegger declares that "the 'doctrine' of a thinker is precisely the unsaid in that which he says." A manuscript note concerning Kant is yet more explicit: "what is said is always wanting, only the unsaid reveals a treasure to us" (*Das Gesagte ist das Dürftige, das Ungesagte erfüllt mit Reichtum*, «Aufzeichnungen zum Kantbuch», appendix to *Kant und das Problem der Metaphysik*, 5. Auflage, Frankfurt: V. Klostermann, 1991, 249). Heidegger's passion for the unsaid is not the fact of an esoteric whim, it flows directly from his conception of phenomenology.

19. Cf. H.-G. Gadamer, GW, II, 219.

20. WM, in GW I, 472 ("Der Begriff der Aussage (. . .) steht nun in einem äußersten Gegensatz zu dem Wesen der hermeneutischen Erfahrung und der Sprachlichkeit der menschlichen Welterfahrung überhaupt"); TM, 468.

21. GW II, 226; *Philosophical Hermeneutics*, 11.

22. Cf. H.-G. Gadamer, "Grenzen der Sprache," *op. cit.*, 89–99 (now in the GW VIII, 350–61).

23. WM, GW I, 472–3 ("In einem ganz anderen Sinne nämlich hat die Sprache selbst etwas Spekulatives—nicht nur in jenem von Hegel gemeinten Sinne der instinkthaften Vorbildung logischer Reflexionsverhältnisse, sondern als Vollzug von Sinn, als Geschehen der Rede, der Verständigung, des Verstehens. Spekulativ ist ein solcher Vollzug, sofern die endlichen Möglichkeiten des Wortes dem gemeinten Sinn wie einer Richtung ins Unendliche zugeordnet sind. Wer etwas zu sagen hat, sucht und findet die Worte, durch die es sich dem anderen verständlich macht. Das heißt nicht, daß er 'Aussagen' macht. Was es heißt, Aussagen zu machen, und wie wenig das ein Sagen dessen ist, was man meint, weiß jeder, der einmal ein Verhör—und sei es auch nur als Zeuge—durchgemacht hat. In der Aussage wird der Sinnhorizont dessen, was eigentlich zu sagen ist, mit methodischer Exaktheit verdeckt. (. . .) Sagen, was man meint, sich Verständlichmachen, hält im Gegenteil das Gesagte mit einer Unendlichkeit des Ungesagten in der Einheit eines Sinnes zusammen und läßt es so verstanden werden. Wer in dieser Weise spricht, mag nur die gewöhnlichsten und gewohntesten Worte gebrauchen und vermag doch eben dadurch zur Sprache zu bringen, was ungesagt ist und zu sagen ist.); TM, 469.

24. Pannenberg, W., "Hermeneutic and Universal History" (1967), in W. Pannenberg, *Basic Questions in Theology*, London, 1970, 96–136. Pannenberg relies on Gadamer's text cited above: "the concept of the statement finds itself in the most extreme opposition there is to the essence of the hermeneutical experience and the linguisticality of the human experience of the world." The criticisms of Pannenberg have been taken up by G. Warnke in *Gadamer. Hermeneutics, Tradition, and Reason*, Stanford University Press, 1987. See also N. Davey, "Hermeneutics, Language and Science: Gadamer's Distinction between Discursive and Propositional Language," in *Journal of the British Society for Phenomenology* (24) 1993, 250–65.

25. On the abstraction, even the "fiction" that the statement is, cf. GW II, 194–95.

26. H.-G. Gadamer, *Vernunft im Zeitalter der Wissenschaft*, 1976, 102–3 (*Reason in the Age of Science*, Cambridge: M.I.T. Press, 1982): "Dieser erste Schritt hermeneutischer Anstrengung, insbesondere die Forderung, beim Verstehen von Aussagen auf die motivierenden Fragen zurückzugehen, ist nicht ein Verfahren von besonderer Künstlichkeit, im Gegenteil, es ist unser

aller allgemeine Praxis. (. . .) Es ist im Gegenteil künstlich, nicht über diese Voraussetzungen nachzudenken. Es ist sehr künstlich, sich vorzustellen, daß Aussagen vom Himmel fallen und daß sie analytischer Arbeit unterworfen werden können, ohne überhaupt in Betracht zu ziehen, warum sie gesagt werden und in welcher Weise sie auf etwas Antworten sind."

INDEX OF SUBJECT MATTER

INDEX OF NAMES